Seasons of Shame

ROBERT C. YEAGER

SEASONS OF SHAME

The New Violence in Sports

Illustrated with Photographs

McGRAW-HILL BOOK COMPANY

New York St. Louis San Francisco
Mexico Toronto Düsseldorf

The author is grateful to the following firms for permission to reprint copyrighted material:

Burgess Publishing Company for the chart on page 234 from *How to Change the Games People Play* by G.S. Don Morris. © 1976 by Burgess Publishing Company.

Random House, Inc., and Curtis Brown, Ltd., for the excerpt on pages 131–133 from *I, Claudius* by Robert Graves. © 1934 by Robert Graves, renewed 1962.

Book design by Anita Walker Scott.

1 2 3 4 5 6 7 8 9 DODO 7 8 3 2 1 0 9

LIBRARY OF CONGRESS CATALOGING IN PUBLICATION DATA
Yeager, Robert C
Seasons of shame.
Bibliography: p.
Includes index.
1. Violence in sports. 2. Sports—History.
I. Title.
GV706.7.Y42   796   79-17041
ISBN 0-07-072255-2

Published in association with
SAN FRANCISCO BOOK COMPANY

For ELIZABETH ROYDE CALLEN

Contents

Photographs will be found following pages 14 and 66.

Author's Note

The subject of sports violence is as difficult as any this writer has examined. Its sources are at once as broad and elusive as human psychology and as narrow and specific as physical damage to necks and shoulders and knees. In this country, the importance of the story has been focused on brutality in big-time football, but the impact of athletic viciousness extends well beyond that limited arena. Other major sports have been wounded, some more seriously than football. Children have been traumatized and fans around the world engulfed by the savagery which rules today's competitive play.

These unfortunate developments might be less important but for the unparalleled influence of modern spectator sports on the young. Thus, if this book is philosophically centered, it is upon teenage and younger players, upon interscholastic rather than professional competition. There has been little attempt in these pages to cover the so-called bloodsports, such as hunting and bullfighting. These activities present their own particular problems and require separate consideration.

This book is for those who, with the author, stand far outside the circle of commercial sports, yet remain fascinated, perplexed, and often infatuated with the mainstream athletics that bring us together as a people. It is deeply hoped that this effort will help make it easier for all of us to stay in the game for fun.

Prologue: Lessons in Games

These are the days of childhood that stick in a boy's mind forever: the long, warm days of late summer, of drying grass and fresh earth smells and soft puffs of hot wind that brush against his face like some prepubescent beard. If he is older than eight or nine, though not yet far into his teens, they also are the days of his early lessons in games. Mastered in play but later practiced in his vocation, his mating, his recreation, these lessons may become the most important of his life. Because they encompass the extremes of experience, games in many ways chart the outer boundaries of emotion itself— pain and pleasure, triumph and defeat, sadness and joy.

Even today, with women involved in sports as never before, this instruction remains part of a largely masculine curriculum. Its precepts can shape a man's achievements and the way he relates to the rest of us. Its discipline often helps him, hardening his spirit against failure, teaching him the values of cooperation and comradeship, preparing him for the rigors of a competitive society. But to a disturbing degree these lessons of late summer also embody a potential for lasting harm. They can teach a youth to be vicious and cruel, to bully a physically inferior foe, to disparage women, to cheat, to prize winning above the game itself, to punish an already defeated opponent, and eventually, when he is older and the glory is great enough, to damage his own body with drugs and surgical grotesqueries.

Can you remember? It is August in a small California town near the Mexican border. The fading afternoon sunlight skims across the schoolyard playground, striking a cluster of boys, silhouetting each one against the stubbly turf, already burned a deep autumn brown. How many are they? Perhaps a dozen, most between the ages of nine and eleven, split into two teams of six players each and grouped around an oval ball.

Among them is a slender, dark-haired youngster who, like the rest, dreams of a plastic helmet, genuine low-top football shoes, and his own set of shoulder and knee pads. Like them, too, he dreams of playing the game in high school.

On this late afternoon, the boy moves over the prickly playing field in bare feet and blue jeans. It is ground he knows well. At the far end of the field a sagging baseball screen clings like a tattered banner to three weathered posts, somehow lending even this sand-lot football contest a sense of rickety importance.

The game itself is like hundreds of others the boy has played, yet it is like no other. The inevitable convocation and adjournment of the huddle, which, after all, is still a boy's huddle—"Didn't ya see me out there in the flat? I wuz wide open!" The count, "R-e-e-e-a-a-a-d-d-y, hut-two-three, hut-hut!" The play, arms and T-shirts flying, the boy feeling his own muscles—small, young, hard. The tug of clothing across his body, the touch of other boys, their shoulders, knees, hipbones, and hands. Crimson earth cakes along the furless ridge above his lips, wet with sweat, saliva, and wind-torn tears.

Again now, the boy moves with the play, across the straw-brown field against the pure blue sky. He turns to look behind. The ball floats toward him in a wobbly spin. He lifts his arms in the beseeching gesture of generations of pass catchers. He has beaten the only defender, a heavier boy, perhaps two years his senior, by something more than five feet. His team is one touchdown behind and, if he can make the catch, he has an open field to the goal. The football slaps into his hands hard and fat, its white cowhide laces pressing just beneath his fingertips. Running free now, he hugs the ball under his nose and inhales deeply. He loves the smell, a mix of leather and dust and the green juice of new grass.

Upfield, the other players still drift toward him, as if in slow motion. The goal is just steps away. Clutching the ball by one end, he points it skyward. He leaps toward the end zone, only dimly aware of the dark, sliding blur closing in from his right. It is too late. A large, strong hand grasps his neck while a closed fist hammers into the side of his skull. The boy drops to the ground, on his knees, his head reeling. A foot crashes into his cheek, its heel catching in his mouth, dragging a thin strand of spittle into his nose. The other players seem far away now, spinning off like sparks in a dream. A bubble of his own blood grows in the powdery, red dirt. A forearm slams into his shoulder once, then again. The ball squirts from his grip and he rolls over, on his back now. The larger boy, the player he thought he had beaten in the game, stands over him, waving the ball he has ripped away. "He fumbled! We win!" the heavier boy screams, his young face already twisted in a sneer. "He fumbled, he fumbled! We win!"

1 Troubles

Any species must risk extinction when aggressiveness finds its fences in ruin and violence an ever-available entertainment.
                                                                —Robert Ardrey

The evil of athletic violence touches nearly everyone. It tarnishes what may be only religion. Brutality in games blasphemes play, perhaps our purest form of free expression. It blurs the clarity of open competition, obscuring our joy in victory as well as our dignity in defeat. It robs us of innocence, surprise, and self-respect. It spoils our fun.

For all these reasons, the shame of sports violence assumes epic dimensions, its sorrows seem even more consummate. The toll extends well beyond a small boy's vanished enthusiasms, though such boys—and girls—are many, and their collective loss large and important. The more tragic cost is physical, tallied in broken bones and torn flesh. From high school on, the careers of an alarming number of players end or are shortened because of crippling injuries.

Never before has the harming of athletes seemed more deliberate, its practice so widespread. Even those who have battled in the trenches of big-time, big-money sports sense a difference in attitude and tactics on the playing field. "When I came into pro ball, I don't think there were many guys who

4

intentionally tried to hurt somebody," says Steve Owens, a Heisman Trophy winner and the first 1,000-yard rusher for the Detroit Lions. "But in the past few years I've seen enough to change my mind. They hit late, spear, and do unnecessary things when officials can't see it. They're trying to hurt people."

That the problem is neither exclusively American nor limited to the playing field provides little comfort. Canada's McMurtry report—an official government investigation of hockey violence prompted by the slaying of a teenage player—concluded that a "sick situation" existed at all levels of that country's favorite sport. The British athletic establishment was rocked by a recent finding that one in four male spectators has joined in soccer hooliganism, an epidemic of sports violence believed to include at least three murders. Elsewhere:

- In Guatemala City, five persons are hacked to death at a soccer match when hometown loyalists, bitter in defeat, descend on the winning team with machetes.

- In Florida, an argument at a high school football game ends when an assistant principal is shot and killed by the rival school's business manager. Seventy miles away, a boys' club football coach narrowly survives a beating by two dozen pipe-wielding spectators, mostly relatives of the losers.

- In Italy, a rugby player emerges from a scrum with much of his left ear bitten off; newspapers in Rome call this the first instance of sports cannibalism.

- In Florida, the facial bones of a major-league baseball manager are shattered in an attack by one of his own players during spring training. Successive World Series end in fan riots, with some of the violence so ugly that video crews are reluctant to film it.

- From Toronto to Minneapolis, stick-swinging cheap-shot artists rule the National Hockey League. Players slam each other into the boards, brawl with officials and fans, and are let off by confused courts which cannot believe a proud sport has been taken over by plain, scofflaw thuggery. "Hooliganism must be eradicated," says one NHL executive, but after years of supposed cleanups and promised crackdowns, hockey violence today seems as bad as ever.

So it goes. Knifings, shootings, beatings, muggings, paralysis, and death become part of our play. Women baseball fans are warned to walk with friends and avoid taking their handbags to games because of strong-arm robberies and purse snatchings at San Francisco's Candlestick Park. A professional football coach, under oath in a slander case, describes some of his own players as part of a "criminal element" in his sport. The commissioner of football proclaims that playing field outlaws and bullies will be punished, but to anybody with normal eyesight and a working television set the action looks rougher than ever. In Europe and South America—and, chillingly, for the first time in the United States—authorities turn to snarling attack dogs to control unruly mobs at athletic events.

Sports officials, parents, and athletes themselves condemn the worldwide wave of bloodletting, but the ugly parade of savage spectator outbursts and player-maiming injuries keeps getting longer. We worry about our children viewing fictional mayhem on television; yet the camera's relentless athletic vigil presents, unexpurgated, every major act of sports viciousness, then endlessly replays it, in full view of millions of hero-worshipping youngsters.

Clearly, children are among the most unfortunate victims of sports violence. "Professional games are allegories," says Robert R. Luby, a health education and safety official for the Detroit public schools. "When overaggressiveness wins the day, it puts the wrong emphasis on the meaning of athletic competition."

We are only beginning to understand how much television magnifies such emphasis. According to a December 8, 1975, report in the *Journal of the American Medical Association,* the average youngster witnesses some 18,000 fictional video slayings by the time he or she is in the mid-teens. Televised acts of sports viciousness may add appreciably to that childhood exposure to violence, some experts believe. The mere televising—and replaying—of such acts in effect condones similar behavior in children who idolize athletes as incapable of wrongdoing. "Violence in hockey is appearing in younger and younger age groups," said a report by Canada's Royal Commission on Violence in the Communications Industry, "because children are being shown on television the way professionals play the game."

What is sports violence? The distinction between unacceptable viciousness and a game's normal rough-and-tumble is impossible to make, or so the argument runs. This position may appeal to our penchant for legalism, but the truth is most of us know quite well when an act of needless savagery has been committed, and sports are little different from countless other activities of life. The distinction is as apparent as that between a deliberately aimed roundhouse and the arm flailing of an athlete losing his balance. When a player balls his hand into a fist, when he drives his helmet into an unsuspecting opponent—in short, when he crosses the boundary between playing hard and playing to hurt—he can only intend an act of violence.

Admittedly, violent acts in sports are difficult to police. But here, too, we find reflected the conditions of everyday life. Ambiguities in the law, confusion at the scene, and the reluctance of witnesses cloud almost any routine assault and battery case. Such uncertainties, however, have not prevented society from arresting people who strike their fellow citizens on the street.

Perhaps our troubles stem not from the games we play but rather from how we play them. The 1979 meeting between hockey stars from the Soviet Union and the National Hockey League provided a direct test of two approaches to sport—the emphasis on skill, grace, and finesse by the Russians and the stress on brutality and violence by the NHL. In a startling upset, the Russians embarrassed their rough-playing opponents and debunked a long-standing myth: that success in certain sports requires excessive violence.

Violence apologists cite two additional arguments. First, they say, sports always have been violent; today things are no different. But arguments in America's Old West were settled on Main Street with six-guns, and early cave-dwellers chose their women with a club. Civilizing influences ended those practices; yet we are told sports violence should be tolerated. The second contention is that athletes accept risk as part of the game, and, in the case of professionals, are paid handsomely to do so. But can anyone seriously argue that being an athlete should require the acceptance of unnecessary physical abuse? And, exaggerated as it may seem, the pay of professional athletes presumably reflects their abilities, not an indemnification against combat injuries.

"Clearly we are in deep trouble," says perplexed former sportscaster and football player Al DeRogatis. "But how and why has it gotten so bad?"

Our involvement in games has not always been so frenzied or, for that matter, so organic. Indeed, organized popular sports occupy a position of little or no importance in the long historical corridor stretching from the Circuses of Rome to the dawn of the present century. Except for crude contests at fairs and some primitive sports of villagers, athletics remained an aristocratic preserve. In America, the Puritans branded games as devil's work and forbade them. It was not until nineteenth-century Englishmen saw a connection between the demands of an industrial society for disciplined, hardy workers, and soccer's ability to train them, that they codified the game's rules and taught them to working-class schoolboys. In the United States, a full flowering of sports popularity awaited a loosening of the country's unbending economic and religious beliefs, the development of public-health measures which could protect large congregations against the spread of disease, and the nurturing of mass communications. This last factor is especially important. Not until July 21, 1920, did radio broadcast its first title fight, the match between Jack Dempsey and George Carpentier; the first World Series broadcast did not reach the airwaves for another five years.

It is in our own time that interest in sports has become a thundering obsession. Consider these figures for the decade from the mid-1960s to the mid-1970s:

SPECTATORS AT MAJOR SPORTS EVENTS

Sport	1965	1974	Percentage Growth
Horse Racing	40,737,000	48,824,000	20
Auto Racing	39,000,000	47,500,000	22
College Football	24,683,000	31,235,000	27
Major League Baseball	23,437,000	30,630,000	31
Harness Racing	26,899,000	29,976,000	11
College Basketball	16,384,000	24,630,000	50
Dog Racing	10,865,000	16,274,000	50
Professional Hockey	2,823,000	12,006,000	325
Minor League Baseball	10,194,000	11,032,000	8
Professional Football	6,956,000	10,236,000	47
Professional Basketball	2,356,000	8,229,000	249
Professional Boxing	1,733,000	2,675,000	53

Source: *U.S. News & World Report*

Our sports stadiums filled as our churches emptied. Our canonizing, in fame and dollars, of athletic excellence came at the same time we pitched aside traditions about family relationships, sexuality, and patriotism. Our frantic pursuit of victory on the playing field coincided with the first major battlefield engagement we failed to win.

In a real-life world of permissiveness and uncertainty, sports preserved our traditional concepts of endeavor and reward. In athletics, the phrase "to the swift goes the prize" still held a direct and uncomplicated meaning. Is it any wonder, then, that professional sports became so important in the working lives of two recent conservative presidents? Or that Richard Nixon, when at last he tried to stretch his hand to America's youth on a cold dawn at the Washington Monument, chose to discuss football rather than international politics? For him as well as for many Americans, games stood as a last citadel of the nation's classic social and economic beliefs.

Violence in sports is an important issue because sports themselves are important—and in ways and to an extent they never were before. It is not enough to say, as so many have, that sports provide a substitute for war. Sports always have done that. It is not enough to blame money or the capitalist system. The ex-slave Diocles received an amount that was probably in excess of $1.8 million in today's money for switching stables at the Circus Maximus. Marxist critics attribute abuses in athletics to Western free enterprise, yet some of the most severe excesses in sports are found among Europe's socialist countries.

What is different is that our athletics have become a surrogate ethic in a secular time. There may be no other faith that binds us quite so universally. Just as winning has become sacred, the perception of athletic foes as mortal enemies has become crucial to success in today's competition. "The contract is either you hurt the opponent or he hurts you," says Harvard psychiatrist Dr. Charles M. Pierce. "The coach must have his men feeling they not only can kill, but that they should kill."

Spectator violence mirrors those feelings. Until recently we might have thought barbarous fans were only to be found in the stadiums of Europe and South America. But on October 18, 1976, the stands exploded in violence at National Football League–owned Schaefer Stadium in Foxboro, Massachusetts. Before the long night of mayhem was over, two men lay dead of heart attacks and forty-nine persons had been arrested. As an ambulance attendant fought to save one of the dying heart attack victims with mouth-to-mouth resuscitation, someone urinated on his back. Countless fist fights broke out, a police officer's jaw was broken, and a man was stabbed as he walked through the parking lot. An elderly woman was hit in the head with a bottle, and a handicapped fan's wheelchair was stolen. Drunks and young toughs roamed in and around the stadium. One youth grabbed a policeman's gun and waved it in the air yelling, "Come and get me!"

Is it surprising that, in the end, the crowds watching sports come to emulate the bloody spectacle they see before them? Violent fan outbursts march step-for-step with increased participant injuries. An estimated twelve million Americans under the age of eighteen suffer from permanent, sports-caused disabilities, says Dr. John L. Marshall, director of the Sports Medicine Clinic at New York's Hospital for Special Surgery. Some disabilities are not serious, he admits, but others, many others, are crippling. Even injuries incurred in practice sessions—variously estimated at 50 to 80 per cent of all sports injuries—are known to be far more numerous than previously thought.

For most of this century, about thirty young people a year have died playing American football. Federal injury data indicate that well over 300,000 youths are treated annually in hospital emergency rooms for football injuries. The Occupational Safety and Health Administration calculates that a football player—high school, college, or pro—is two hundred times more likely to be injured than a coal miner. "I see the bad injuries, the blown-out knees," says University of Washington team physician Steve Bramwell, a former gridder for the Huskies. "If somebody had sat me down and told me about all the injuries when I was a player, it would have scared me to death."

Efforts to reduce the carnage in football have created painful ironies of their own. Hailed as a significant safety innovation when introduced in the late 1940s, the hard-shell plastic helmet later became associated with hostile styles of play and skyrocketing head and neck injuries. Coaches seized upon the development as a chance to use the head as a battering ram in blocking and tackling. Dangerous enough even for well-muscled college players, such techniques carry deadly risks for more slender-necked high school competitors. Despite repeated physician warnings, however, high school pigskin authorities persisted for years in allowing head tackling and blocking. Their intransigence helped fashion a national tragedy: besides causing paralysis, head and neck injuries are blamed for more than 80 per cent of high school football fatalities during the post-1960s era.

It should come as no surprise that young athletes have been schooled systematically in violent and dangerous techniques. They too live in what Michael Novak calls the Kingdom of Ends. It is the temple of football's great, gap-toothed deity, the late coach Vince Lombardi, where injuries are borne as sweet sacrifices to victory. Each winter weekend, before millions of television's faithful, that spirit again proves everlasting. A vicious purposefulness crowds into every corner of professional play. "I express America in the ring," a ranking heavyweight observes before a boxing match. "America wasn't built on going to church; it was built on violence." Looking at today's athletic scene, few could disagree.

Some may choose to concur with historian Richard Hofstadter's observation that "there is nothing new in our violence, only in our sudden awareness of it." But that, of course, goes right to the point. We live in an age when ninety million people witness the illegal violence in a single American football contest, when rugby fans in Italy carry Molotov cocktails and steel bars into their stadiums, when both players and officials have been stomped to death on soccer fields in Latin America, and when "games" have become an instrument of international terror and even a cause for war. The time for scholarly detachment would seem to be past.

Some say we all should become free-spirited Frisbee throwers, that we should drop competitive sports completely. But that would ignore the basic need in most of us to occasionally test ourselves, to engage in friendly contests with other members of our species. Even the so-called alternative sports of the early 1970s—jogging, bicycling, and Frisbee, too—are becoming increasingly competitive as the decade draws to a close. Watch when a group of children playing near a lake discovers a pile of smooth-sided stones. Soon they are skimming them across the water's surface, trying to see who can get the most skips. We seek games, we love games—all of us do.

To oppose violence in sports is not to condemn sports themselves. On the contrary, to condemn brutality in our play is to recognize how important our play has become. But a future which depends on cooperation in allocating energy resources, protecting the environment, and avoiding nuclear war, almost certainly will require some rethinking of our ideas about competition. Today we live at Puritanism's distorted apex, an affluent era whose central ethic is self-centeredness. Win-at-all-costs, what's-in-it-for-me athletics are a part of that. In times to come, however, Americans may well need the strength of character and sense of community which carried their grandfathers through hardship. The old school sports values of teamwork, fair play, and mutual respect could prove not only helpful, but necessary.

Admittedly, this vision of the future presents sports with a heavy burden. But we must ask ourselves where else the values of our society will be found better preserved. In a government riddled with epidemic corruption? In a business community whose quest for security has long since killed its appetite for free enterprise? We simply cannot afford heresy in our athletics. To a great extent, probably more than is prudent or many of us care to admit, sports is the single faith we still share.

"I've started daydreaming about Merlin Olsen," writes Jerry Kramer, the great Green Bay Packers offensive guard, in his book *Instant Replay.* "I see myself breaking his leg or knocking him unconscious, and then I see myself knocking out a couple of other guys, and then I see us scoring a touchdown, and always, in my own dreams, I see myself the hero."

Jerry Kramer may have been a noble warrior in another time, but now we must choose new heroes. The survival of our games, perhaps of our souls, depends on it.

Darryl Stingley, far left, tries to make a leaping catch of a pass just before his collision with Raider defensive back Jack Tatum (32) in the second quarter of a game between Oakland and New England, August 13, 1978. Stingley was rendered a quadriplegic in the incident.

Drake running sensation Johnny Bright (circled) is shown being slugged by Oklahoma A & M defensive tackle Wilbanks Smith in this sequence of photos, which won a Pulitzer Prize for the *Des Moines Register.*

PEANUTS

I'M DOING AN ARTICLE ON VIOLENCE IN SPORTS...

IS THERE ANYTHING THAT YOU THINK MIGHT HELP CUT DOWN THE VIOLENCE?

♡ SMAK! ♡

MORE KISSING!

The violence of pro football is reflected in the equipment worn by quarterback Dan Pastorini of the Houston Oilers, for a 1978 game with the Miami Dolphins. Pastorini wore an impact-softened flak jacket to protect his three broken ribs, a brace to protect his strained knee, and an elasticized pad to ease the pain of a perpetually sore elbow.

Bobbie Allison, left, and Cale Yarborough chose the Daytona 500 in 1979 to show how far auto racing had slipped from its beginnings as a gentleman's sport.

This video replay shows Los Angeles Laker Kermit Washington in the act of striking Rudy Tomjanovich of the Houston Rockets on December 9, 1977.

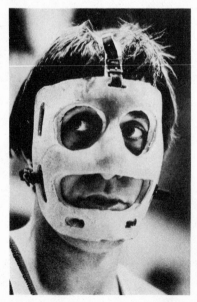

In January 1979, Rudy Tomjanovich wore a modified goalie's mask after being reinjured in Detroit. His 1977 slugging by Kermit Washington, a physician later testified, had left the Houston player with more severe facial injuries than he had seen in years of treating auto accident victims.

The Atlanta Flames's David Shand (fist raised) and the Detroit Red Wings's Nick Libett demonstrate the kind of violence the National Hockey League evidently considers "minor." The players each received a two-minute penalty for this 1979 fight.

Politics is Bill Bradley's life today, but this 1975 picture shows the former New York Knicks player mixing it up with Rick Barry, then of the Golden State Warriors. Barry got the best of the match but the Knicks won the game, 99–98.

2 **Players**

A game is a machine that can get into action only if the players consent to become puppets for a time.

—Marshall McLuhan

The sound of the shattering of Darryl Stingley's young life hung above Oakland Coliseum like the sharp clap of a very large popgun. "You could hear it all over the stadium," recalled a spectator later. "Everybody there knew it had been one hell of a hit."

Stingley, a twenty-six-year-old wide receiver for the New England Patriots, had gained forty yards on two successive plays against the Oakland Raiders. Leaping toward an overthrown pass, he literally was demolished at the 12-yard line. Stingley had run a dangerous crossing pattern in which the receiver twists back toward the quarterback while cutting across the defensive backfield. He may not have seen Jack Tatum before colliding with the feared, black-and-silver–helmeted defensive back.

The blow fractured the fourth and fifth vertebrae in Stingley's neck and damaged his spinal cord. In a single, tragic

15

flash of fate, Darryl Stingley, whose six-foot, 195-pound frame accounted for nearly one-third of his team's passing yardage the year before, faced what could be a lifetime battle against paralysis.

Game films later showed Stingley may have contributed to his injury by inadvertently ducking his head before contact. But the first reaction among the 53,335 fans in Oakland that warm August night had been to cheer Tatum for his devastating play. The press had been crowing about Tatum's hard-hitting but legal exploits for years. Named, perhaps unfairly, as one of pro football's ten "meanest" players by *The Sports Page,* Tatum was fined $750 for alleged roughness in a 1976 game with Pittsburgh and set an unofficial NFL record by knocking out seven opponents in one season.* So proud was football's establishment that Tatum's most dazzling coldcockings were included in highlight film clips. In his novel *Semi-Tough,* writer Dan Jenkins created Dreamer Tatum, who put his opponents to sleep with his tackles. In the novel, Billy Clyde Puckett describes the fictional Tatum:

I'll tell you Dreamer Tatum is a stud sumbitch on the football field . . . Dreamer Tatum is what we call a pisser. I mean that sumbitch will make your helmet ring when he puts it on you.

But all the macho backslapping ceased when the sports world found itself staring down at the fallen Darryl Stingley. Most journalists paid careful attention to legality, pointing out that what had been done lay well within the rules. Tatum himself remained characteristically taciturn. "You hate to see anybody get hurt," said the three-time winner of all-league honors, "but I was just doing my job."

Tatum's NFL bosses had more reason for concern. Two days before the tragedy *Sports Illustrated* had launched a

* See Notes and Bibliography.

major series on football brutality, and publications from *Reader's Digest* to *Penthouse* were questioning the rising violence in sports, especially football. Assurances that a player's broken neck had been broken "legally" failed to address the question of whether such a horror could be prevented. What rules permit such "legal" atrocities? Could existing equipment and uniforms be changed to reduce the incidence and severity of injuries? The game went on that night—would it have been halted if Darryl Stingley had been killed?

One reason for the increasing concern about sports violence is that so many more of us are affected. Big-time college football was concentrated in a handful of elite eastern schools when eighteen gridiron deaths in 1905 convinced President Theodore Roosevelt that he should call a White House conference to make the game safer. Today, football claims relatively few additional lives each year, but the participants who are permanently mangled number in the thousands. In 1905 there were an estimated 159 serious pigskin injuries, according to the *Annals of American Sport.* Today, as many as 50,000 knee injuries alone require surgery each year, most of them involving boys aged fifteen to nineteen.

They may not be life-threatening, but that many knee operations surely merit our concern. Not too long ago, surgeons were happily carving cartilage out of athletes' knees at the drop of their forceps. The result was a gimpy army of later-life quasi-cripples. Even today, with far more sophisticated diagnostic, repair, and transplant techniques, a typical knee ligament operation on a high school football player results in some permanent defect, costs thousands of dollars, and requires long periods of hospitalization and recuperation. As Dr. Allan J. Ryan, editor-in-chief of *The Physician and Sportsmedicine,* points out, the complex nature of the knee and the wide variety of procedures and ability of surgeons in treating it make it impossible to achieve the uniformity of results possible, for example, in appendectomies. "Anybody who has had knee surgery," says Dr. Ryan, "knows that no matter how successful it is, there is almost always some kind of residual annoyance, perhaps worse."

A letter in *Sport* magazine from a young football player adds first-hand testimony to Dr. Ryan's words:

Last year I had my fourth knee operation. I can only bend my left leg about 60 degrees. I've had my left kneecap removed, my cartilage removed, my ligaments sewn back together three times. I had three blood clots that had to be surgically removed. The arthritis in my knees and other joints is getting worse and as a result, I probably take more aspirin than I should. My right knee has bone chips that cause my knee to lock and I often fall down when I'm walking. I've had 18 casts on my legs and can't even count the number of times my legs have had to be drained of fluid. One doctor has recommended fusing my left leg perfectly straight and another wants to totally replace my left knee joint with some kind of metal joint. I already have enough metal in me to start a junkyard. I've been doing leg therapy for seven years now. And I'm only 20 years old.

The Consumer Product Safety Commission has estimated that nearly one in four football injuries requiring hospital emergency treatment involve broken bones. The commission calls the game the most dangerous sport played in America. A normal college season ends with 70,000 players from nine hundred schools on the injury list—and that may be just the beginning of a human toll higher than most realize.

A study of nearly three hundred professional and college football players by Dr. Hasib Tanyol, a Philadelphia internist, found that more than 25 per cent suffered from hypertension, an incidence of high blood pressure more than twice that of the general population and four times the rate among long-distance runners and track athletes. The average life expectancy of Americans who had been college or professional

football players, adds Dr. Tanyol, is fifty-seven, a full fourteen years less than their average fellow citizens.

It would be different if the suffering in athletics were limited to football. The problem, however, is not that a lone
sport in one country is experiencing an unprecedented wave
of viciousness, but rather that nearly all sports in all parts of
the globe are. And the victims have spread well beyond the
confines of the playing field. "I saw a man almost kicked to
death ten feet from me," wrote Frederick Baron, an American studying in England, in describing a soccer match for the
New York Times. "Fighting broke out, with big boots kicking,
chains flying and blood flowing like water. After the game,
there were fights outside the stadium, cars overturned and
liquor stores and shops broken into and looted. The city
hospitals were packed with casualties." Indeed, last season
some 6,000 spectators were ejected from British soccer
stadiums, and an average of 100 fans a week were jailed.

"Nobody can put their finger on the cause of it; no sport
seems free of it," is how John W. Joyce, security director for
the National Basketball Association, assessed the new violence in sports. And, he might have added, that includes
events well outside the holy trinity of football, baseball, and
basketball.

American cyclist Gerald Ash suffered a broken collarbone
after he and a partner were run off the track at Munich, Germany's world cycling championships in 1978. Their Czech
opponents, who collected a gold victory medal for
"sportsmanship," had deliberately forced the Yanks onto the
track's infield grass, where they shot out of control and
crashed. In auto racing, the 1979 Daytona 500 ended in a
nationally televised brawl between three-time Winston Cup
champion Cale Yarborough and the Allison brothers, Donnie
and Bobby, competing drivers in the race. Yarborough accused the brothers of forcing him off the track only half a mile
from the finish line, and the three wound up in a kicking,
punching, helmet-swinging battle. After viewing films of the

incident, race officials placed both Yarborough and Donnie Allison on probation, but a few weeks later the pair were at it again, crashing side by side while they battled for the lead in another stock car race. This time three other drivers went to the hospital. But if events such as these demonstrate how far automobile racing has drifted from the days when silk-scarved aristocrats sat at the wheel, it should be remembered that Rumania's Ilie Nastase and America's Jimmy Connors introduced the raised middle finger and NFL-style butt wiggle to the once genteel galleries of tennis.

Taken by themselves, few of these incidents would merit undue concern. But the fact that taunting, fist swinging, and dirty play have invaded hitherto peaceful sports seems worthy of alarm. Even basketball, invented in 1891 by Dr. James A. Naismith to boost membership in the Springfield, Massachusetts, YMCA, recently has provided savage examples of sports violence. In an insensitive October 1977 issue on pro basketball entitled "The Enforcers," *Sports Illustrated* described one player, Kermit Washington of the Los Angeles Lakers, as "a nice quiet person who lifts weights and sometimes separates people's heads from their shoulders." A short time later, Washington did just that.

The incident began with a fight between Washington, a muscular, six-foot-eight, 230-pound forward, and the Houston Rockets' seven-foot center Kevin Kunnert. Enter Rudy Tomjanovich, Houston's best player, an eight-year veteran with a reputation as a peacemaker, a man who had never been in a basketball fight. Hoping to break up the altercation, Tomjanovich rushed full speed toward the battling players, just in time for Washington to unload a devastating right hand from somewhere around nail level in the hardwood. "I hit him instinctively," Washington said later. "I had no idea who it was. I just saw him coming at me and swung. Now that I've talked to other people, I understand Rudy wasn't going to fight. It was an honest, unfortunate mistake."

That honest mistake crushed Tomjanovich's face into a

fist-shaped dish that caved back almost an inch into his skull. In a subsequent lawsuit filed by the Houston player, his injuries were listed as fractures of the nose, jaw, and skull; facial lacerations and a brain concussion; loss of blood and leakage of spinal fluid from the brain cavity. Facing surgery, his jaw wired shut, the Rockets team captain was out for the season. For his part, Washington drew what was believed to be the biggest one-time fine in sports history—$10,000—and a suspension without pay for sixty days, a potential loss of another $50,000.

In truth, Washington had been singled out as an example by the NBA, whose courts had become arenas for an estimated fifty brawls a season. Only weeks before, the previous record NBA fine of $5,000 was levied by Commissioner Lawrence O'Brien against Laker Kareem Abdul-Jabbar, who broke his right hand belting Milwaukee Bucks rookie Kent Benson.* "I will use all of the powers of my office to prevent violence within the NBA," pledged O'Brien. Hand checking was banned and a third referee added for 1978–79, but the move brought storms of protest and resulted in an average of only one additional foul called per game. Meanwhile, the suspicion lingered that muscling under the boards, elbowing, and fights had helped sell thousands of eight-dollar tickets. If not, why not simply outlaw any contact?

The 1977 baseball season got underway with an unprecedented jaw wiring of its own when Texas Rangers manager Frank Lucchesi was slugged before the start of an exhibition game.** His assailant: disgruntled utility infielder Len Randle. Hospitalized with a triple fracture of his right cheekbone, Lucchesi also suffered a concussion, lacerated lip, and back injuries. Elsewhere around major league diamonds the story was much the same: a Massachusetts father said his son was struck in the eye by a baseball purposely thrown from the

* Jabbar claimed he had been repeatedly elbowed by the rookie player.
** See Chapter 7, "Victims."

bullpen by a Baltimore Oriole pitcher; locker room squabbles soured clubhouse relations for the New York Yankees and the Los Angeles Dodgers; and Billy Martin, the Yankees ex- and *in futuro* manager, a man whom violence seemed to fol- low like a shadow, could, depending on the time and the occasion, weep in grief or swing with abandon.

Perhaps more than in other American sports, however, baseball's difficulties seem centered in the stands. The ugly rain of bottles, bricks, cans—and sometimes knives and iron bars—has become torrential. A recent benchmark was set on a cheap beer night at Cleveland's Municipal Stadium in 1974, when a game between the Indians and the Texas Rang- ers ended in a riot by hundreds of fans who fought with themselves and players from both teams.

The Cleveland melee erupted during a game the local team was losing. Ordinarily, however, baseball crowds misbehave most when they're happy, as when New York Mets rooters ripped up 6,500 square feet of sod to celebrate a pennant victory at Shea Stadium. Violence at Candlestick Park was never worse than during the summer of 1978, when the San Francisco Giants were enjoying their first run at a division flag in many years. The 1977 World Series ended in a barbaric wrangle by victorious Yankee fans that left thirty persons, including twenty policemen, injured. The 1978 Series ended in a postscript riot by fans—winners all—when their return- ing Yankee team landed at the airport.

Thus far we have not yet considered hockey, perhaps the world's most vicious sport for participants. Writer Alan Goldfarb recounts a memorable scene from an especially vio- lent, penalty-ridden game in which three major fights, one a near riot, left four players in need of stitches. Watching from his private box, Conn ("If you can't beat them in the alley, you can't beat them on the ice") Smythe, the president of the Toronto Maple Leafs, turned to a companion and said: "If they don't put an end to this sort of thing, we're going to have to print more tickets." Eddie Shore, a superstar on defense for the Boston Bruins from 1926 to 1940, paid for his title as the "Babe Ruth of Hockey" with a body sutured and resutured with nine hundred stitches—Shore's nose alone was broken fourteen times. Gordie Howe, the Detroit Red Wing all-everything for twenty-five years and more recently part of a father–son team with the New England Whalers, has had five hundred stitches in his face.

Minnesota county attorney Gary Flakne, writing in *Trial* magazine, described a battle between the Boston Bruins' Dave Forbes and Minnesota North Star Henry Boucha: "The butt end of Forbes's hockey stick struck Boucha just above the right eye. The force of the blow caused Boucha to drop to the ice, stunned and bleeding profusely. Forbes then dropped his stick and pounced on the helpless Boucha. He punched him in the back of the head with his clenched fist, then grabbed the back of Boucha's head by the hair and proceeded to pound his head into the ice until Forbes was restrained by another North Star player."

According to Flakne, who unsuccessfully prosecuted Forbes for aggravated assault with a dangerous weapon, the fight started when the Boston player skated up behind Boucha and punched him in the head with his hockey stick. Boucha subsequently required thirty stitches and three operations to repair a fractured eye socket, and Forbes became the first athlete in our time to stand trial for his conduct during a regular season game. The incident had thousands of witnesses, but the trial ended in a hung jury, Forbes's attorney having successfully argued that such fights have become standard fare in hockey play.

Sports violence breeds imitation. If chop blocks, spearing, and gang tackling work for professional and college teams, you can count on seeing the same techniques at high school and Pop Warner games around the country. A recent link between otherwise separate arenas of athletic savagery has been the "sneak Sunday." This is the hidden haymaker delivered against a relaxed, defenseless opponent in the gentlemanly belief that what your foe doesn't see coming is sure to hurt him. That's the kind of blow, thrown by Pittsburgh defensive lineman Joe Greene, that found its target in two successive Denver players during a nationally televised NFL playoff game. Baseball's Lucchesi claimed he was looking the other way and had one hand in his pocket when he was pounded by Randle. Greene's assault closely followed the demolishment of Tomjanovich, and within days a virtually identical college incident hospitalized UCLA player Raymond Townsend for yet another sports-caused jaw wiring.

In a September 4, 1978, *Newsweek* essay entitled "The Violent Game," Pete Axthelm compared the cases of Darryl Stingley and Ron Turcotte, a popular, Triple Crown–winning jockey paralyzed from the waist down after a spill earlier that summer. Axthelm contended that sports such as football and horse racing carry self-contained dangers that must be recognized by those who would participate. He denied that today's athletes are any meaner than those of the past and argued that sweeping changes in football's blocking and tackling rules could ruin the sport "at the expense of everyone who is earning a living at it." Never mind that neither of the athletes he wrote about were still in that category. To Axthelm, the real message in what befell both is "that an athlete's career expectancy can be short, with a sickeningly sudden ending. Some stars may seem grossly overpaid. But in high-risk sports like football and racing, boxing and hockey, players are gambling their bodies against a few years of productivity. Happily, the odds are vastly in their favor."

Even ignoring the fact Turcotte was making a standard $35 jockey fee when he went down and that, at $55,000 a year, Stingley ranked among professional football's more moderately paid receivers, Axthelm's argument bristles with illogic.

The NFL projects its casualty rate at 100 per cent—that is, during any given season an injury occurs for each of its 1,200 players—hardly a good wager regardless of the payoff. But let us not mourn those who receive at least some financial reward for their skills. Figures now emerging from injury studies suggest that sports are far more physically hazardous than previously believed. And the vast bulk of young victims are paid nothing at all for gambling with their bodies. Some of the most serious injuries result from abuses which, while "legal" in the tortured sense that word has taken in our play, could easily end in arrest and conviction if they occurred off the playing field.

Darryl Stingley attracted nationwide attention because he was a well-known NFL player. But the spinal cords of amateur football players have been ripped and bruised by the dozen. The nation's high school and college gridirons became factories for paralysis during the 1960s and 1970s. Paraplegic injuries (waist-down paralysis) strike more than thirty players a year on American gridirons according to *Blood and Guts,* a 1979 treatise on sports violence by Australian journalist Don Atyeo. In the period 1971 to 1977, according to the University of Pennsylvania's National Football Head and Neck Injury Registry, an average of more than ninety players a year broke their necks playing football, nearly a third of them (32 per cent) suffering quadriplegia (neck-down paralysis). Eighty-one American football players were rendered quadriplegic during just three seasons ending in 1977, the last year covered by the Registry's figures. In reporting its findings in the April 6, 1979, *Journal of the American Medical Association,* Registry researchers underscored the distinction between tragic but happenstantial neck injuries of the kind sustained by divers and gymnasts and the type found in football, where players have been schooled in "executing a maneuver where the head was used as a battering ram; the initial point of contact was made with the top or crown of the helmet in a high-impact situation. Thus, rather than an accidental, untoward event, there occurs the deliberate implementation of a technique that places the cervical spine at risk of catastrophic injury."

In a 1977 report in the *Journal of the American College Health Association,* the same authors,* documented a dozen severe neck injuries in a single football season in the states of Pennsylvania and New Jersey. At the time, they called their findings "an indication of the probable emergence of a significant national health problem." Following are just a few cases from their files:

• E.H., seventeen, injured in a varsity interscholastic football game. "The patient was on the kickoff team, attempting to block an opponent head first . . . he was rendered quadriplegic, with permanent motor and sensory deficit . . ."

• A.P., sixteen, playing defensive back in a junior varsity game, "made a tackle striking the ball carrier with his head . . . was immediately rendered quadriplegic . . ."

• R.R., twenty, playing defensive back in an intercollegiate game . . . "made a tackle, sustained a fracture /dislocation of C-5 on 6 [fifth and sixth cervical, or neck, vertebrae] and was rendered quadriplegic . . ."

• J.S., fifteen, "participating in an unsupervised sandlot pickup tackle football game. He was running with the ball and in attempting to head butt a tackler, sustained a dislocation of C-3 on 4 . . . patient remains functional quadriplegic, being unable to ambulate independently, feed himself or have bowel or bladder control . . ."

---

* Dr. Joseph S. Torg, director of the University of Pennsylvania Sports Medicine Center in Philadelphia; Dr. Raymond Truex, Jr.; Theodore C. Quedenfeld; Albert Burstein; Alan Spealman; and Claude Nichols III. Much of the Registry's early work was done at Temple University.

A continuing thread in this tragic legacy has been the benign neglect of establishment writers such as Axthelm, who in the same essay in which he pooh-poohed concerns about the incidence of athletic violence, could not resist heaping praise on the Dallas Cowboys' ability to "beat up on rival backs." Attorneys Harry M. Philo and Gregory Stine, writing in *Trial* magazine in January 1977, put the issue bluntly: "The jockstrap power structure in and around the financially powerful football business has effectively hidden from players and parents the grave risk of quadriplegia. Brain concussions in football are all too frequent, and the number of spinal cord injuries is on the increase."

In truth, so many weaknesses exist in our system of sports medicine that it is difficult to say how much of the blame should be placed on cover-up and how much on sheer ineptitude and inadequacy. The President's Council on Physical Fitness and Sports admits it has no precise idea of how many Americans participate in athletics. The two major sources of sports injury data are still in their infancy.* The only national tally of football deaths is based on local newspaper reports; fatalities must then be classified as to whether they were "directly" or "indirectly" caused by football.

The first nationwide sports injury survey sponsored by the Department of Health, Education, and Welfare, delayed for

---

* The Consumer Product Safety Commission's National Electronic Injury Surveillance System (NEISS) gathers football injury data from 119 selected hospital emergency rooms. The National Athletic Injury Reporting System (NAIRS), a fee-for-service computer network, collects continuous athletic injury/illness information from participating schools. Unfortunately, both systems have drawbacks. NEISS was not designed to address the entire spectrum of injuries, and NAIRS has been criticized as being too expensive and sophisticated for ready application at the secondary level (only about a dozen high schools in the nation participate), the area in which the most devastating injuries occur. The registry of interscholastic football deaths—a grim log kept by the National Federation of State High School Associations and the American Football Coaches Association—indicates a decline in fatalities during the past few seasons, according to NFSHSA. But because of what it mysteriously calls the "sensitivity" of its data, the federation no longer releases its figures without prior assurance as to how they will be used.

years and hamstrung by a niggardly $75,000 budget, finally became available in 1979. According to its 1975–76 data, more than one million injuries a year—111,000 of them major—occur in high school and college athletic programs, with tackle football accounting for half of all varsity sports mishaps. "Casualties may have reached unacceptably high levels," warned former HEW secretary Joseph A. Califano, Jr. More attention to safety rules, better training of coaches, and improved equipment could have prevented many of the injuries, he said.

The HEW study did not estimate the number of nation-wide football fatalities. But an extrapolation of data sampled at some 1,500 schools suggested that more than thirty high school youngsters may have died playing the game during the year of the survey. If accurate, that figure would substantially exceed recent football death estimates by national high school authorities, who claim just over ten deaths a year were directly tied to gridiron mishaps during 1973–77, about half the rate of the previous decade.

For the present at least, providing less speculative figures may prove difficult indeed. A precise estimate of those being killed and maimed in sports requires a national, mandatory computer network capable of tracking deaths and injuries at every school. Even then, experts trying to evaluate the impact of deliberately hostile or dangerous styles of play face a difficult task. It is not, however, an impossible one.

In 1979, investigators at the Institute for Athletic Medicine in Minneapolis completed a rigorous study that for the first time attempted to relate injuries and illegal play. Researchers Susan Gerberich and Dr. James Priest used a sophisticated questionnaire involving almost 4,000 players in taking a comprehensive look at high school athletic care in Minnesota. Their preliminary findings included page upon page of hand-scribbled notes by football players themselves, telling of the continued use of deadly head tackling and blocking despite a two-season-old national ban on such techniques. The Gerberich–Priest preliminary findings also turned up disturbingly high concussion rates—14 per cent of the players were either knocked unconscious or suffered loss of memory or "awareness" at some time during the season.

Statistics, studies, and reports, however, cannot begin to relate the incredible human calamity of a young athlete who becomes paralyzed.

> Who's the quickest team? We are!
> Who's the smartest team? We are!
> Who's the strongest team? We are!
> Hut-two, hut-hut! Hut-two, hut-hut!

The high school practice field is within earshot of Rob Mudd's family home in Stockton, California. But when the ritual sounds of August—the grunted chants, the slap of young bodies and hard armor, the incessant screech of coaches' whistles—drift up the street, they echo like a bad melody. If Rob is listening, it will be from his wheelchair. A sophomore football player, he had celebrated his fifteenth birthday just twenty-one days before he tried to bring down an older varsity player with a "face-to-the-numbers" tackle in a practice session. When the play was over, Robert Francis Mudd, Jr. remained on the ground, paralyzed from the neck down.

It is difficult to imagine a more depressing human condition than teenage paraplegia, especially in a young athlete who has dreamed of a lifetime of physical activity. Totally dependent, confined to a wheelchair, the ex-player must deal with the knowledge that his world, as well as his body, has withered away. He possesses neither the emotional maturity nor the sense of larger purpose that might bring some small comfort to an older, similarly handicapped military veteran. There will be none of the public outpouring of sympathy—to say nothing of the $1,000 a month, eighteen-months' lump-sum salary payment, and other NFL-paid financial benefits—received by a Darryl Stingley. The future stretches into endless decades of tiny movement.

"You get bored, you don't have any friends, and there's not much to do," Mudd said after the accident. "I like the outdoors. I used to hike and hunt and fish and play sand-lot baseball. I still go out and watch them shoot and shoulder the gun sometimes, but it's not like it used to be." Carol Mudd could not conceal a mother's bitterness toward the sport that locked her son's body in a lifetime prison: "You think, what kind of life is he going to have? will he meet someone? will he be able to get married? It's just a catastrophe, and there's no other way to put it."

Almost every serious study has correlated football's paralyzing head and neck injuries with increasing use of the helmet as an instrument of intimidation. The 1944 Army team of Felix 'Doc' Blanchard and Glenn Davis was the first ever outfitted with plastic helmets. Though it had some initial detractors, the hard-shell helmet—together with multiple-bar face masks and rules requiring that players wear mouthpieces—had by the dawn of the 1960s established the head as football's ultimate weapon. Rather than learning to block and tackle with their shoulders, players were taught the new techniques of butt-blocking and stick-tackling. They speared headfirst into pile-ups, enemy quarterbacks, and downed running backs. Neck injuries increased four- to fivefold and by the 1960s accounted for more than 90 per cent of deaths caused directly by football.

The trouble is that bulling the neck and establishing initial contact with the forehead or crown of the helmet shifts the brunt of the blow to the cervical vertebrae, far more vulnerable to serious injury than the lower thoracic (middle) and lumbar (lower) regions of the spine. A fracture above the

fourth cervical vertebra often means death; below that vertebra the same neck injury can result in quadriplegia or
paraplegia.
To determine the punishment absorbed by players'
skulls, Dr. Stephen Reid of Northwestern University at-
tached special recording equipment to linebacker Joe
Schmidt's helmet during the 1962 Pro Bowl. The electroni-
cally signaled impacts reached 5,780 times the force of grav-
ity with an amazing 400 G's getting through to the player's
head, roughly twenty times the level at which jet fighter pilots
normally black out (20 G's). Even spring-loaded blocking and
tackling dummies, which travel as little as three or four feet,
are touted by their manufacturers as being able to "hit like a
280-pound lineman."
Obviously, it is one thing when such forces are absorbed by
the eighteen-inch neck of a pro footballer and quite another
when the participant is a high school player. As he approaches
his mid-teens, a player's ligaments and cartilage are still growing, his vertebral end plates may not mature for several years,
and his neck itself may contain less musculature than that of a
comparably aged female. Nevertheless, in a study of nearly
350 Iowa high school football programs by a team of respected physician researchers, neck conditioning was found
to be "poorly emphasized," a kind way of saying that coaches
spent an average of less than five minutes a day on neck
exercises. The same men, of course, were urging their charges
to drive their skulls into blocking sleds and tackling dummies
as well as "into the numbers" of human opponents.
Not surprisingly, a subsequent study by the same Iowa
group suggests as many as one in three prospective college
freshmen players display X-ray evidence of neck injury prior
to playing *any* collegiate ball. A survey of fifty-one colleges
turned up 378 head and neck injuries among football players,
nearly seven per school. "Unless changes in techniques are
taught and rules are enforced, continued neck injuries and

catastrophic paralysis will put football in severe jeopardy," warns Dr. Harley G. Feldick, University of Iowa team physician and one of the authors of the Iowa studies.

Fred Rensing was a rock-hard, 230-pound freshman guard at Indiana State when a fateful play during a punt return drill exploded his dreams of the future. A dislocated vertebra and bruised spinal cord rendered him a quadriplegic on the final day of spring practice. "I hit him in the right breastplate," Rensing said in recalling a classic face-to-the-numbers tackle. I didn't feel any pain at all. The only thing that seemed weird at first was a buzzing sound in my head. Then I felt like I was falling backward in slow motion."

After years of warnings by physicians, head tackling and blocking have at last been prohibited by high school authorities. It remains to be seen whether the new rule can be effectively enforced. States such as Idaho and Massachusetts, whose interscholastic federations sponsored a hard-nosed campaign to convince coaches and officials to return to shoulder-first contact, can probably expect good results. Elsewhere, however, the lack of information on head and neck injuries and infrequent levying of penalties make any early assessment difficult at best. "The jury is still out on whether the rule is effective," admitted a spokesman for the National Federation of State High School Associations in early 1979. Meanwhile, Minnesota researchers Gerberich and Priest were compiling evidence that it was not.

"Unless the rules are enforced, unless you have a coach saying, 'The first kid I see doing this is off the field forever,' the rules aren't going to do any good," comments a Consumer Product Safety Commission official who headed a status report on football helmet hazards. The report's gloomy conclusion: that a large reduction in injuries can be accomplished only by changing the actual styles and conditions of play. "There simply must be more control over butting and spearing," the CPSC official said. "It is a risk that cannot be controlled by further changes in equipment." The only real solution may be one nobody wants to hear: that tackle football be banned in secondary schools and college and professional players forced to adopt shoulder-first tackling techniques.

The brutalizing of our sports, however, extends well beyond the gridiron, or the basketball court for that matter. As a prominent psychiatrist suggests, violence shows signs of becoming purely recreational, capable of being enjoyed in the same way we might sample a snack before dinner. In the space of a few recent winter weeks, a time when television athletics alternate between a steady stream of yawners and an orgy of what one writer calls "trashsports," viewers were treated to a gourmet's banquet of savagery. On successive Saturdays, a power lifter tore his hand apart on "Sports World" and a weightlifter squashed his legs under a 500-pound barbell. ABC showed a wrist wrestler breaking his arm on "Wide World of Sports" and seasoned the effect with slow-motion replay. The same network endlessly repeated film clips of fan and player violence in stretching a réchauffé "Sports Journal" feature into three weeks, then cut to the main entrée—a sequence showing boxer Duane Bobick getting smashed flat in South Africa.

Meanwhile, on rugby fields in Australia and New Zealand, authorities were investigating a wave of nine deaths and scores of serious injuries they blamed on increased use of the head as a battering ram, scrums packing too low, and out-and-out, fist-swinging violence. Like soccer, rugby long has been thought to be relatively free of such injuries because of its absence of heavy headgear and other armor. But the Sugadaira Summer Clinic in Japan, a treatment center for hundreds of rugby players who compete in nearby tournaments, reports head and neck complaints now constitute 36 per cent of all injuries. And rugby isn't the only sport experiencing unaccustomed casualties. In American horse racing, eight riders were rendered paraplegic and two killed in an unbelievable twenty-month period during 1977 and 1978. "This is a tremendous percentage rise, considering that we list only forty-eight permanently injured jockeys since we started keeping figures in 1944," says Nick Jemas, head of the jockeys' guild.

Career-halting injuries such as those suffered by basketball player Tomjanovich figured prominently in Commissioner O'Brien's decision to launch the NBA's investigation of violence. In the NFL, team physicians, including the Rams' Dr. Robert Kerlan, reported a steady increase in the kind of wounds that clearly reflect the savageness of battle—broken arms, hands, shoulders, cheekbones, and legs.

Given the violence in sports competition, is it surprising that painkillers, stimulants, and anabolic steroids have become so inextricably a part of athletics? The sports establishment can argue that violence is no worse today than it ever has been, a position which depends on the shaky contention that athletes somehow have escaped the troubles which beset the rest of us. But it is difficult to dispute the mushrooming use of drugs in sports of all types. The widespread use of drugs represents two parallel outgrowths of professionalism: first, the desperate search for an artificial competitive advantage; second, the economic necessity of players to stay in the game, whether or not their bodies need time off to heal.

As much as anything else, drugs have signaled the new violence in our games. According to the *Chicago Sun-Times,* football players have been known to rip apart their lockers in cocaine-induced frenzies before a big game. During the last years of his career, a famous baseball player was unwilling to take the field without first snorting coke. Drug busts have rocked pro hockey and the NFL, and all indications suggest the problem is worldwide. Scottish soccer star Willie Johnson flunked a test for stimulants in 1978, becoming the second player so barred from his sport since 1966. Estimates of the amphetamine use among bikers in 1978's Tour de France ranged as high as 50 per cent. Indeed, the tour's leader, Belgium's Michel Pollentier, was banned from the event and fined after trying to cheat his way through a drug test—he had concealed a rubber pouch of old urine under his armpit with a tube running to his palm. Finnish runners "pack" their blood; American football players swill down steroids. Pills, powders, injections, drops. One might visualize a new international shield of sports: crossed hypodermics above an apothecary jar and a snorting spoon.

Some say the drug phenylbutazone, an anti-inflammatory agent, may be to blame for horse racing's lengthening list of brutal mishaps. Though "bute" is not a painkiller per se, many jockeys believe it can give an animal a false sense of well-being, allowing it to put too much weight on an injured limb. Some are convinced bute also retards healing and reduces bone density, which might explain why more horses seem to be snapping bones—like the four-horse spill at Pimlico which killed jockey Robert Pineda and sidelined Ron Turcotte's brother Rudy with a broken collarbone.

In his book *Ball Four,* ageless pitcher Jim Bouton says he tried bute to ease the pain of an aching elbow. Later Bouton joined Whitey Ford in switching to dimethylsulfoxide (DMSO), a drug absorbed so rapidly that rubbing it on the arm brings an immediate taste to the mouth. DMSO subsequently was banned by the FDA. "Word is it can blind you," writes Bouton. "I've also taken shots—Novocain, cortisone, and xylocaine. Baseball players will take anything. If you had a pill that would guarantee a pitcher 20 wins but might take five years off his life, he'd take it."

"First it was toke, then coke, then drop a little of this and that," Steve Kiner, now with the Houston Oilers, told the *Oakland Tribune.* "Next thing you're doing it all week long." Kiner has since brought his own problem under control, but drugs nearly wrecked the career of the two-time All-American from Tennessee. In one game when he was with New England, the six-foot-one, 225-pound linebacker, frozen sky high on drugs, never moved from position during a wild play in which athletes from both teams scrambled for a loose football. "I must have taken 10,000 beans [uppers]," said Kiner later.

Drugs can ignite deep-seated fires of hatred and anger, thereby adding to the psychological climate of violence. Some players use amphetamines to deliberately provoke their own temper tantrums before a game, says Dr. Arnold Mandell, former psychiatric consultant for the San Diego Chargers. Because of chemical changes they cause in the brain, uppers can transform even mild-mannered pro players into killers for a few hours, he says, insisting amphetamine abuse is rampant among professional and high school players.

Mandell, a respected researcher and a professor at the University of California School of Medicine in San Diego, told a 1978 news briefing at the National Amphetamine Conference in San Francisco that some players on the San Diego team were jamming 80 to 100 milligrams of amphetamines—more than six times the amount in a typical all-day diet pill—down their throats before games. Besides hyping their hostility levels, the pills serve to mask pain, according to Mandell. The heaviest users were older players who took the pills only on game day and then only because they felt they had to—"They told me it was a matter of survival."

A post-game drug depression can be "severe and prolonged," says Dr. Mandell. "It magnifies and is magnified by the agonies of bruises, pulled muscles, cracked ribs, trick knees, strains, the works. It causes impotence, irritability, insomnia, and self-torture." Dr. Mandell tried to curb the Chargers' use of pep pills with counseling and by making the players themselves responsible for rationing their prescriptions over the season. Today he feels drug use is so tightly interwoven with the violence of the game that only extreme public pressure can bring it to an end.

"The Warriors, the Trail Blazers, any sports organization, they'll ask the athlete to take the drugs," says Derrick Dickey, a former member of the Golden State Warriors. "If they think you're not willing to help the ball club win by playing with a certain amount of pain, they can no longer use your services."

The drug-dispensing practices of the Portland Trail Blazers were a major reason cited by star center Bill Walton in requesting release from the Oregon team. Walton claimed he played his last 1977 game on a broken foot injected with xylocaine, a fast-acting painkiller. Walton's brother has charged that another player, forward Bobby Gross, was so numbed by the same drug that only by hearing the cracking bone could he tell when he broke his own leg. Former Oakland Raider wide receiver Mike Siani charged team management and doctors with making a cruel decision to shoot him up with painkillers so he could remain on the field with two dislocated toes. The Raiders' owner, Al Davis, is obsessed with victory—"and if it takes an injured player to go out and play numbed up, then that's what it takes," charged Siani. Since traded to the Baltimore Colts, Siani claims his foot still has not completely healed.

The teams, of course, routinely deny such charges. And, as easy and attractive a target as establishment owners and management present, the problem of drug abuse is far more complicated than most facile criticism would suggest. Players do not abuse drugs simply because money-hungry owners want to win. They abuse drugs partly because a pharmaceutical priesthood has been telling them since childhood that drugs can provide a "scientific" solution for almost any illness, athletic deficiency, or pain. Mostly, however, players abuse drugs because of their own intumescent cravings for money, victory, and recognition. A system devoted to winning above all taints not only its managers, it unites all its constituencies in a desperate coming together for an edge, any edge. If your opponent is using drugs that hype him up and make him, at the moment of athletic combat, the stronger foe, then the choice is clear-cut—either use drugs or accept defeat When competition becomes its own fanaticism, all the w ips of moderation come off.

Former San Diego running back Paul Lowe told of being threatened with fines unless he took pep pills and steroids. Lowe, who testified at America's first official government inquiry into athletic drug abuse—held in 1970 by California's Legislative Subcommittee on Drug Abuse and Alcoholism—later asked for and was given amphetamines as a player for the Kansas City Chiefs. "I thought I performed better with them," he said. The same subcommittee heard that half of the University of California at Berkeley football team had tried amphetamines and more than a quarter (28 per cent) had used steroids.

More recently, Washington Redskin Bill Brundige decided on painkilling injections to help his team into the 1977 playoffs. Brundige subsequently required an operation, was sidelined for the entire 1978 season, and may never play again because of the hobbling pain in his left foot. "I did it because I felt I had to do it," Brundige told the *Washington Post*'s Leonard Shapiro. "I felt an obligation to the guys I was playing with . . . but it was my choice. And every athlete at one time or another has to make a choice." Added Redskin wide receiver Charlie Taylor: "There are times as a professional athlete where you have to protect your job. You can't wait six weeks for mother nature to do her stuff."

Former San Francisco 49er quarterback John Brodie took Dapprisal—a combination amphetamine–barbiturate since withdrawn from the market—for two years to relieve the tendonitis in his arm. Brodie believes his use of the medication drifted into a continuing pattern when he became convinced "that my whole existence depended on my ability to throw a football. When I realized that my whole existence ¹idn't depend on that, I was okay. Football and a lot of other things began to look better."

There have been cases of addiction and excessive use. Joe Gilliam, the talented young quarterback who for a time threatened to replace the Pittsburgh Steelers' Terry Bradshaw, fell victim to drug abuse. Gene "Big Daddy" Lipscomb, a member of the same team a decade before, died of an apparent overdose. In the past year, three American basketball players died in Rome from reported drug overdoses.

But the real dangers for most players are far more subtle. Consider Evonne Goolagong, hailed for her courage after playing—with the help of a painkilling procaine injection—an entire Virginia Slims Tournament with severe blisters, a damaged arch, and bursitis at the base of her Achilles' tendon. Nothing was said of the risk—or the wisdom—of numbing the area before strenuous competition. Joseph D. Godfrey, team physician for the Buffalo Bills, believes that precontest anesthetic injections virtually ensure that players will hurt themselves more seriously. "You don't give aspirin and then tell a man to go bang his head," the doctor told *The Physician and Sportsmedicine* magazine in June 1978. "This is worse. It invites damage by reducing inhibitions."

"Drugs should be used only to cure, control, and comfort," believes Dr. James M. Glick, a San Francisco orthopedic surgeon and sports medicine specialist. "They should never be used to increase performance." *The Physician and Sportsmedicine* has warned repeatedly against direct tendon injections of the type given Goolagong, yet such treatment continues because medications pumped directly into a muscle or joint can help get a player back into action faster. In the opinion of most physicians they also boost the likelihood of more serious injuries. In

Goolagong's case the apparent result was searing pain during the Wimbledon matches and the prospect of prolonged recuperation.

The quest for a chemical advantage has led thousands of athletes to abuse anabolic steroids, hormone compounds initially developed to fatten cattle. Despite evidence to the contrary, many athletes claim the steroids add dozens of pounds of plastic muscle to their frames and make them stronger and faster as well. Doctors warn that steroids have been linked to at least three fatal diseases, including cancer of the liver, and that even small doses (as little as 10 milligrams per day), taken for only a few months, have been known to cause liver damage. In males, steroids shrink testicles and interfere with sperm production; in females, the drugs' effects include masculinization, disruption of puberty, irregular menstrual cycles, and enlargement of the clitoris.

Nonetheless, an estimated 99 per cent of the world's top body builders use steroids, and high school football players have been known to gulp doses of up to 60 milligrams per day. At the end of 1978, Europe was embroiled in steroid scandals involving some of the continent's most prominent male and female runners, gymnasts, swimmers, shot-putters, and discus throwers. Five world-class athletes, including Russia's Nadia Tkacenko, world record holder in the pentathalon, were banned permanently from competition for flunking steroid tests.

Renate Neufeld, twenty, an Olympic-class East German sprinter who defected to the West, claimed she was forced to take steroids as part of her training. In her statement, the first by a major East German athlete to confirm widespread rumors of hormone abuse in that country, Neufeld cited side effects including hardening of her leg muscles, periodic voice loss, hair growth on her upper lip, and frequent irregularities in her menstrual cycle.

As they swallowed steroids, football players grew in physical stature, an increase in size blamed by some for directly contributing to the game's escalating violence. Today's average professional linemen stand almost seven inches taller and weigh nearly a fifth more than they did thirty years ago. But football players today also carry a greater percentage of blubber than in the days of Sid Luckman and Johnny Lujack. "In our quest for giant-size players," asked a pair of St. Cloud University researchers in Minnesota, "are we placing too much emphasis on body weight alone, thus inducing the athlete to add more than desirable amounts of body fat in a misguided effort to weigh more?" When Alan Page, the Minnesota Vikings' dozen-season star lineman, started a jogging program, his weight dropped to 220 pounds, and he was traded away—his position filled by a 263-pound replacement. Another steroid-related question: does a connection exist between excess weight and the high incidence of hypertension recorded among football players? "The tendency," wrote *Rip Off the Big Game* author Paul Hoch in summing up widespread use of the drugs in football, "seems to be toward the production of plastic supermen with no balls."

Playing field violence has never been more clearly depicted than in federal judge Samuel Conti's San Francisco courtroom in July 1977. The case: a $2 million slander suit against Steeler coach Chuck Noll by Oakland Raider George Atkinson. A strong safety with a tough-guy reputation on and off the field, Atkinson sued Noll after the coach branded him as part of a "criminal element" in the NFL. Noll's statement followed a September 12, 1976, Oakland–Pittsburgh game in which Atkinson struck Steeler wide receiver Lynn Swann, one of pro football's smaller players and the previous victim of three concussions, from behind. Swann sustained another concussion and was forced out of the game. "George Atkinson's hit on Lynn Swann was with intent to maim and not with football in mind," charged Noll. "I'd like to see those guys thrown out of the league. They put a guy's whole career in jeopardy."

The trial opened with one of Atkinson's attorneys describing football as "a violent . . . physical-injury producing, legally approved method of combat" whose "warriors" bend the rules "based upon the conduct one finds on the field at any given time." A parade of plaintiff witnesses testified to the brutality of the game, including fifteen-season former Raider center Jim Otto. Big, kind-hearted "Double O" estimated he had been the victim of as many as twenty concussions, some of them serious enough to bring on temporary bouts of amnesia. Doctors had warned that he should quit the game to preserve his intelligence, said Otto, but he played anyway. He blamed illegal late hits for most of his nine knee operations and once was kicked so viciously in the side that he had to be carried from the field. Fouls, testified Otto and others, were committed on almost every play, usually without penalty.

Commissioner Pete Rozelle of the NFL had sought to keep the matter out of the courtroom "in the interests" of the game. Now he took the stand, attempting to reconcile his own official finding that the Atkinson hit had been "devastating and illegal" with a public claim that most NFL violence was not "criminal." At every step the evidence seemed to contradict him. Game films reeled off a montage of illegal late hits, forearm smashes to the head, players being snatched up like flour sacks by huge defensive behemoths and thrown down after the whistle. A videotape of Atkinson breaking New England tight end Russ Francis's nose in four places during a playoff game drew a gasp from the courtroom. Lance Alworth, for a decade perhaps the game's greatest outside receiver, testified that premier pass catchers are harassed by defensive backs, who intimidate foes with continuous verbal abuse and "by hitting you as much as they feel they can get away with." In his own case, said Alworth, he accepted the violence as part of the game. "But, the better I got, I felt like the dirtier the players tried to get with me."

Nothing, however, could compare to the remarkable testimony of Chuck Noll. Under the aggressive questioning of plaintiff attorney Daniel S. Mason, the Pittsburgh coach may have offered the most ironic indictment ever made of a major sport.

MASON: Well, let me—let me ask you, coach Noll: at the beginning of this examination, you said that Atkinson and Tatum . . . out of the twelve hundred players in the National Football League, two; Mr. Atkinson and Tatum are criminals because they willfully and they wantonly violate the rules. And I asked you, coach Noll: is there anybody else? And you said: I can't think of anybody. But now you say that: . . . . yes, Mel Blount [a Pittsburgh player] took his forearm when the play was over, and he went behind Cliff Branch—who weighs some 45 pounds less than him—and he took that arm, and in a propelling motion, smashed it against the head of Cliff Branch. And the play was over.

Now, coach Noll, to be fair—and you are fair minded—can we add Mel Blount to this list? Is he one of Noll's NFL criminals?

NOLL: You have the chalk, sir.

MASON: Well, let me ask you: I want you to tell me, coach Noll. You have started what is known as a club in the NFL. And that club is called the criminal element of the NFL; and Mr. Atkinson is part of it, and Mr. Tatum is part of it. We want to add to that if that's the proper and correct thing to do.

Is Mel Blount a criminal element?

NOLL: Every time an official throws a flag, he's accusing a player of what I said.

MASON [after a brief exchange]: Can we add to this list?

NOLL: Yes.

MASON: Is Mel Blount a criminal?

NOLL: Put it up there.

MASON: Is he—

NOLL: Yes.

MASON [after a mutual exchange of charges and bickering]: Is Glen Edwards "aggressive"?

NOLL: Yes.

MASON: Is he "hard hitting"?

NOLL: Yes.

MASON: Does Glen Edwards play for your team?

NOLL: Yes.

MASON: Is he part of the criminal element?

NOLL: He falls into the same category . . . If you want to go on, and make lists, you can add anybody you would like.

MASON [following an exchange over the words "willfully" and "wantonly" and whether Edwards could be called "courageous"]: Tell me, Mr. Noll, was Glen Edwards courageous when he smashed Ken Anderson in the face with his fist, as Ken Anderson was running out of bounds in Cincinnati? Was that courageous? [According to earlier testimony, Anderson was sidelined for the season.]

NOLL: It was a very hard tackle.

MASON: It was a hard tackle. It was a smash to the face. [Another exchange.] Now, you saw Ernie Holmes smash Pete Banazak on the ground that day in the film, didn't you? Do you remember that play?

NOLL: I remember that play, yes . . .

MASON: . . . the Pittsburgh Steelers' technique of defensive tackling says that when a player on the Oakland Raiders is being tackled, Ernie Holmes's job is to come around and take his fist, and deliberately club . . . the runner, as he's being tackled by another player. Is that what you are saying? It was part of the tackle and Ernie Holmes was helping?

NOLL: I didn't say that at all, sir.

MASON: You didn't say that.

NOLL: That's not close to what I said.

MASON: You remember Commissioner Rozelle sending a letter to Ernie Holmes on that play, don't you?

NOLL: Yes, I do.

MASON: He said he deliberately clubbed him. You recall that, Coach Noll?

NOLL: Yes, I do.

MASON: You don't recall that you said: yes, you agree, Ernie Holmes took his fist, deliberately clubbed Banazak in the face when Banazak was on the ground.

NOLL: Well, the film that I just reviewed and saw yesterday, he didn't take his fist and do it . . .

MASON: He did it with his entire arm, didn't he? It wasn't just his fist, but it was his entire arm. Do I stand corrected?
NOLL: I know it wasn't his fist; I don't know exactly what part of his body.

After four hours of deliberation, the four woman–two man jury rejected Atkinson's suit. Steelers attorney James Martin MacInnis hailed the decision as a vindication of Noll "that could serve as an impetus to end unnecessary violence in football." In truth, of course, it was nothing of the sort. For the first time, professional football players in America had undergone hostile cross-examination under oath about conditions in their sport. The picture which emerged was smeared with the dark emotions of men who long ago gave up any pretense of knowing the meaning of play. The game they said they love was shown to depend on hair-splitting legal definitions to legitimize brutal injuries. Noll escaped at least partly because a plaintiff's attorney got him to admit that virtually the entire sport was corrupt.

Signs exist, however, that the law is closing in on the savage excesses in our sports.* For one thing, courts appear more

* In an August 17, 1979, decision that could have far-reaching implications, a federal court jury awarded Houston basketball player Rudy Tomjanovich $3.3 million in an injury suit against his assailant, Kermit Washington. Not only was the amount $700,000 more than Tomjanovich had sought—a relatively uncommon occurrence—but the jury also found specifically that Washington's team (the Los Angeles Lakers) had been negligent in handling players "with a tendency for violence." The team, the jury said, "failed to adequately train and supervise its employee" (former Laker coach Jerry West testified that nothing was said before or after the incident to Washington about controlling his temper). The Lakers, according to the jury, were "negligent . . . by retaining Kermit Washington [subsequently traded] if they became aware that he had a tendency for violence." Washington testified he saw a "blur coming directly at me. I didn't know who it was. The blow was a reaction." Though further court action was scheduled—the Rockets filed an accompanying lawsuit seeking recovery of lost earnings while Tomjanovich was sidelined—Houston general manager Ray Patterson predicted the initial jury decision would help clarify the difference between violence and normal, physically aggressive play in the NBA. "In the past the distinction separating acts like this and the game itself was quite hazy," he said. "I think 90 per cent of NBA fights are not that at all. In 90 per cent of the fights one person is trying to defend himself. The aggressor should be punished more often."

willing to distinguish between injuries which must be assumed as a risk of the game and those for which a player
cannot be held responsible. The nation's football helmet
manufacturers face between $116 million and $150 million in
negligence megasuits, a figure the industry claims exceeds its
own annual gross by 500 per cent. Helmet maker Riddell,
Inc. of Chicago paid $40,000 for liability insurance in 1975;
three years later the company expected premiums of $1.5
million.

Minnesota county attorney Gary Flakne dragged Davey
Forbes before the bar despite a decision by then National
Hockey League President Clarence Campbell to suspend
Forbes for ten games (this for a blow that very nearly took his
victim's eyesight). At the time, Campbell called Flakne's action embarrassing to hockey and insisted that civil authorities
were not equipped to discipline participants for behavior during games. But Flakne argued that, by bringing the case to
trial, the sports world had been put on notice. "The mere act
of putting on a uniform and entering the sports arena should
not serve as a license to engage in behavior which would
constitute a crime if committed elsewhere," Flakne said, after
the case ended in a hung jury. "If a participant in a sporting
event were allowed to feel immune from criminal sanction
merely by virtue of his being a participant, the spirit of maiming and serious bodily injury, which at present occurs all too
frequently in a sport such as hockey, may well become the
order of the day. It is ludicrous to think that anything short of
criminal sanctions will deter conduct that is criminal in its
character."

The issue is gathering a desperate momentum. Violent de-
lights have violent ends, Shakespeare said. Sports are no different. Professional and world-class athletes today are out-
stripping evolution. In almost all sports players now weigh
more and have gained windbreaking speed. Athletes today
are, quite simply, the strongest, fastest, biggest race of giants

the world has known. Physically, it is a small step from grabbing a face mask and jabbing at an opponent's eyeballs, from slashing at a foe with a hockey stick or throwing a Sunday in the key, to—in Noll's words—playing with the principal intent to maim. If moral and legal constraints fail to keep pace with the incredible development of players' bodies, how long will it be before the superdome freaks start killing each other?

There are places where this already is happening. In Mexico not long ago, Felix German Torres, a twenty-five-year-old soccer player, made an obscene gesture at opposing University of Guadalajara players during a hotly disputed contest. They surrounded him en masse, kicking and beating him in the head and chest until he died, strangling on his own vomit. Not far away, a "friendship game" was held between a pair of rural amateur soccer teams. Only four minutes remained in the contest when referee José Morales, forty, called a foul against the hometown club of Otumba and awarded the visitors a free penalty shot. Rocks and stones were strewn near the playing field, and four of the Otumba players decided to use them. They pelted Morales with the stones until he crumpled against the sun-burned grass. Then they beat and stoned him until he was dead.

3 Coaches

There is no room for second place. I have finished second twice in my time at Green Bay and I don't ever want to finish second again. There is a second-place bowl game, but it's a game *for* losers, played *by* losers. It is and always has been an American zeal to be first in anything we do, and to win and to win and to win.

—Vince Lombardi

The lights come up in the makeshift screening room just as the last of the flickering, black-and-white stacks of corpses have been shoved into the long rows of trenches that will serve as their graves. Richard Alagich, thirty-two-year-old Sydney, Australia, soccer coach, turns to his players. "Just imagine that was your father, mother, son, or daughter," he says, "and go out and avenge them." Alagich has shown his team film clips of the shooting and mass burial of hundreds of Jews at Auschwitz in preparation for a grudge match against the Amelita Eagles, a traditional rival. "The idea," he explains later, "was that they should seek revenge for the concentration camp victims." Outraged, Jewish leaders warn against cheapening the dreadful lessons of World War II. But the only lesson of importance to Alagich has been proven: his team, losers to the Eagles earlier in the year, wins the rematch, 1–0.

The pursuit of victory has not always been so maniacal, nor has the behavior of coaches bordered so closely on psychosis. There was a time, at least in the amateur ranks, when good sportsmanship counted for more than an out-of-fashion caveat. No better example exists than the famous "fifth down" game between Cornell and Dartmouth in 1940.

Undefeated, ranked number one nationally, Cornell had been a two-plus touchdown favorite. But the Big Red was trailing, 3–0, when it drove to the Dartmouth five with less than a minute to play. Dartmouth held off Cornell for four plays, but the referee mistakenly awarded the offense an extra down. Cornell quarterback Walt School made the most of the break, completing a touchdown pass to Bill Murphy, and the game ended, 7–3.

In the ensuing outcry Dartmouth protested, but even some of those present at the game, played in a raging snowstorm, believed offsetting penalties had been called, giving Cornell the extra down. But when Cornell coach Carl Snavely and athletic director Robert Kane reviewed the game films, the circumstances were indisputable: Cornell had won illegally, on the last play. Kane and Snavely spoke to the university president and players and told them the school had no choice but to give up the victory. The decision was wired to Dartmouth coach Red Blaik and the concession publicly announced; only bookies refused to accept the switch.

How difficult it is to imagine the same spirit prevailing today. Think of the incredulous surprise, the disbelief, if the Oakland Raiders had offered to concede their last-play 21–20 win over the San Diego Chargers in 1978. The victory came on a fumble play that everybody, including the Raiders, admitted was illegal. Still, the win stood in the record books. In the twisted philosophy of professional football, the Raiders had come out on top; the legitimacy of their victory was beside the point. "That last play's in our playbook," bragged

Oakland guard Gene Upshaw after the contest. "It's called 'Win—at any cost.'"

Is it surprising that cruelty and superstition have accompanied such an attitude? After losing to Navy for five years straight, the entire Army football team met secretly at West Point's Michie Stadium in the middle of the night, slit their left thumbs with razor blades, and pressed their spurting digits onto a football. The team carried the red-stained pigskin to every season game in 1977, and their blood oath paid off in a 17–14 win over the Middies.

Baylor University coach Grant Teaff popped a five-inch earthworm in his mouth—then spat the creature aside—to inspire his players during their 1978 game with favored University of Texas (Baylor won 38–14). But Larry Canady, football coach at Eau Gallie High School in Florida, went even further. He chomped the heads off live frogs to build his team into a frenzy. "Our kids love it," Canaday remarked. "They say look how wild the coach is, let's get wild too."

Canaday's inspirational tactics reportedly included slicing his own head open with a razor blade; nonetheless, they had earned him high praise among parents for developing hard-hitting, emotion-charged teams. In fact, Canaday's stunts had been common knowledge around the small community for years, but when local newspapers and radio stations started spreading the story, school authorities ordered the coach to stop.

Parents of Canaday's team members rushed to his defense, some even bringing him frogs for future motivational decapitations. "I don't see the harm in it," one mother told a local newspaper reporter. "After all, he didn't *eat* the frogs." Added the father of another player: "I have no objection to it. It gets down to a question of where do you draw the line. Certainly if he brought a dog out there and cut his head off, we'd all be against it. But I think he's kept it within limits." The coach complied with the school officials' order, but insisted his techniques were being singled out by "certain intellects as an excuse to pick on football."

Indeed, Canaday's practices do seem gentle compared to those reported in Florida's *St. Petersburg Times* a few years ago. The story announced the resignations of twenty-eight scholarship football players at Florida State because of the school's brutal winter hardening drills. As recounted by James A. Michener in *Sports in America:*

The class, presumably voluntary but actually obligatory, if anyone wanted to keep his scholarship, met five times a week for six weeks, in a bare room in which a chicken-wire false ceiling had been suspended four feet from the floor. Under this, pairs of wouldbe football players were shoved to engage in what amounted to almost mortal combat, which was continued until one emerged clearly victor. Then the loser had to face a fresh combatant, and stay under the wire clutching and clawing and spitting blood until he finally defeated someone . . . the final loser, who had been able to conquer no one, was forced to rise at dawn next morning and race up and down the steep stadium steps ten or twenty times.

Coaches stand at the center of such atrocities because they are the teachers of sports. But coaches in most major sports, even at the amateur level, are under tremendous daily pressure to produce victories. Excuses, even proof that a loss came as the result of an opponent's illegal play, cannot justify defeat. Athletic viciousness thus becomes a tool of self-preservation, the encouragement of violence a part of player training. Former Washington Redskins coach George Allen once said following a brawl between his team and the St. Louis Cardinals that he "loved the fight . . . if we didn't go out there and fight, I'd be worried. You go out there and protect your teammates. The guys who sit on the bench, they're the losers." Allen admitted encouraging an intra-clubhouse bout during his first tour as coach of the Los

Angeles Rams "just to get 'em going, just to get 'em all together . . . It's all part of winning."

At the hockey-violence trial of Dave Forbes, his Boston Bruins coach Don Cherry conceded his pregame pep talk may have helped hype up the atmosphere that ended in the savage attack on Henry Boucha. "It has always been my philosophy to win at all costs," Cherry testified in recalling his locker room speech. The coach felt his own future was at stake: "We'd been losing games. We really had to win. The pressure was on me, and if the pressure is on me, it's on the players."

Vince Lombardi drove his players without mercy to prove his theory that "winning isn't everything, it's the only thing"—a line first uttered by John Wayne in the 1953 film *Trouble Along the Way*. In training camp, Lombardi was the brutal master of the "two-a-day," morning and afternoon exercise sessions that included torturous "up–down" grass drills in which players run in place, knees high, and then, on the "down" command, fling themselves face forward onto the turf. He taught his players to deny pain and to conceal their injuries from families, friends, even wives. A true Green Bay Packer never quit because of injury, even if, as Jerry Kramer recounts in *Instant Replay,* that meant playing with broken ribs.

In a very real sense, Vincent Thomas Lombardi politicized victory on the playing field in the same way Douglas MacArthur politicized victory in combat. Long before both, coaches and generals had played and fought to win. In the 1940s and 1950s there had been Frank Leahy and Paul Brown in football, Casey Stengel in baseball, and Kentucky's immortal Adolph Rupp in basketball. But Lombardi brought to winning a moral rightness, and he made losing seem somehow cowardly and traitorous. It was Lombardi who lifted the pigskin sport to the level of a holy war and made losing the equivalent of death. He froze innovation in football, turning the game inward, back toward the fundamental plays that carried less risk of mistake. For his brand of football, Lombardi demanded that players concentrate on basics—a running back would practice endlessly passing the ball from his left hand across his body to his right hand, and linemen would repeat minute blocking changes dozens of times. But most importantly, Lombardi insisted upon groveling obedience and told his troops to offer football their souls. "To play this game you must have fire in you," said Lombardi, "and there is nothing that stokes fire like hate." The result? Kramer tells how he felt toward the Dallas Cowboys' defensive end George Andrie, who recovered a Green Bay fumble and scored during the 1967 NFL championship game:

Forrest Gregg tackled Andrie just as he crossed the goal line, and I was only a step or two behind Forrest, and I suddenly felt the greatest desire to put both my cleats right on Andrie's spinal cord and break it. We had been victimized by these stupid plays—scooped up fumbles, deflected passes, blocked kicks, high school tricks—so many times during the season that I felt murderous. I'd never in my career deliberately stepped on a guy, but I was so tempted to destroy Andrie, to take everything out on him, that I almost did it. A bunch of thoughts raced through my mind—I'd met Andrie off the field a few times and I kind of liked him—and, at the last moment, I let up and stepped over him.

The Lombardi ethic may not be as fashionable as it once was, but it still can be seen in the contorted, angry faces of Little League, Pop Warner, and junior hockey coaches and in the boot-camp style of professional training camps.

The working environment of most coaches is a temple-pounding, heart-stopping killer, a pressure cooker that can, and often does, translate into violent behavior on and off the field. The self-immolation of Woody Hayes, his career finally bursting into flames at the 1979 Gator Bowl, followed years of brush-fire temper tantrums. Only a year before, millions of television viewers saw the Ohio State University coach slam

down his telephone, then charge an ABC television cameraman during his team's loss to Michigan State. The picture
swung wildly out of control as Hayes aimed a punch at the
cameraman's midsection. The blow was blocked, but some of
Woody's other victims haven't been so lucky: in 1959, a
Hayesmaker slammed a local sports writer against a locker
room wall after Ohio was defeated by USC; in 1973, Art
Rogers, a *Los Angeles Times* photographer, reportedly had his
camera crammed into his face by Hayes; in 1976, Hayes
allegedly grabbed a Michigan State student newspaper reporter by the throat and just two months before the Gator Bowl
incident, Hayes threatened a Columbus, Ohio, newscaster,
then walked out in the middle of a televised interview.

Other coaches, by far the majority, take the tension out on
themselves. The University of Colorado's Bill Mallory
slammed the blackboard so hard during a half-time talk that
he fractured his hand. Ara Parseghian told reporters he was
emotionally exhausted when he gave up his coaching post at
Notre Dame. "My doctor didn't order me to quit," said Parseghian. "But I found myself taking blood pressure pills,
tranquilizers, and sleeping pills, and that's not right. So I
backed off and said, 'What the hell is happening?' It's not a
twelve-month job; it's more than that. You can't understand
the demands of this job until you walk in the shoes of the man
who has it."

A festering ulcer that burned its way through the lining of
his stomach forced John Madden, the Oakland Raiders' 103-
game-winning coach, into retirement in 1979. Often
exhausted, wracked by internal bleeding and painful stomach
spasms, Madden could no longer get through a day without
Maalox. According to one report, the popular coach nearly
collapsed after his team's 1978 playoff loss to Miami and had
to be helped to the Raiders' bus.

Basketball coaches may well face the most searing trial of
all. Played in tiny, packed arenas, before highly partisan fans,

and with outcomes more closely tied to referee's calls than either baseball or football, basketball can generate nightmarish tensions. "You just want to pick up a baseball bat, turn off all the lights, and start swinging at anybody and everybody," said former Boston Celtics coach Tom Heinsohn in explaining the pressure to keep pace with the Washington Bullets a few years ago.

Of 202 top college basketball coaches in 1967, only twenty were still in their jobs in 1978, according to a recent Associated Press survey. Typical was University of Detroit coach Dick Vitale. Though still in his thirties and a self-described "tough Italian," Vitale was forced out of college coaching because of severe stomach disorders. Three bouts of internal bleeding, in which he lost two, four, and six pints of blood, respectively; a stay in intensive care; and a final, major intestinal attack convinced him to leave the game rather than "stand on the sidelines and rip my guts." When Vitale returned to basketball, accepting a job with the NBA's Detroit Pistons, he lasted less than two games before being hospitalized again. Indeed, one of the NBA's winningest coaches, the Denver Nuggets' Larry Brown, resigned early in 1979 because of "very severe physical problems."

Pete Newell, former basketball mentor at the University of San Francisco, Michigan State University, and the University of California at Berkeley, left coaching under doctors' orders after making a name for himself as the game's number-one towel chewer. "The towel was a psychological crutch," says Newell, now general manager of the Los Angeles Lakers. Newell would use half the towel to dry his hands, but kept the other half soaked in water to suck on. "Later I found that I could avoid technicals by saying what was on my mind into the towel. Ultimately, I was chewing on it, and it became my trademark." Ironically, Newell's most serious health problems were caused by not eating. Lack of nutrition due to pregame tension brought him "perilously close" to a complete physical breakdown, Newell told *The Physician and Sportsmedicine* in January 1976.

Medical researchers in South Carolina monitored thirty football and basketball coaches in 1969. During games, their average heart rate jumped sixty-three beats per minute, nearly doubling the typical normal rate of seventy-two beats per minute. Studies at Brigham Young University's Fitness for Life Program found that head basketball coaches experienced heart rates as much as 44 per cent higher than their assistants. The BYU researchers recommended all coaches take part in exercise programs to prevent heart attacks. In fact, when Michigan's Bo Schembechler and Ohio State's Woody Hayes squared off, the rivals did so as heart patients. Schembechler underwent quadruple coronary bypass surgery at the age of forty-seven and Hayes suffered a heart attack in preparing for his twenty-fourth season at OSU in 1975. They were the lucky ones. The Oakland Raiders' conditioning coach, Alvin Roy, fifty-nine, and UCLA's Mike Mikolayunas, thirty, a quarterback and receiver coach, died of heart attacks on the same day—April 27, 1979.

Perhaps because of their own suffering, many coaches regard the denial of pain by their players as crucial to a winning attitude. "The harder you work, the harder it is to surrender," said Lombardi, who warned players weary of his body-breaking workouts not to give up. "Once you learn to quit," he said, "it becomes a habit."

Not surprisingly, this attitude has led to some dangerous myths about training, leading to regimens which may well achieve the coach's purpose of turning a player into a raging animal—if they don't kill him first. The most pernicious of these myths concerns hot-weather training and the withholding of water.

Joe Kuharich was called "the Barracuda" at the University of San Francisco in the early 1950s. When he took his club to 115-degree Corning, California, for hot-weather training,

Kuharich added oatmeal to the team's water to prevent players from drinking it. Kuharich himself once described the effort of his waterless regimen on a burly fullback who looked as if he had been turned to stone. "He got into a crouch and just froze there—he'd lost all the salt in his body. . . . For a while, we thought he'd had it."

The fear was not unreasonable. Heat stroke has killed more than fifty football players in the last decade and ranks second to spinal injuries as a cause of death among high school athletes. "When the football player or [military] recruit has died of heat stroke, it is common to find evidence of punitive drills, carelessness, ignorance or a 'don't give a damn' attitude," reported Dr. James P. Knochel in the August 11, 1975, *Journal of the American Medical Association.* Dr. Knochel, professor of internal medicine and associate chief of staff for research at the Veterans Administration Medical Center in Dallas, identified seven "old coaches' tales" that could kill a football player. Topping the list: hot-weather practice sessions and withholding water.

While physicians generally agree such punitive training practices are less widespread today, they remain in use by a disturbing number of coaches.* Players still wear excessive clothing on hot days, practice when the temperature and humidity far exceed allowable limits, and work out during the worst heat of the day. "It would seem that whatever disaster befalls a young man, it is regarded as some type of heroism, like a soldier dying in action," says Dr. Knochel. "Despite all the warnings, coaches have sent their players, particularly large linemen, to run laps in plastic sweat suits because they returned to fall practice in an overweight condition. Players have developed temperatures in excess of 108 degrees and died. Yet there was little if any repercussion toward the coaches involved. What would happen if a construction fore-

---

* See Howard Cosell report in Chapter 7, "Victims."

man ordered his men to wear impermeable clothing while working and they died of heat stroke?"

Imagine the consternation among the Los Angeles Rams medical staff when newly rehired coach George Allen, one of the most successful men at his trade, turned out to be a hot-weather conditioning devotee. Taking command in the summer of 1978, Allen quickly instituted a grueling schedule of "two-a-days" that lasted almost three hours longer than those of his predecessor, Chuck Knox. Practicing at a hot, smog-choked camp in the heart of the Los Angeles basin, Rams players were placed on the reward system for water— they had to earn each drink. Team doctors begged Allen to institute water breaks. On a single July afternoon, seven players collapsed; all required emergency treatment because their body liquids had dropped to the dehydration point. "George just rams the accelerator down to the floor, like Mario Andretti," one L.A. player told the *Los Angeles Times.* "If the car lasts, it lasts; if not, he just throws it away and gets a new car." In this case, the car got a new driver: Allen was fired after just two games of the exhibition season, his spartan training methods an important reason for his dismissal.

It would be one thing if these practices were merely foolish, but they are part of a misguided approach to training that endangers the lives of thousands of players annually. In his *JAMA* report, Dr. Knochel cited other ways of killing a football player besides holding drills in the heat of the day and denying water. Among them: encouraging the use of salt tablets in large numbers, even in the absence of water; giving obese players diuretics for fast weight loss; requiring players to wear full uniforms on hot, humid days; prolonging wind sprints until players vomit, have muscle cramps, or collapse; looking the other way when players take amphetamines. Sadly, these practices are actively employed in training programs around the country and each year claim the lives of a number of teenage athletes and military recruits. One can only

guess at the outcry that would have resulted had a member of
the Los Angeles Rams perished in George Allen's smoggy
oven in Fullerton.

In their extensive study of high school teams in North
Carolina, Carl S. Blyth and Frederick O. Mueller found that
fewer than half of the coaches gave water to their teams at
recommended thirty- or forty-five-minute intervals during
preseason practice, despite blazing mid-August heat. The
largest group, 34.1 percent, gave water only once during
practice, and, incredibly, one coach gave no water at all. Of
the coaches who gave salt additives, the majority did so at the
wrong times. The study also suggested that rough Monday
workouts, often scheduled as punishment for a loss the previous Friday night or Saturday, were clearly associated with
higher injury rates.

Perhaps more intriguing, it was found that teams coached by
physical-education majors experienced no fewer injuries than
those led by coaches who had majored in Romance literature,
history, or Oriental art. In fact, the lowest injury rates occurred
on teams with coaches who had minored in physical education.
"Our data failed to establish a significant relationship between a
coach's possession of a degree in physical education and a lower
injury rate among his players," said the researchers. "Perhaps
the universities and colleges preparing physical education
teachers should re-evaluate their criteria."

Few coaches have sophisticated knowledge of sports medicine, let alone proper conditioning and training methods. In
1978 only seven states*—two fewer than in 1970—required
that public school coaches be certified as to their competency
in the prevention and treatment of athletic injuries, according
to the *Journal of Physical Education and Recreation.* In other
states, faculty members without basic first-aid training
shoulder at least some of the coaching load. Some states don't

---

* Pennsylvania, Minnesota, Nebraska, Iowa, Wyoming, South Dakota, Indiana.

even require that coaches be certified teachers or, for that matter, employees of the school system.

Coaches were the first providers of health care in most cases of athletic injury, according to the Department of Health, Education, and Welfare report released in 1979. "Unfortunately," the report said, "the attention of coaches generally focuses on the practice or competition rather than on health care problems." The difficulty of the situation was underscored by another finding of the HEW study: fully 80 per cent of high schools and one-third of colleges with football programs did not have athletic trainers.

"Faced with a constantly expanding demand for sports programs at the same time school funds and enrollments have declined, we have gone backwards rather than forwards," says Gordon Jeppson, former program administrator for the National Association for Sports and Physical Education. Now physical-education chairman at Iowa's Simpson College, Jeppson believes the professionalism of coaches is intimately tied to an end to violence in sports. "Many of the problems occur because of something a coach initiates," he says. "Hopefully, well-qualified coaches would be less likely to enflame the situation, particularly in basketball, where there is a tendency toward constant protests of official decisions and excited outbursts. Coaches trained to recognize how their behavior affects participants in a game or the crowd could go a long way toward cooling things off and controlling their own inner pressures to win."

Even a simple understanding of sports injuries could reduce the brutal toll of some games. Iowa state researchers found medical consultation had not been obtained in almost half of the high school neck injuries they analyzed. X-rays rarely were taken, and in only a few cases were coaches even aware that neck injuries had been sustained. Less than 2 per cent of serious or fatal brain injuries in football have been traced to congenital defects or pre-existing tumors, yet the coaches' initial statements after such injuries often attribute the cause to abnormalities at birth.

In the annual survey of high school football fatalities, deaths are categorized in such a way that many fatalities, heat stroke and heart failure among them, escape classification as "directly" the result of football. "It appears quite logical to me that such fatalities are directly the consequence of football," says Dr. Knochel, "whether they are from heat, head injury, spinal-cord injury from a broken neck, or cardiac arrest . . . The term 'indirect' as applied to football deaths resembles statements such as 'Hand guns don't kill; people do.' "

Sports health care rates a low priority at most schools. Injured players in West Virginia were being carted from football fields to nearby hospitals in the same vehicles used to haul corpses by local funeral homes, according to a survey a few years ago by *The Physician and Sportsmedicine.* Everyone from school custodians to bakery-truck drivers acted as athletic trainers; in rural areas, doctors often were not even in attendance at varsity football games. At one small Oregon school, splints made by the school's shop class were used to mend athletes' broken arms and legs. "Pretty barbaric," was the magazine's terse summary.

Conditions today have improved somewhat for the general populace, with a rapid growth in sports medicine clinics and an increasing number of qualified athletic trainers. While this may be good news for middle-aged joggers, it hasn't really changed things for their teenage kids. Traditionally locker room outsiders or little fellows who couldn't make the team, trainers only now are emerging into full professionalism, and their presence is still to be felt in schools. Something less than fifty National Athletic Trainers Association–certified trainers are currently employed by American high schools, just a bit more than 1 per cent of NATA's nationwide membership. Only a few high schools have coaches on staff who have been certified by the association.*

"School administrators assume that every coach is qualified to handle athletic injuries—it's amazing how few are," comments an NATA-certified coach in southern California. When he first assumed his post, the coach said, at least half the ankle injuries were being incorrectly treated because coaches routinely taped all sprains in the same direction, regardless of which foot was injured or whether an inside or outside strain was involved. Many coaches persist in gorging their teams with huge steak dinners before games, despite evidence that carbohydrates require far less energy to digest. When it comes to injuries, says the California coach, most of his colleagues "don't know jack—they've had a two-unit class in college called 'Athletic Injuries' and that's it." Indeed, the federal government's first nationwide sports injury study found that 47 per cent of coaches in a sample survey were ill-prepared to provide sports health care, despite being relied upon to do so in 77 per cent of the high schools surveyed.

Conditions may be even worse in community sports programs outside the schools. A four-year, three-volume legislative study of youth athletics in Michigan, perhaps the most extensive ever undertaken by a governmental body in the United States, concluded in 1979. After sampling responses from thousands of youngsters between the ages of five and seventeen, the study concluded that school and community sports programs had done "little to provide for the health of

---

* NATA, which functions for trainers much the same as the AMA does for physicians, requires that certified members pass rigorous examinations in proper sideline procedures for immediate treatment of injuries, injury recognition and prevention, rehabilitation of injured athletes, proper fitting of equipment, and wrapping and taping for prevention of and protection against injuries—not to mention an advanced mastery of all aspects of first aid.

the athletes who participated in them . . . only 22 per cent were required to have physical examinations prior to participation, only 10 per cent had a medical consultant assigned to the leagues, less than one-half had adequate athletic training services, 27 per cent were not covered by any kind of insurance, approximately 75 per cent did not have a pre-season conditioning program . . . " A predictable result: nearly 30 per cent of the injuries to boys were broken bones.

"The alternative to contracted and periodic medical care is no care at all, and this seems to be the case to an alarming degree throughout the state," said Dr. Richard W. Redfearn in surveying athletic health care in Michigan schools. A biomechanics specialist at MSU's College of Osteopathic Medicine in East Lansing, Redfearn reported that less than half the 216 high schools he studied possessed a simple airway passage device, crucial in providing oxygen—thus preventing brain damage and possible death—in head and neck injuries.

While the slightest incorrect movement of a player's head in a case like Darryl Stingley's can mean paralysis or death, Redfearn found that 70 per cent of such emergencies were first handled by coaches who may not have had any medical training at all. "In Michigan, there is no accrediting agency to establish a minimum plateau of education, training or experience for a high school coach," Redfearn reported. ". . . The status quo has prevailed because of fiscal limitations and a willingness to allow high school players to live close to the edge of potential physical danger."

A willingness to allow high school athletes to live close to the edge of potential physical danger. Surely these words are as chilling as any written about sports, yet ample evidence exists to support Redfearn's contention. High school football officials waited more than a decade after physician researchers had warned them of the risks of hard-shell-helmet head blocking and tackling before outlawing the technique prior to the 1977 season.* Effective enforcement of the new regulation remains open to serious question. And "face-to-the-numbers" continues in college and pro ball despite reports from ex-players like Jerry Kramer and Jim Otto of their spines (and their height) being compacted by as much as two inches after years of ramming their skulls into opponents.

"Coaches love to recount examples of players who have played with serious injuries," writes Dave Meggyesy, former St. Louis Cardinal linebacker, in recalling his experiences at Syracuse University under legendary coach Ben Schwartzwalder. "Ben's favorite story was about Jim Ringo [later an All-Pro center with the Green Bay Packers]. According to Ben," Meggyesy recounts in *Out of Their League,* "Ringo played one game his senior year with infected boils covering both legs. Ben would emphasize that both Ringo's legs were covered with pus and blood when he came into the locker room at half time. According to Ben, Ringo did not once speak of the pain. He simply bandaged the draining boils, put on a clean pair of pants and went back out to play a great second half . . . In the Catch-22 world of football, as in war, this passes for reasonable behavior."

Players are encouraged not only to ignore pain, but to conceal it. The Denver Broncos withheld the true condition of quarterback Craig Morton, suffering from a hobbling hip injury, during the 1977 playoffs, and the Minnesota Vikings have, when the occasion demanded, been less than frank about the health of their former signal-caller, Fran Tarkenton. University of Nebraska football coach Bob Devaney, with

* "The practice of head-blocking and head-tackling known as 'spearing' must be examined carefully. Almost 61 per cent of the players with head injuries and 44.1 per cent of those with neck injuries were taught to spear . . . One must question the place of spearing in high school football."—Richard H. Alley, Jr., M.D., writing in the *Journal of the American Medical Association,* May 4, 1964.

"In surveying the group of 208 direct fatalities sustained during the 1947–1959 interval a slowly progressive shift occurred, with a . . . corresponding elevation of the mortality rate due to head and spinal cord injuries." —Richard C. Schneider, et al, "Serious and Fatal Football Injuries Involving the Head and Spinal Cord,"*JAMA,* August 12, 1961.

Alabama's Paul "Bear" Bryant concurring, cautioned a conference of university sports-information directors in 1978
against publicizing "things like injuries to key players that
aren't asked about."

Cruel training techniques, inadequate health and emergency care, the denial and concealment of injury—these are
the long strands of neglect which weave through the violence
in our sports. A brutality that begins with a lack of concern
for proper medical care in athletics, asks us to reject or
ignore the suffering of ourselves and others, quickly works its
way from the practice field into the stadium or arena. The
acceptance of savagery is contagious. Non-violent athletes are
forced to include a repertoire of viciousness among their own
skills. Basketball players learn to use their elbows and, if
need be, their fists. Basepath runners slide spikes-high, and
pitchers graze killer fastballs past men's ears. "Good" holding, "leg-whipping," and the well-timed forearm smash become part of the gridiron manual of arms. During a nationally
telecast football game in 1978, the commentator observes—with a passing note of regret—that one of the
teams is deliberately coached to clip, an outlawed, behind-
the-back tackle that can result in crippling knee injuries. A
team physician for the Atlanta Falcons explains why quarterback Steve Bartkowski leaves a game after someone has hung
onto his face mask: "People are taught to go for the eyeballs,
and they don't get caught."

Coaches have tolerated this new and hurtful illegality; it is
they who must help end it. Coaches are and should be the
parish priests of sport—the first to celebrate our progress, our
sternest critics when we fail. They are our teachers and, if we
grew up in a household where traditional male roles were
obscured by divorce and uncertainty, often our fathers as
well. Yet we have placed tremendous burdens on our
coaches. As sociologist Harry Edwards notes, we have asked
them to assume total liability for outcomes over which they
exert only limited control. We expect them to maintain abso-

lute values in academic settings where their colleagues have rejected those same qualities wholesale. We have undermined their disciplinary powers and placed them in stress-laden environments, under constant scrutiny by the media. Most of all, we have insisted, implored, demanded, that they win.*

Now we must hope that coaches will, like firm but gentle patriarchs, help lead us out of the wilderness. In its lengthy series on football brutality in 1978, *Sports Illustrated* expressed great pessimism that coaches would assume such leadership: "How many ribs were crushed and spleens ruptured before spearing [driving the crown of the helmet into a downed player] was disallowed? How much longer before the helmet is legislated out of the hit business entirely? How many ligaments were torn before crackback blocks were outlawed?"

It may be true that coaches have been notoriously resistant to change and that many remain so. But it is equally true that they have a big stake in seeing to it that a system of rules survives. The regulations in a sport comprise its structural spine, the form around which individual performers are free to shape their art. The corruption of that framework carries the risk that our games will lose their form and art and collapse in charade. We already have seen this happen in some sports, notably professional wrestling and roller skating, and there is reason to believe the same process may be underway in professional hockey and football. "If you wish to know what a man is," suggests an old Yugoslavian proverb, "place him in authority." If it is too much to depend on our coaches for compassion, perhaps we can rely on their own self-interest.

---

* "Less than seven wins will be considered unsatisfactory and a win over Navy is mandatory." That was an ultimatum beyond his contractual obligation to perform satisfactorily in his job, contended Army coach Homer Smith when he resigned in 1978. West Point, 4-5-1 going into the game, lost its December 3 contest with the Middies, 28–0, and Smith quit the next day.

Former Ohio State coach Woody Hayes, left, at the moment he struck Clemson player Charlie Bauman, as seen by an ABC-TV monitor. An instant later, Hayes's uncontrolled fury turned against one of his own players. The incident occurred in the 1978 Gator Bowl.

Texas Rangers manager Frank Lucchesi required plastic surgery after a slugging by infielder Lenny Randle. Here Lucchesi is shown recuperating from a triple fracture of his right cheekbone.

Chris Chambliss was besieged by fans after blasting a ninth-inning home run to capture the American League pennant for the New York Yankees in 1976.

Yankee Reggie Jackson and a few teammates had a harrowing run back to the dugout after winning the 1977 World Series in New York against the Los Angeles Dodgers.

Only incredible luck prevented this 1976 crash of a light plane in Baltimore's Memorial Stadium from becoming one of history's worst sports tragedies. The aircraft plummeted into the seats at 5:05 P.M. Only minutes before, thousands of fans had watched the Pittsburgh Steelers beat the hometown Colts, 40–14.

The ninth-inning "cheap beer" riot in Cleveland during a June 4, 1974, game between the Indians and Billy Martin's Texas Rangers was a harbinger of the fan violence that would sweep baseball parks in other cities, particularly New York.

This knife-wielding spectator was grabbed as he charged an umpire in a Babe Ruth League game in Sarasota, Florida, in 1978. The would-be assailant got away before police arrived.

Brazilian soccer great Pele had to be carried from Nickerson Field in Boston in 1975, after rampaging mobs left him with a pulled knee muscle and a twisted ankle.

Soccer fans panic in the worst stadium riot in history on May 25, 1964, in Lima, Peru. Peruvian authorities reported that 318 died, many from trampling and asphyxia.

A fraction of an inch more and the steel dart that lodged in the bridge of Peter Brookes's nose might have cost him an eye, authorities said. Brookes, a seventeen-year-old Manchester United supporter, was hit during a 1978 fight at the soccer stadium in Liverpool, England.

United Press International

The relative calm at London's Wembley Stadium during soccer cup finals in April 1923 is sadly missing at English soccer matches today. Because of its sheer size, the largest soccer crowd in history—estimated at 300,000—spilled out onto the playing field. But cool heads prevailed and only a small force of police preserved order among the thousands of fans.

Radio Times Hulton Picture Library

New Games: in Boffing the object is to pummel the daylights—and the hostility—out of one another with harmless styrofoam sabers.

New Games: Earth Ball is a tournament favorite. In a variation called Orbit, participants keep the huge ball in the air with their feet.

4 Fans

. . . And the small brawls became one big brawl, and the big brawl became a wholesale fight with a long roll call of dead and wounded. The episode was reported at Rome and Nero took it up. In the end, the ringleaders of the tumult were exiled, and amphitheatral shows were banned for ten years.

—Jack Lindsay, in *The Writing on the Wall, An Account of Pompeii in Its Last Days*

The great stadium riot at Pompeii, which preceded the eruption of Mt. Vesuvius by two decades, exploded during a horseback riding competition between rival youth groups. Before it ended, corpses stretched across the amphitheater floor and men in breastplates and plumed helmets fought with lances and swords in the corridors and stairwells. Some rioters were disgruntled war veterans, angry because the emperor had paid them in land rather than cash; others were rowdy youths, caught up in the emotions and violence. Afterward, official Rome tried to hush up the entire incident, but without success. The outburst was immortalized in frescoes, sketches, and history books.

Nineteen centuries later, on May 24, 1964, to be exact, referee R. Angel Pazos, standing on the floor of Peru's National Stadium in Lima, nullified a home-team goal during the final minutes of a pre-Olympic soccer playoff against Argentina. Peru was trailing, 6–1, when Pazos signaled the rough-play foul. Two Peruvian fans immediately scrambled over a wire barrier to the field, flailing their fists and screaming oaths, and thousands in the stands let out an ominous roar. Concerned for the players' saftey, Pazos halted the game. The events which followed ushered in a new era of spectator violence.

Screaming in rage, the crowd of nearly 50,000 persons surged out of the bleachers, hurling stones and bottles, smashing stadium windows, overturning benches, and leaving parts of the arena in flames. Mounted policemen lobbed tear-gas bombs, fired shots in the air, and released attack dogs in hopes of driving the fans toward the exits.*

When part of the crowd, a mob of nearly 12,000 persons, started tugging down the fence around the playing field, police opened up with tear-gas grenades and bullets, killing at least four persons on the spot. Now in complete panic, the fans rushed for the exits, only to find most still closed. Pushing and shoving, the mass of people became a grinding stampede, crushing those in front against the locked iron gates. The gates snapped under the pressure, but many people were trampled. Crawling and running over the broken, bleeding bodies of the dead—stacked six high in some places—the multitude spilled out into the street, turning over cars, sacking stores, and setting fire to a bus, numerous autos, two office buildings, and a small industrial plant. So many corpses lay inside the stadium that private cars were commandeered to haul the bodies to hastily established morgues in local hospitals. Outside, the crowds swirled in quickly gathering pools. "Revenge!" they cried. "Down with the police!"

* Pazos and the players found safety in a locker room beneath the stadium. From there they dashed into buses that sped to a remote part of the city.

Heavy police reinforcements finally brought the uprising under control. But all that Sunday night relatives streamed by the rows of dead, laid out in hospital corridors or any place there was room. The government launched a full-scale investigation, promised pensions to the families of riot victims, and said the state would pay for burial expenses. Even so, thousands of student Communists took to the streets, denouncing the action by stadium police. A long file of angry fans marched to the presidential palace, seeking official intervention in declaring the game a tie. Pope Paul VI, describing himself as a long-time sports enthusiast, pleaded with fans everywhere to help prevent similar tragedies; sports, said the pontiff, "must be without passion in the athletes and the public." It took nearly ten hours to complete mass burial rites, according to the *New York Times.* Jeeps, military trucks, and funeral cars clogged traffic around Lima cemeteries for miles. The toll in history's worst recorded sports riot: 318 dead, more than 500 injured.

"Every man has a mob self and an individual self, in varying proportions," wrote D. H. Lawrence. All across the globe, sports are driving people crazy, and no one seems sure exactly why. Shouting "I don't want to live anymore," a West Berlin man hurled himself through a second-story window when his team was defeated by Austria, 3–2, during the 1978 World Cup matches; a Catholic nun, member of the Merciful Sisters order, half-strangled a man who cheered the Austrian victory in a cafe near Frankfort. When her mate watched World Cup action on television rather than helping her in the kitchen, a French housewife blasted the luckless man's brains out with a shotgun.

In 1969, El Salvador and Honduras broke diplomatic relations and engaged in a brief "soccer war," triggered by the neighboring Central American nations' World Cup rivalry. When El Salvador won the second match (tying the three-game series at 1–1), rioting Honduran crowds attacked Salvadorians living in their country, sending a stream of more than 10,000 fleeing refugees into El Salvador and Nicaragua. Tensions were so high that the third and final game (El Salvador won, 3–2) was moved to Mexico City, hundreds of miles to the north. Even in that neutral territory, uneasy authorities assigned nearly 2,000 armed police to the game.

It would be less frightening if what we were seeing could be dismissed as deranged behavior limited to Europe and South America. Conditions may be worse in those places, but barmy off-the-field behavior exists in the United States too.

Consider the aura of extracurricular violence which pervaded every aspect of the 1979 Super Bowl. In a stroke of mindless programming, CBS television scheduled *Black Sunday* for prime-time screening shortly after the Super Bowl's final gun. That meant at least a week of pregame publicity about the movie, in which terrorists hijack a blimp and attempt a mass murder at the Super Bowl.

Captain Mike Cosgrove, head of host city Miami's twenty-four-member antiterrorist unit, spoke openly with the press about his fears over the game's potential for large-scale mayhem—and the training and weaponry his force could use to stop it. "Terrorism is coming," Cosgrove said as the NFL's promotion-conscious brass writhed in agony. "You're going to see it; it's just a matter of time." Pro football commissioner Pete Rozelle denied precautions for the game were anything other than routine, but a cordon of explosives experts with specially trained police dogs examined every inch of the stadium prior to kickoff. Standing by: a helicopter, Cosgrove's SWAT team, and more than two hundred uniformed and private police.*

---

* As it turned out, the worst Super Bowl violence happened outside the stadium. When Raymond L. Wilson, thirty-five, was denied admission to a special Super Bowl television party at Kelley's Bar in Louisville, Kentucky, he returned with a .45-caliber submachine gun. He opened fire on the tavern's two dozen patrons from outside the building, killing one person and seriously wounding two others.

"It was a tragedy," recalls Wayne Williamson, athletic director of the Hillsborough County school system in Florida. "I
knew both men and they were fine gentlemen." Williamson is
talking about Rudolph Burgess, forty-four, former business
manager at Tampa Bay Tech, and Hall Griffin, an assistant
principal at Hillsborough High. Burgess shot and killed the
forty-six-year-old Griffin during an argument at a football
match between the arch county rivals. The game, it may be
noted, continued uninterrupted. Now, in an interview more
than a year afterward, Williamson has dismissed the October
17, 1975, incident; it was, he insists, "just a freak thing."

Six days earlier and less than a hundred miles away, Edward
Murphy, a thirty-two-year-old boys' club football coach, had
won a four-hour battle for consciousness after a savage beating
by more than two dozen pipe-wielding spectators. The pack fell
upon Murphy after their team of twelve-year-olds, the South-
west Boys' Club Blazers, was defeated, 2–0, by his team of
twelve-year-olds, the Kissimmee Boys' Club Midgets. The
attackers did not leave until someone shouted Murphy was
dead. Three other Kissimmee coaches and a parent were
beaten. "The way they were swinging those pipes and clubs,
it's a miracle nobody was killed," said Alan Baker, one of the
victims. "I've never seen anything like that mob."

In Baltimore, it is December 19, 1976. Ben Roth hears a
buzzing sound and glances up. He may be the first person in
Memorial Stadium to spot the blue-and-white Piper
Cherokee as it swoops in above the rows of bleachers at the
north end. For a long instant on that late Sunday afternoon,
Roth simply gapes in disbelief. The small plane's engine
chews at the air less than fifty feet above the playing field, its
landing lights blazing at the assistant stadium manager and his
grounds crew. "Hey!" Roth shouts to the men tugging a tarp
over the field. "Get out of the way! This guy's coming in."

The aircraft, piloted by Donald N. Kroner, thirty-three, a

former commercial flier with a history of minor psychiatric difficulties, plows into the upper-deck seats, where, moments before, thousands of Colts fans had seen their Super Bowl hopes dashed in a 40–14 loss to the Pittsburgh Steelers. "We were very lucky," Jack Danahy, the National Football League's director of security, says later. "If it had happened six minutes earlier, we could have had one of history's worst sports tragedies on our hands."

As it is, Kroner and two policemen escape with minor injuries. But within hours it will be known that Kroner actually buzzed the stadium several times that afternoon in *two separate planes,* and an aircraft matching the Cherokee's markings made repeated low-flying passes over the field in the days immediately preceding the contest. Kroner openly boasted about a stunt he was planning at the stadium and hired a photographer to preserve the incredibly irresponsible act on film.

For days following the incident, those who protect the multitudes in their athletic arenas are struck by a sour-tasting sense of impotence. True, remedial action is quick to follow: Kroner is charged on three counts of reckless flying and destruction of property. Security—reflected in a circle of hovering police choppers at the following Super Bowl—tightens in the skies above stadiums. But the Kroner episode is unprecedented, and its grisly potential puts sports cops everywhere on notice. The madness in athletics differs little from that which has scarred the rest of society. Whatever is brutish and insane *out there,* sooner or later spills over, *into here.*

"There is no question about it," says Dr. David Bachman, Chicago Bulls team physician and director of Northwestern University's Center for Sportsmedicine, "the trend is toward more raucous behavior among the fans. Our [National Basketball Association] physicians' group is very concerned about this because of the increasing number of complaints by players. If attitudes don't change, we're going to have to do like they do in South America: put a fence and a moat around the playing field to keep the fans away from the players."

Why is it happening? Dr. Arnold Beisser, a Los Angeles psychiatrist who has counseled major league baseball on the subject of fan rowdyism, believes violence may become an inextricable part of our games. "The developing generation does not have the same horror about violence that traditionally we have had," says Dr. Beisser. "We have emphasized violence, and where violence once was a safety valve for people, it is now an accepted thing." The result: many fans today, especially the young, see violence in a "recreational" context.

Dr. Thomas A. Tutko, a San Jose State University psychologist who specializes in athletics, blames violence in the stands on a general social climate which breeds hostility and aggression. The key, the psychologist suggests, is a shared addiction for stimulation, a craving to glimpse the edge of experience. "And violence," contends Dr. Tutko, "is the most powerful stimulant of all."

Dr. Tutko views the increase in overtly aggressive fan behavior through the lens of recent history—the Vietnam War, urban unrest, and worker alienation. He theorizes that spectator behavior changed at about the same time the rest of the country did, and for many of the same reasons. "Until the last few years, America thought of herself as a reacting nation— we had to be the people who were attacked first. This evidenced itself in sports as well as foreign policy—baseball, a relatively passive game, was our national pastime."

By the middle of the 1960s, the situation clearly had changed: whether the battleground was Hamburger Hill in Vietnam or Municipal Stadium in Cleveland, goal achievement required at least the willingness to use force. The Lombardi ethic was formulated as strategy, and through no coincidence, football became the most popular game in the land.

Gridiron fans are especially likely candidates for aggressive behavior, believes Dr. Tutko, if only because they themselves represent an exclusive, self-selecting elite. "The price and availability of tickets are such that only the most competitive members of society are the ones who get in."

Dr. Edwin Schneibman, a University of California at Los Angeles expert on death and suicide, suggests some fans may be drawn to football for the same reason 30,000 people paid twenty-five dollars a head to watch Evel Knievel narrowly avoid death in a rocket cycle over Idaho's Snake River Canyon. They are obsessed with a vicarious need to experience risk and danger. Others argue that increasing social and economic distance between athletes and their supporters somehow has created in fans both resentment and a desire to get closer and interact with the players. "Fans used to go to the park to see players and to support the team," says the operations manager at one southern stadium. "Now spectators want to share the limelight with players."

Newsday's Steve Jacobson describes a frightening scene being reenacted around the country, especially before urban high school basketball games. As players clamber aboard their bus in high spirits, Jacobson wrote in a 1979 article for his newspaper, the driver tears open a sealed envelope:

It tells him where he is taking the team to play. It has been a carefully guarded secret. The team is going to play a home game, but they don't play at home anymore. All games are played on neutral sites.

It's too dangerous to play in front of the home fans. Too dangerous for the players, too dangerous for the referees, too dangerous for college recruiters, too dangerous for the fans and too dangerous for those responsible for crowd control.

In Pittsburgh, fans have smashed wrestlers over the head with chairs and choked and assaulted usherettes. At a New

York Jets football game in 1978, a security guard was tossed headfirst from the grandstand when he tried to break up a fight among fans. Early in 1979, an excited fan grabbed and twisted the painfully fractured thumb of Larry Bird, Indiana State's All-American forward; "I dropped him with a punch in the mouth," said the six-foot-nine star. The second game of the 1977 NBA championship series between the Philadelphia 76ers and the Portland Trail Blazers wound up in a 100-fan scuffle with players and coaches. Brazilian soccer star Pelé was roughed up so badly by American spectators after first joining the New York Cosmos that the team's management threatened to cancel his United States appearances, despite holding the bag on a multimillion-dollar contract. And few Chicagoans will forget the 1976 College All-Star contest, perhaps the first major American football game called off because of fan violence. During a rain delay, fans rushed onto the field, harassing players and officials. As lightning raked the sky, gangs of rowdies risked electrocution to tear down the steel goal posts. "Will mob rule become a way of life in our nation's athletic arenas?" asked *Chicago Tribune* sports editor Cooper Rollow following the incident.

More Americans are sports spectators today than ever have been spectators of anything in history. According to the *World Almanac,* a regular-season record of 40.8 million fans paid to see major league baseball games in 1978, and the figures were headed even higher in 1979. More than 11 million persons jammed into NFL stadiums during the 1979 season. About 9 million fans pay to see National Hockey League contests each year.

Spectators have paid dearly for their obsession with games. Their financial stake is not only large and personal, it has shaped the choices available in their lives and communities. As local taxpayers, spectators have heavily subsidized the construction and operation of sports stadiums and arenas, at the expense of alternate uses of public funds.* As if that weren't enough, the federal government has underwritten escalating ticket prices by allowing corporations to buy huge blocks of tickets and write them off as business expenses.

Fight to Advance the Nation's Sports (FANS) was sponsored by Ralph Nader in 1977 to combat financial and spectator abuses. An early investigatory target: scalping at the 1978 Super Bowl. FANS found that two-thirds of the tickets at the biggest single sports event in America probably were purchased illegally, at prices as high as $400 each. FANS charged that ticket-scalping players, owners, and team officials reaped huge profits and side-stepped their high-bracket taxes thanks to cash-under-the-table ticket sales. Scalping even extended to hotel rooms: one New Orleans businessman paid $1,600 for two nights in a seedy hotel, the organization said. "The bottom line for the average fan," FANS quoted a ticket agent as saying, "is that in some cities [he or she] doesn't have a shot at getting a decent ticket at face value, no matter what he does."

A pair of reserved seats at National Football League contests can exceed $250 a season; a private box at Yankee Stadium rents for as much as $19,000 to $30,000 a year. At such prices, fans cannot be blamed too harshly if occasionally they become belligerent and resentful. The message, says Michael Novak, author of *The Joy of Sports,* is "O.K., we came out, we paid our money, but we know what you're doing and here's what we think about it."

The competitive scramble to witness athletic contests in person lends even their secondhand experiencing a sense of tremendous importance. Irate football fans jammed local

---

* At the same time New York taxpayers were heading toward an unprecedented fiscal crisis in the 1970s, remodeling costs for Yankee Stadium were soaring from $24 million to $240 million, counting interest. The project was promoted as a way to rejuvenate the neighborhood around the stadium. In fact, buildings in the area remain in ruins and thousands are unemployed (see Chapter 5, "Hucksters").

television stations all over the country with protest calls when CBS and NBC decided the coronation of Pope John Paul I was more important than NFL football. When unfortunate events dictated that Pope John Paul II would be coronated a few weeks later, at least one fan, a San Francisco man, mounted a petition drive demanding that the historic ceremony be shown on a replay basis to avoid interfering with gridiron telecasts.

Fan: short for fanatic, sometimes a synonym for frenzy. In Denver, the term "Broncomania" is used to describe the fever generated by pro football's only Rocky Mountain team. In 1973, a man unsuccessfully attempted suicide after the Broncos fumbled the ball seven times in a loss to the Chicago Bears. "I have been a Broncos fan since the Broncos were first organized," he wrote before squeezing the trigger, "and I can't stand their fumbling any more." One citizen of the mile-high city charged his former wife with "extreme mental cruelty" when she allegedly forged a request transferring his season tickets to her name. At a Denver bistro named the Arabian Bar, a fan pulled a gun and started shooting when it was suggested that the television set be switched off in the closing minutes of a 1977 match between the Broncos and the Baltimore Colts. One patron was killed, and two others, who wanted to play the jukebox, were wounded.

The classic model for a spectator outbreak traditionally is supplied by a contest—such as the one in Lima—in which tempers slowly build during a losing effort in a crucial match, then hit flash point in a close and negative referee's call. But the puzzling thing today is the lack of evidence that disappointed fans are the ones who go berserk. Denver was winning easily when gunfire ended the disagreement in the Arabian Bar. When the New York Mets captured their first World Series championship in 1969, their fans launched an ugly "Fun City" tradition of savage rejoicing, smashing seats, stealing signs, and ripping out more than 6,000 square feet of sod.

The Oakland Raiders threw a come-one, come-all victory party after capturing Super Bowl XI. "Fifteen thousand people showed up," recalls John F. Ream, an Oakland deputy chief of police, "and half of them were hoodlums and toughs." The result? For the first time in the Oakland Coliseum's ten-year history, a major show of force was needed to preserve order. "We were fantastically outnumbered," said Ream afterward. "We had seventy-five officers there. I can police the whole city of Oakland with that many patrolmen, but inside that stadium they could not begin to control things." Officers used their nightsticks, but when fans began storming the field, Ream sent in a "last resort" squad of thirty motorcycle cops.

Most Bay Area sportswriters dismissed the disturbance as a few isolated fist fights, but that didn't jibe with the fan's-eye view of Dwayne Bracey, eighteen, who watched as the "celebration" became a melee. "There were fights everywhere, people were bleeding, police were hitting people across the head with billy clubs. Wine bottles, beer cans, and firecrackers were being thrown onto the playing field. It was gruesome." A little girl sat with blood streaming down her face; she had been struck by a flying metal towel container thrown from the upper deck. "Fans" poured onto the field toward the players, while people in the stands tossed bottles at the motorcycle cops.

Young toughs roamed the stadium in packs, mugging and beating victims in lavatories and passageways. Afterward, the violence continued into the night, with more beatings outside the coliseum, a spree of windshield smashings in the parking lot, and the upturning and ripping up of benches from their moorings. Riding home, white bus patrons were shoved around and slugged by gangs of black punks. When the night was over, ten persons had been hospitalized and fourteen arrested, figures that by Ream's account reflected only a fraction of the problem. "It wasn't any victory celebration," summed up Thearon Lawton, eighteen, another fan who attended. "It was a riot."

New York's brutal baseball crazies became legend in less than a decade. Their worst excesses inevitably accompanied success on the playing field. By 1976 the situation had spun so far out of control that Chris Chambliss required a police escort to make his way around the bases after slamming a pennant-winning home run against the Kansas City Royals. The playoffs were delayed seven minutes when Royals manager Whitey Herzog was struck by a flashlight battery. The Cincinnati Reds, the Yanks' opponents in the Series a few days later, hired special security guards solely to protect their families; some players even refused to allow their wives to attend the games because of possible fan reprisals.

By 1977 tensions were running even higher, especially since the Bronx Bombers were facing their old arch rivals, the Dodgers. Security concerns were such that Los Angeles players made a secret, nighttime landing at a deserted cargo hangar rather than risk coming in at one of Kennedy Airport's three main passenger terminals. Dodger pitchers were afraid to run near the stands during pregame warmups, and fears of fan-tossed bricks, batteries, and bottles prompted security advisors to reroute the small auto which ferries pitchers to the mound.

Yankee Stadium officials hired 300 extra private guards, and a special contingent of the city's finest added another 350 officers. In other words, a peace-keeping force larger than the entire police departments of El Paso, Texas; St. Paul, Minnesota; and Fresno, California, had been called upon to preserve order during a few baseball games. None of it would be enough. "You could have a security force of 1,000 out there and it wouldn't stop them," said a Yankee Stadium spokesman.

In the ninth inning of the second game, Dodger right fielder Reggie Smith suddenly slumped to the turf, struck on the top of the head by a rubber ball. Smith, who left the game complaining of spasms down his neck and back, returned to finish the Series—and to dodge apples, ice cubes, and beer cans. In the final game, a golf ball missed his head by an inch and he was struck in the testicles by a potato. "This is a different breed of fan," Smith said later. "They said they'd kill me, and they talked about my heritage. These people want to hurt you. It's frightening. You feel like you're in a cage out there."

Appropriately enough, the Series ended in a disgusting brawl, the Yankee victory blackened by charges of police brutality and injuries to at least thirty persons. Twenty more were arrested for disorderly conduct, larceny, and assault. One youth, clubbed by police, lay near third base with blood oozing from his head for nearly half an hour. But what millions of Americans would remember most was the sight of Reggie Jackson, a tiny figure on their television screens, running in terror from the outfield to the dugout, slamming one fan flat as he rammed through the gathering crowd, chopping at another with his right hand; Reggie Jackson, a five-home-run hitter in the Series and everybody's Most Valuable Player, frightened more than he would admit by an uncontrolled mob of swarming, grabbing, screaming, fighting "fans."

Fortunately, 1978's Dodgers–Yankees replay ended in Los Angeles, but that didn't stop an estimated 6,000 to 8,000 Yankee faithful from showing up at Newark International Airport for their team's return. The crowd broke through barricades and stormed the runway, ignoring orders from police, who tried briefly to hold them back. Meanwhile, the Yankees circled helplessly in their jetliner, marooned for nearly forty minutes while the entire airfield came to a standstill. Finally, the cops turned fire hoses on the crowd and cleared an escape route for the team's chartered buses.

For obvious reasons, team management has avoided taking a stand on the raucous behavior of their customers. Commenting on the playoff madness after Chambliss's homer in 1976, Yankee owner George Steinbrenner drolly observed, "I can't fault our fans at all. If I was on the field with them, I probably would have joined in." Others have suggested that the unruliness of New York Series spectators was a direct reflection on clubhouse relations of the team itself. By 1978 the Yankee dugout had become filled with super-salaried, ill-tempered prima donnas led by a manager who had difficulties of his own in controlling his fists. "That was no celebration when the fans ran wild after the final game," wrote author Novak. "That was a rebellion against the cynicism of Steinbrenner and the players, a scream of outrage against the profaning of something good."

In any event, as providers of the sports industry's bread and butter, even obnoxious fans can expect kid-glove handling by top management. Clamping down on the rowdies is a sensitive matter; nobody wants to alienate the folks who buy the tickets. An important, if not controlling, consideration: the possibility that fan outbursts and subsequent scuffling with police may themselves become part of the event, a spectacle which catches up other fans, who then take sides—inevitably against authority—and stir up an already charged atmosphere. "When you're dealing with tens of thousands of people," Bob Fishel of the American League told *New Times* in November 1977, "you've got to be sure that you don't make a bad situation worse. Sometimes people ask me why—when spectators go out onto the playing field—we let them stroll around for a minute or two, hoping they will come off by themselves. The answer is simple. Fans like to root for the underdog. If they see an overweight police officer chasing some kid all over the outfield without being able to catch him, it creates even more of a disturbance. It fosters disrespect for the law. So we try to let the intruder come off by himself, and that's when we make the arrest."

In a private survey of professional-sports executives by Burns International, the security company, more than 75 per cent cited "disorderly patrons" as their biggest problem; fourteen of the seventeen top managers and owners thought unruly fans were worse than they were a decade ago. Fifteen thought spectator drinking was excessive, and fourteen said they try to screen out beer, liquor, and other bottles and objects that might wind up as airborne projectiles. Even so, it's hard to stop a determined fan. After the 1978 World Series games at Yankee Stadium, beer cans, wine bottles, and whiskey pints were piled in clumps around the playing field like so many glass and tin burial mounds.

In more than a few instances, however, the sports establishment has no one to blame for its troubles but itself. Team and stadium owners have sometimes shown surprisingly little regard for their customers. Older stadiums generally have far too few restroom facilities for any reasonable standard of human comfort, their builders having made early decisions to reduce expensive plumbing in favor of paying concession stands. Walter O'Malley originally planned to open Dodger Stadium in Los Angeles without a single drinking fountain—the better to boost his park's beverage sales—until a public outcry forced him to back down.

Oakland's Raiders failed miserably at organizing the sale of their 1977 Super Bowl tickets, forcing fans to stand a chilly night watch outside the coliseum for tickets that would be sold on a first-come, first-served basis. Police had to quell fist fights in the lines, while fire trucks doused blazes set by fans trying to stay warm. Since nobody thought to provide portable toilets, fans unwilling to yield their positions urinated in line or found a stand-in while they defecated in the parking lot. For the poor souls who stuck it out but were unable to obtain the tickets, the effect was sometimes traumatic. "One guy was carried away babbling incoherently," wrote a reader to the *San Francisco Chronicle*. "Another woman was crying uncontrollably and I tried to console her. She said her husband was going to beat the hell out of her for not getting the Super Bowl tickets."

There have been some ingenious efforts to curb in-stadium problems. In Minneapolis, grounds crews coat goal posts and stadium beams with STP to slow down rowdies intent on a climb, mounted police patrol the parking lots, and detoxification vans are on hand for fans who drink too much. At the 73,000-seat Superdome in New Orleans, guards were hard-pressed to cover the huge facility's two hundred exits; now they scoot around in golf carts. The Cincinnati Reds appointed a Designated Security Officer to protect players and their families during the 1976 Series against the Yankees. At Hackensack, New Jersey's new Meadowlands Stadium, planners made sure the first row of seats was a twelve-foot drop to the playing field. And the National Hockey League requires eight-and-a-half-foot-high protective Plexiglas around penalty boxes and has ordered canopies placed over passageways to shield players and officials.

Outside the United States, 200,000-seat Maracana football stadium in Rio de Janeiro, the biggest outdoor sports facility on earth, was designed specifically to discourage fan violence. A twenty-five-foot-wide, fifteen-foot-deep moat, rimmed with jagged glass, isolates the playing field from the stands. Police armed with tear-gas guns stand guard around the moat; players and officials reach the field through underground tunnels that run from locker rooms to a trap door in the turf. Indeed, a heavy steel door in the dressing room at Peru's National Stadium in Lima is credited with saving the lives of the escaping players and referee in the tragic 1964 riot described earlier; pursuing fans pounded on the door, but they could not pry it open.

In the United States, snarling attack dogs were on duty at the next home game to prevent a repeat of the October 1976 outbreak at NFL-owned Schaefer Stadium in Foxboro,

Massachusetts—scene of a massive melee by New England Patriot fans (see Chapter 1, "Troubles") a few years ago. Schaefer manager Daniel J. Marcotte went even further, hiring an additional three hundred security officers and, for the first time in stadium history, halting beer sales in the stands. "We'll make this a family-type stadium yet," pledged Marcotte.

Even so, evidence of the limited effects of such precautions can be found on the floor of any stadium or arena in America. Spectators are heaving everything they can pick up with an abandon undreamed of a decade ago. Frank Torpey, security director of the National Hockey League, puzzles over the tendency of hockey fans in recent years to throw objects less often, though *what* they toss has been more vicious than ever. Ball bearings, open switchblade knives, even a steel dart have turned up in after-match inspections of the ice. "If throwing a steel dart doesn't show premeditation, I don't know what could," says Torpey.

A few years ago, the security bosses of big-league sports were chilled by a film called *Two-Minute Warning,* an action drama in which a football stadium becomes a shooting gallery for a sniper. Privately, most admit no way exists to predict, much less halt, such behavior. The psychotic loner remains the most dangerous of all criminals, no less so in our arenas.

• Hours before his team is to take the field against the Philadelphia Phillies, the phone rings in Pittsburgh Pirate Dave Parker's hotel room. "Come down in the lobby and I'll kill you," says the caller.

• Before a contest between Penn State and Pittsburgh, half a dozen letters arrive at the home of Penn quarterback Chuck Fusina's mother in McKees Rocks, a small community near Pittsburgh. The letters say Fusina's mother will be slain if he plays.

• Shortly before a Chicago Bears game, a stadium switchboard operator reports a racist call threatening running back Walter

Payton. If the attack is unsuccessful, warns the caller, he will turn his weapon against the crowd. During the contest, spectator Donna Fantozzi, thirty-nine, suddenly feels a burning sensation in her right arm. She has been shot with a small-caliber bullet.

• Swedish tennis star Bjorn Borg poses in an Israeli army uniform during a visit to the Middle East in 1978. Later a brown envelope arrives at Sweden's national news agency, proclaiming a death sentence on Borg by the Italian Red Brigades. At first Borg dismisses the threat, but within hours he has a change of heart. He will not play in his homeland, Borg announces, for at least a year.

Each of the foregoing incidents weakens an already crumbling explanation for fan violence, namely that hostility released through sports somehow reduces aggression that otherwise would pop up somewhere else. "People's emotions are similar to steam locomotives," wrote psychiatrists Richard C. Proctor and William M. Eckard, two proponents of that idea, in the March–April 1976 *American Journal of Sports Medicine.* "Spectator sports give John Q. Citizen a socially acceptable way to lower his steam pressure by allowing him to spin his wheels and toot his whistle." In his classic work *On Aggression,* Konrad Lorentz suggests we seek athletic spectacle because of a deep need for an emotional outlet, an outlet that in today's "civilized" world must often be suppressed.

New evidence increasingly disputes such ideas. Many authorities, Britain's former minister of sport Denis Howell among them, trace increasing aggression and hostility in the stands directly back to the darkening conflict on the field. Rather than releasing precontest tensions, overly aggressive games add to them, with the emotions of players and fans moving together in a concert of imitation, bound by a shared, reciprocal need to express and carry out violence. For example, nearly three-fourths of the spectator outbursts by hockey fans during a 1963–1973 period studied by York University professor Michael D. Smith were triggered by "assaultive behavior," most of it player versus player.

Hostility among male spectators at an Army–Navy football game, perhaps one of the most competitive contests in the country, was rated by two Canadian psychologists. Using standard hostility scales, Jeffrey H. Goldstein and Robert I. Arms analyzed 150 fans before and after the contest, then compared the results to a control group of 81 persons attending an Army–Temple gymnastics meet. If the displacement theory were correct, both groups of fans could be expected to show a decrease in aggressive feelings. What happened? Just the reverse. Post-game hostility scores were nearly 20 per cent higher for football fans but showed no significant increase in the subjects attending the gymnastics meet.

In explaining their findings, Goldstein and Arms noted that both contests required sitting for two or three hours in a large crowd which frequently broke into cheering and applause. The gym group was smaller and more scattered, and there were no cheerleaders, roaming vendors, or bands. But the psychologists found the crucial differences were between the events themselves: "A football game involves multiple players in direct physical contact with one another, while a gym meet involves individual performances in which no contact occurs. *It seems likely, therefore, that the increase in hostility is due to the nature of the observed event; watching an aggressive sport leads to an increase in hostility among spectators . . .*" (emphasis added).

Imitation research on children and adolescents has thrown further doubt on the idea that violence observed is violence released (see Chapter 8, "Kids"). And several investigators have documented evidence of stress among spectators both during and after games. Far from their emotions evaporating while they watch a coolly remote athletic contest, spectators closely interact with what happens on the court, arena, or playing field. Their cheers direct violent impulses against the opposing squad, then bounce back again. They supply athletes on their own teams with a mandate for aggression which they themselves feel.

Most of us learn to be fans. We get used to the idea that only the best players take the field. Teachers and classmates train us in developing a "we–they" feeling about opponents at other schools. Is it surprising that this relationship thrives on resentment as much as enthusiasm?

There may be some validity in arguing, as did Clark Whelton in *New Times,* that the precise reasons for fan misbehavior are less important than deciding on ways to bring it to an end. Everybody knows standards of public conduct have slipped alarmingly in recent years, Whelton noted, adding, "there have always been people who got a kick out of hurting or disturbing other people . . . the immediate question is not how to understand, but how to prevent them from injuring others."

Nonetheless, in the long run at least, the explanations for such gross public misconduct seem important. If it is true, for example, that middle-class males make up the bulk of professional-sports spectators, then what does their growing anger tell us about their frustrations? The distinction between imitative violence and violence as catharsis is important because the latter has been used for years to justify every kind of playing-field excess. Whelton has a point: it seems unnecessary to establish elaborate theories to explain the behavior of fans who harm players and other spectators. But neither is it sufficient to merely condemn their actions. The escalation in such incidents makes understanding their origins more important. Things can get worse; we need look no further than Great Britain to see just how bad that can be.

Postscript 1: GREAT BRITAIN

"A kid had a potato with razor blades in it thrown at him."

"Villa fans turned over milk van. Milk bloke seriously hurt. Fan stabbed with bottles."

"Friend got a brick in face."

"Friend bought and threw bottles. Boys beaten up in toilets. Forty-eight-year-old man stabbed eight times. Saw a fan hammer a chisel in another's head."

"Badly cut by razor boots—only provocation was being members of opposition team."

"Had bottle smashed over head."

"I was with a group of friends in the opposing side's end—a mate pulled a knife and said, 'Come on then.' He stabbed three of their leaders, and we had to defend ourselves as they pushed down at us."

"Smashed phone boxes, fights on terraces; beat up and bottled. Unfairly beat up by police. Broke windows."

Drawn from hundreds of eyewitness accounts,* these comments by young residents of England's West Midlands area describe what one newspaper has called Britain's leading bloodsport—violence by soccer fans. "Football hooliganism is all but over," predicted one respected commentator in 1974. Five years later, however, a new soccer season opened with spectator viciousness still rampant. There were fist fights, knifings, and property destruction. On two occasions, steel darts thrown by rival team supporters pierced the skulls of teenage boys. Fans tried to knife a goal-tender on one London team, the Queen's Park Rangers, and authorities shut down some fields completely because of rioting. Indeed, Great Britain, that island of civility, already had experienced its first soccer murders.**

---

* A 1976 study by the Westhill College of Education included 1,200 interviews with young men and women involved in or direct witnesses to soccer hooliganism.
** A young Blackpool fan was stabbed to death in 1974, and a seventeen-year-old fan died beneath the wheels of a train, where, authorities believe, he was pushed by rivals. Others have suffered severe injuries; a policeman sustained a fractured skull at a game in 1975.

A look at the past made the scene all the more disturbing. Before reinforcements arrived, a single policeman, mounted on a white horse, cleared thousands of fans from the pitch (playing area) when London's Wembley Stadium opened for World Cup finals on April 27, 1923. Wembley had been designed for 125,000 persons, but as many as 300,000 showed up for the match between the Bolton Wanderers and West Ham United. The first attraction at what was then the world's largest sports arena had drawn the biggest soccer crowd in history.

"The day was perfect," reported the following day's *London Times,* "and, by irony of fate, the superb organization of the many railway lines converging round the stadium was the crowning factor in producing such a crowd that it was impossible for any arrangements there to be carried out according to plan."

Surging through the stadium's inadequate entryways, the great crowd swept up from nearby underground stations by sheer momentum, pushing straight through the protective barriers and swarming over the field. More amazing, however, was what did not happen. Though a number of fans received minor injuries, there were no stabbings, muggings, rapes, tramplings, or gang fights. The unwieldy crowd simply dispersed. "The bulk of them," reported the *Times,* "though suffering intense discomfort, kept their places and eventually had the satisfaction of seeing the final played to a finish . . . One's main impression of events at the stadium was the amazing good humor and patience of the officials, of the police, and of the crowd itself. Probably no other crowd in the world would have behaved so well under the circumstances, which looked as if they would make the playing of the match an impossibility."

It is hard to imagine the same scene taking place today. Scores of fans frequently are arrested even before an English soccer game gets underway. In a 1977 match between British and Scottish teams, the entire contest eventually was abandoned to brawling fans. One youth was hospitalized after being kicked unconscious by a gang of rowdies, three others were stabbed, and forty-five more were hauled off to jail. Fights continued outside the stadium, cars were overturned, and liquor stores and shops were broken into and looted.

After a 1977 contest in Luxembourg, British fans smashed windows, dented cars, and started fights in bars. The principality vowed it would never play Great Britain again. Liverpool fans returning from a match in Düsseldorf, Germany, robbed a duty-free shop, trashed cafes, slashed upholstery, and smashed windows on two chartered trains. In Britain itself, hospitals typically are packed with casualties after a soccer Saturday. "The government has to do something," said one team manager after one youth was thrown to his death— apparently by rival soccer fans—from a railway platform into the path of an oncoming train. "They [hooligans] are crucifying the game."

Eighty-four per cent of soccer fans cited hooliganism as a serious problem in *Public Disorder and Sporting Events,* a 1978 study by the government-sponsored Social Science Research Council (SSRC). "Highly publicized disorder is an embarrassment to the football league and the Football Association, especially on international occasions," the sixty-page report stated. "The minister for sport is harried by continual questions from the press and demands for preventive action by the House of Commons."

Soccer hooliganism occurs twice as frequently now as during the pre-1960 period, the report suggested. But the kinds of action that could do most to effect immediate help— rebuilding and modernizing stadiums to improve their design and accommodations, for example—are financially beyond the resources of most clubs. Further police action or tightening the laws, the report concluded, would accomplish little. And any permanent solution almost certainly would require

long-term improvement in the country's depressingly stag-
nant economic and social climate.

Soccer rowdyism has "always been our escape from the
unhappy things about reality," says Chris Lightbown, a re-
formed "skinhead" who now writes for the *London Sunday
Times*. "That could be home or school or slums, or all three.
With soccer there is no contact with anything except soccer.
And violence is part of the game."

"In my day knives were flashed but not used like now,"
Lightbown told magazine writer Dorsey Woodson. "Now I
know for a fact that guns are being flashed . . . the ritual of
fighting has broken down. We depended on the coppers to
act as referees; they kept us from killing each other and they
gave us protection when we needed it. Today the police and
the fans fight each other."

As a "skinhead" in the late 1960s, Lightbown was a
member of the last easily identifiable, organized hooligan sect
to appear. Named for their close-cropped hair style, they
wore clothing of subdued colors and heavy, hob-nailed,
high-top shoes for fighting. The skinheads and their
predecessors—the "mods" and the "rockers"—staked out the
ends of the stadium, called terraces, as their private domain.

In the terraces—the "kop" in Liverpool, the "Stretford
End" in Manchester, the "Dreaded Shed" at Chelsea, the
"Mile End" at West Ham—the most fervid fans stand and
scream, waving long scarves bearing their favorite teams' colors. It is also in the terraces that initial battles usually erupt as
combat patrols from opposing ends move in for "aggro." Says
Lightbown: "These kids have blown the bluff on authority: at
home, in school, and now out in society. They recognize no
controls. But as far as stopping the violence at British soccer
games—forget it. It is part of what a lot of soccer fans have
expected—and eliminating it just isn't on."

More than anything, the establishment has succeeded in
welding the hooligans into a cohesive unit, argue the authors

of *The Rules of Disorder,* published a few weeks after the SSRC report. Spiked iron grills, steel security fencing, and wire mesh seal off the "ends." In some stadiums spectators are kept from the playing field by dry moats, roving police, and patrol dogs, as well as binocular-equipped spotters with two-way radios. At one London field, officers watch the fans on a bank of closed-circuit television monitors, zeroing in with zoom lenses at the first sign of trouble. "The net effect of the fortification around the ends, and of the strategies to keep people in them, is, of course, the highlighting of their distinctive nature," concluded Oxford University social psychologist Peter Marsh and *Disorder* co-authors Elizabeth Rosser and Rom Harré. "The police and officials have succeeded in delineating fans' territories in a way that the fans themselves could never have done."

A young hooligan's "career" begins as early as age nine and can extend beyond his teens, the researchers found. Beginning as a "novice," or preteen onlooker, the upwardly mobile youngster can go on to join the "rowdies," seventeen-year-olds who wear "aggro" outfits—baggy trousers, heavy boots, and, increasingly, elaborate hair styles—and provide most of the visible action. A hooligan's "declining" years can be spent in dignity as a member of the "town boys," highly respected ex-rowdies, mostly in their late teens or twenties. Within each category, separate roles exist for "chant" or "aggro" leaders and "nutters." The latter earn their reputations—and often early jail sentences as well—with an appetite for violence which abandons reason—as happens, for example, when a single nutter challenges an entire crowd of rival fans.

Humor is a strong element in hooliganism. As Marsh and his colleagues point out, soccer roughnecks can be "actors of wit and style; they are entertainers." Anybody can steal merchandise from a shopkeeper, they note, but not anybody can playfully waltz up and down the street before giving back the goods—and without getting caught by the infuriated owner.

Hooligans gain honor from such escapades. For a season at Oxford United a 16-year-old named Geoff was famous for his wicked acts. One day a rival fan threw a lump of dog feces at him. In retaliation Geoff climbed up onto a terrace overlooking the offender and his friends, who were drinking tea, and urinated on them—onto their "heads and into their tea and all over," according to one of Geoff's comrades, "and it's raining a bit as well so they don't notice. Me and some others, we run down and were watching this and we're killing ourselves. But Geoff, he don't shout or anything—he just waits for a bit till they finish their tea and then he shouts out, 'Enjoy your tea then,' and as they look up he pisses a bit more and they go barmy."

Marsh and his colleagues believe soccer hooliganism is carefully controlled and, in the main, harmless. In their view, outbursts at soccer matches are richly ceremonial, purposely designed to inflict low rates of injury and death, and distinctly reminiscent of conflict among underpopulated primitive tribes*: "The ritual on the terraces, then, seems clearly related to the age-old problems of proving that one is better at being a man than one's rival . . . aggro, we would suggest, has always been an integral part of human cultures."

As compelling as they may have seemed to sociologists, however, the Marsh group's conclusions found a mostly unreceptive audience among the police officials, politicians, and soccer managers trying to deal with England's lengthening list of sports-related fist fights, knifings, train trashings, and vandalism. "I'm afraid this is well-meaning liberalism," one reformed rowdy told a British journalist. "When I used to stand behind the goals it was just the fist and the boot. Now it's all about blades and cutting. The real nutters have got to be rooted out."

Though few could disagree with his portrayal of English

---

* Despite their thorough familiarity with bird life and flight, Stone-Age New Guinea tribesmen use unfeathered—and hence highly inaccurate—arrows during battle.

youth reacting to lives of boredom, newspapers ridiculed Marsh's comparisons between primitive tribesmen and the rituals of the terraces. The SSRC report noted that soccer violence already has outlasted similar phenomenon—Teddy Boyism, "mods" and "rockers" fights, and the persecutory ethnic violence known as "Paki (Pakistani) bashing."

Soccer's deep roots in nineteenth-century trade unionism assured working-class men of an important role in the fortunes of their home teams. When a fan suggested strategy at a local pub or brought a prospective player by for a tryout, he was regarded as a respected participant, actively aiding in the team's development. By the same token, the income and life style of the player differed little from that of a journeyman steel worker or mill foreman.

Post–World War II prosperity affected Great Britain as profoundly as it did the United States. In the process, the face of English soccer was permanently altered. With higher salaries, team members became active in special associations that set them apart from their former constituents. Players came to see the game as a way out of the country's grinding factory towns, and fans recognized the distinction in their chants and songs:

> In their Nottingham slums,
> In their Nottingham slums.
> They look in the dustbin for something to eat,
> They find a dead cat and they think it's a treat,
> In their Nottingham slums.

Training and strategy became more specialized and scientific, placing, as sociologist John Clarke writes in *Football Hooliganism: The Wider Context,* "a premium upon the avoidance of defeat as much as on the accomplishment of success." Club managers turned to balloon races, female cheerleaders, and gladiatorial salutes to rev up interest in the games. "Sudden death" contests and greater emphasis on international competition were introduced in the 1960s. Television turned English soccer into a melange of zooming close-ups, replays, and special angles.

By the 1970s some psychologists were suggesting that hooliganism might be reversed with greater emphasis on participatory sports for the young and on more sports facilities and youth athletic progams. But to others it seemed the cycle already had spun too far. When officials at Kilbowie Park in London tried to stage a Christmas goodwill match between Clydebank and St. Mirren a couple of years ago, they offered prematch festivities, entertainment, lotteries, and free pictures of both teams in an effort to preclude violence. The result? A sprawling riot in which hundreds of fans fought running battles on the terraces, eventually spilling onto the playing field and forcing a lengthy delay in the game.

And whether the causes of hooliganism can be traced to the sociology of English factory life or, as appears to be the case in Scotland, a mixture of religious hatred and prolonged economic depression, police costs to contain soccer violence currently reach into the hundreds of thousands of pounds annually—paid for by people who can ill afford it. As the situation has worsened, some stadium authorities have begun issuing identity cards to soccer fans. "The weekly lists of injured police officers and innocent members of the public tell the real story," said James Jardine, chairman of England's national law officers' association. "So does the trail of damage to property, which runs into thousands of pounds most Saturday afternoons."

Fully a quarter of the young males surveyed in the Westhill College report admitted taking part in soccer violence. "Our findings," concluded the study's authors, "suggest the 'only-a-minority-are-affected' approach should be subjected to careful examination in public debate . . . We have no desire to contribute to panic or despair. But if our sample is at all representative, it seems that a not inconsiderable section of the youth population is being brought up with first-hand contact with football hooliganism and vandalism as part of their education . . ."

Weathered, stained with smoke and grease, the graffiti in London's Liverpool Street underground station said it as well:

Skins run them every Sunday down the lane—Skins rule Teds

Fulham Skins Kill the Fucking Dg

North London Skins Kill South London Teds

Soccer violence is by no means limited to England. In Glasgow, Scotland, on June 2, 1971, sixty-six spectators were crushed to death in a stampede following an emotion-packed contest between the traditional rival Celtics (Catholic) and Rangers (Protestant). In Italy, "fans" carry stones, bricks, iron bars, and oranges into stadiums, sometimes concealing their arsenals in carrying bags and even small suitcases. Ninety-six people were arrested before the Rome–Lazio game a few years ago; police caught spectators sneaking Molotov cocktails and flare guns into the stadium. Dozens of persons routinely are injured; fans regularly attack players and referees and set torches to benches, billboards, and each other. Squads from the paramilitary *carabinieri* stand vigil at Italian stadiums, tear-gas bombs fitted to their rifle muzzles. High wire fences and moats keep the fans away from the game itself.

None of this has diminished soccer's popularity. The cheapest seats cost about eight dollars at most first-division matches in Italy, and soccer stars are the gods of modern Rome. Players regularly are bought and sold for more than $2 million; the asking price for World Cup star Paolo Rossi has been reported at nearly $7 million. "The clue to Italian soccer violence," says one observer, "is that the fans often get poor value for their money. They see their side get an early goal and then the shutters go up on an afternoon of sullen, slog-

ging, defensive play. The fans know their heroes get stagger-
ing wages for this rather negative activity . . ."

West Germany, dominant in European soccer for several
years, controls its fans, but only by using what many would
consider extreme police measures. Instead of "soccer special"
trains as there are in England and other countries, spectators
are dispersed throughout ordinary coaches patrolled by railway guards. From the moment they arrive at the stadium,
potential troublemakers are accompanied by police, sometimes fifty or more. A mobile van with a mounted television
camera travels in front, ready to videotape any outburst.
Police conduct body searches at the turnstiles, and, inside,
officers scan the crowd with television cameras linked to monitor screens in a central security command post. Plainclothes
officers move among the spectators with walkie-talkie radios,
and police reinforcements are stationed behind the stands.
Fans who make trouble can be banned, fined, and slapped in
prison. German authorities claim the stiff measures have resulted in a 50-per-cent decrease in violence by soccer fans.

Elsewhere, control efforts have been notably less successful. Soccer riots regularly mar matches in France and Greece
and have occurred in the Soviet Union. Though Communist
newspapers give only sketchy accounts of such incidents,
bottle-tossing, stone-throwing outbursts have been reported
in the North Caucasus and Siberia. In 1975 a stampede of
unruly fans at a Soviet–Canadian ice hockey match in Moscow left as many as twenty fans dead (an official toll was not
released) and many more injured.

Postscript II: AN AMERICAN STADIUM, 1978

"This is not an easy detail," the police lieutenant is saying,
traces of his Irish heritage still evident in his speech. "There
are 60,000 people out there and only a few dozen men in

blue. Make a wrong move and you can have fifty to a hundred people against you. Just like that."

Diarmuid Philpott stands in a glass-enclosed security command booth at one end of the stadium's long, narrow press box. With him are Chuck Wood—the large, affable commander of the ball park's fifty-member private security force—and two younger men, walkie-talkie-equipped spotters. All four pick up their binoculars and begin scanning the crowd.

An American professional football game is about to begin. Fans, thousands of them, still file into the stadium's bright orange seats. The loudspeaker blares a metallic request for silence in memory of those slain in the People's Temple insanity just twenty-four hours earlier. Hundreds of balloons, carrying the home team's colors of red and gold, swirl upward against a dark putty sky. This is Candlestick Park, San Francisco, but it could be anywhere. The wind here is chilly and the mood is hard. The club, luckless in ten of its last eleven games, has the bad fortune to face the division-leading Los Angeles Rams. The fans are tired of losing.

The past 150 days have been unusual, even in a stadium known for trouble. Since the early summer, when for a magic time it looked as if the town's baseball team might win its division pennant, the park has seen a long season of drunken fights, bottle and cherry-bomb tossing, strong-arm robberies, attempted rapes, and shootings. The iron grating and long, looping strands of barbed wire on its light stanchions testify to the facility's often uneasy relationship with the public. Management doesn't like the police to talk about it, and the cops themselves try to play it down, but Candlestick hasn't always been a nice place to take the wife and kids.

Especially on Monday nights. That's when the fans who normally booze it up at tailgate parties get a chance to toss down a few more on their way in from work. That's when the presence of national television crews add—in a way nobody seems quite able to understand—to the climate of hostility. And that's when packs of rough young thieves prowl the park's dark tunnels and corridors. A principal target: the passageways leading to the stadium's private mezzanine boxes. More than a few women have been rudely jostled in the darkness by punks, only to discover their purses stolen when the group moves on. Another ploy: snatching a purse, portable radio, or pair of binoculars from beneath the seats which line the aisles. This kind of thievery can be swift and easy, especially if the victim is absorbed in the game and the loot is grabbed from behind.

If that were all they had to worry about, the stadium cops could count themselves lucky. But the old, reliable "rip and run" has taken on some much rougher forms lately. Concession clerks depositing the day's receipts now are accompanied by armed guards because of repeated closing-time heists. Gangs of young toughs have taken advantage of night contests by rolling non-working clunker autos into the path of autos driven by departing fans. Then the brazen thieves worked their way down the line of waiting motorists— stopped for what seemed to be someone with car trouble— clobbering drivers and passengers and stealing what they could grab.*

At least these attacks can be explained by economic motives. For much of the recent violence, however, there is no apparent explanation at all. A local doctor, writing anonymously to the *San Francisco Progress* (October 12, 1977), described his trip home from a football game:

Upon driving out of the main parking lot gate, we turned left and within three blocks were confronted by about eight kids who were blocking the right side of the road. My first thought was that they were just playing in the street, but a quick glance around showed they were armed with rocks, aimed at my car . . . I realized it was them or us. I gradually inched forward through the group. They never said a word, just solemnly stared at us. All this time they were

---

* Candlestick is not the only crime-ridden stadium (see "Notes and Bibliography").

throwing huge chunks of broken concrete at us. The windows were broken, the auto body dented and scratched, but we fortunately sustained only minor cuts from flying glass.

After being stalked and rammed by a mysterious auto that tried to trap him and his companion in a dead-end street, the physician finally arrived at a nearby police station. Two other Candlestick fans already were there, filing reports about how they had been terrorized by packs of rock-throwing youths. Another version of the same game, say police: dropping garbage cans from local freeway overpasses onto the hoods of departing fans' autos.

Many of the park's purse snatchings, auto boostings, and robberies can be traced to a mostly poor and black area about a quarter of a mile from its borders. But given a choice, says the lieutenant, he would gladly take the ghetto kids over the white, suburban troublemakers who hang out in Candlestick's sections 59 and 61. These are the vicious drunks, the fighters, the ones most apt to cause serious injuries by tossing cans and bottles from the upper decks. They are the ones who heaved so many cherry bombs during baseball season that umpires had to clear the players from the field. They are the drunken, cursing fans who suddenly can become a mob when a cop tries to make an arrest. "Maybe they identify with the violence they see on the field; I don't know," says Philpott. "But we sure get some unbelievable, ring-tailed bastards up there."

Cops blame the park's problems on affluence and boredom in suburban kids and on resentment among disadvantaged ghetto youths. The truth is nobody fully understands why stadiums have as much trouble as they do, much less how to stop it. Philpott thinks 75 per cent of Candlestick's trouble could be eliminated by an outright ban on liquor. Booze would still find its way into the stands, but such a move might help reduce some of the park's nastier problems.

Like guns. Recently stadium police disarmed an intoxicated local television newscaster waving a loaded .38 in the stands, and a reserve officer, hearing a loud thump as he pulled out of the parking lot, found a thick slug of lead, a spent bullet, smashed into his car frame. A young woman has just removed the plastic colostomy bag at her waist, the result of painful abdominal surgery, after being shot at a baseball game four months ago. "It's hard to believe," says the police lieutenant, "but we have a lot of people bringing firearms in here."

Crime still touches only a fraction of the fans. A typical football Sunday begins as many as four hours before kickoff with happy times in the stadium parking lot. Three-quarter-inch steaks sizzle under camper awnings, and miniature footballs sail through the air. Everybody in sight seems to be clutching an Oly or a Coors. The small bottles of hard stuff— the diminutive half pints of Seagram's, Smirnoff, and White Horse—wind up inside the park, shoved under seats and out of sight. After the game some fans try to keep the spirit alive, but by then the booze and the fun are played out. One man urinates openly next to his car. Another lobs a dead beer can across the pavement. A girl, red-eyed, wanders among the parked autos, unaccountably sobbing. The cars, the ones lucky enough to reach the exit road, are crammed bumper to bumper, five abreast, starting an hour-long journey to the highway, about a mile away.

For now, however, Philpott watches from his post in the glass security booth. He looks out at the blanket of brown and yellow hats and maroon knit caps and stretched rubber ponchos. He counts himself lucky. His small force has survived the past six months with relatively few injuries: one officer with a severe facial bruise from being slugged during a minor riot at a baseball game; another with two broken bones in his leg; a third knocked dizzy when a bottle bounced off his skull; a young officer still on sick leave due to a possible heart attack suffered in chasing a would-be rapist; and one other man with a serious knee injury sustained while trying to run down a suspected robber. "Considering the kind of year it's been," the lieutenant sighs, "we've come through all right so far."

The stadium scoreboard flashes a sign: FOR THE SAFETY OF THE PLAYERS, THE 49ERS REQUEST THEIR FANS TO REFRAIN FROM THROWING ANY OBJECTS ON THE FIELD. The crowd roars when a Ram punt receiver momentarily bobbles the ball, then is smothered on his own 17. Two plays later they are cheering again: John Cappelletti, the Rams' running back, has unaccustomedly fumbled.

"Unit 14, Unit 14," one of the young private-security men, dark and balding, squawks into his walkie-talkie. "We have a woman down. She's fallen in the south tunnel." The telephone rings. The man listens and picks up the walkie-talkie again. He rests both elbows on the narrow window counter that serves as the small booth's only desk. "The owner's box wants somebody for O.J. and DeBartolo, somebody with a blazer. They've got people all over the place down there."

Superstar Simpson, sidelined with injuries, has been invited to watch the contest with the club's unpopular owner, Eddie DeBartolo. An explosive combination? Fans tore at Simpson's clothes and tried to mob him in Houston at the beginning of the season. The Candlestick cops aren't taking any chances: two guards are assigned permanently to the great running back whenever he plays.

Chuck Wood cranes his neck around, peering through the glass roof at the darkening sky. A spattery, windblown rain has been falling since the night before, and Wood could not be happier. "We're lucky the weather's lousy; we'll have less trouble," he says. "Just keep your fingers crossed it lasts."

The game is late and tight, 28–21, with the Rams leading. Philpott seems paler, his manner more strained than when the contest began. A close Rams game can mean ugly fans, especially if the 49ers lose.* The larger private force includes two nine-man tactical squads, but Philpott's twenty-two regular police will have to handle any real trouble. If a problem gets too big the lieutenant can call for reinforcements, but outside help almost certainly would arrive too late. Even inside the stadium, it can take an officer ten minutes or more to reach another part of the stands.

Far across the stadium grounds, in the parking area that lines Candlestick's landfill boundaries, Sergeant Mario Busalacchi swings his big patrol car off the perimeter road, past the yellow Volkswagen with its sprung door and oddly gaping wing window. Ahead, seven officers cluster around a beat-up Chevy sedan. A pile of FM radios, tape decks, microphones, and cassette tapes lie in a tangle on the back seat. Stuffed into a corner of the front seat are a set of prying tools and a tiny black revolver. The haul has cost half a dozen fans perhaps one or two hundred dollars each, more counting the damage to their cars. In the background, beyond the huge stretch of pavement and yards of cyclone fence, Candlestick looms like a plump, yellow-ribbed basket.

Somebody asks Busalacchi how old they are—the skinny, gaunt-faced white kids in the other patrol car. The large, curly-haired veteran yanks open the door with the bars across the window, then turns back to his questioner. "Thirteen and sixteen."

A brief, buffeting wind sweeps in from the bay, punctuating the momentary silence with damp-sounding slaps. Unexpectedly, there is a sudden and sustained roar. The 49ers have scored, and their fans are cheering.

---

* As it turns out, the game will end quietly, despite San Francisco's eventual 31–28 loss. Only five bookings are logged, one a drug-confused young man who yells in delirium in the stadium's cramped holding cell; he has risked his life in a headfirst dive from a dugout roof.

5 Hucksters

Call it moneyball. —*Sports Illustrated*

"Abrasions, contusions, scrapes from the floor and sticks, broken arms and legs, groin and leg pulls . . . the fans just go crazy watching." The promotion director of a now-defunct Long Island pro lacrosse team was listing a few of the sport's alluring mishaps. Despite injury rates that would make a professional football club wince, for a while the National Lacrosse League seemed certain to catch on. Played on a wooden floor similar in size and shape to a hockey rink, professional or "box" lacrosse* is a sport of unparalleled fierceness. And unlike wrestling or roller derby, the viciousness in box lacrosse is real. Players are free to crosscheck, slam each other with their sticks, break ribs, knock out teeth, and slash flesh. Box lacrosse is violence packaged for a purpose: to sell tickets. What's more, as the ex-promoter told *The Physician and Sportsmedicine,* "They [players] still love to play."

* Lacrosse is played by teams of ten players each, using three-foot-long strung sticks, on a 120-yard pitch divided in half, with a round goal area at each end. Scoring is accomplished when the game's orange-sized rubber ball is passed or rolled into the net.

104

Underfinanced, the NLL folded. But examples of success-fully merchandised athletic savagery abound. Violence not only sells athletics, sports violence sells products—from beer to books.

"Experience more bone-crushing tackles than any player in football," pledged the Advent Corporation in national magazine ads touting its giant-screen color television sets. A Massachusetts man expressed delight with his $2,400, six-foot boob tube. "The most dramatic part," he testimonialized, was seeing "the ferocity of the tackle, which you experience, life-size, in front of you."

"How close do you want to get?" snarled a *Sports Illustrated* subscription ad above a teeth-bared, eye-squinting, close-up of a growling football player. "Do you want to go nose-to-nose with the honchos?" challenged the copy, practically shoving the magazine's prospective readers in the chest. "*Sports Illustrated* will get you there, alive and kicking," it continued, for full coverage of "America's longest running hit."

Even the world of book publishing will gladly spill a little plasma for sales. The advertising for Ira Gitler's chronicle of ice hockey, *Blood on the Ice,* could not have been more explicit. For $7.95, the reader could expect the game's "whole, exciting, terrifying, bloodthirsty history, from the turn-of-the-century to today—complete with action photos. From the first fatality in 1907 . . . you are there at the fights and brawls, at the fiercest stick play and body checking. . . ." The hockey establishment has long admitted that the game's vicious fights pack arenas. Obviously, they can help sell books as well.

In Arizona, some taverns promote fighting matches be-tween their customers to boost patronage, an activity out-lawed in most parts of the country. Opposed by its own state athletic commission, the Arizona beer bouts nonetheless go on, featuring free-swinging boxing between friends, strangers, and sometimes women. Most combatants enter the contests without benefit of ringside physicians or prematch physicals. The two- and three-dollar seats barely cover expenses, one bar owner told the *Los Angeles Times,* but the fights still turn more profit than the club's four nights of live rock music and dancing. "The boxing crowd drinks more," he said. "The people are the macho types . . . I make the money on the bar."

Violence is one half of America's great commercial equation. Along with sex, it is used to sell products as well as sports in subtle appeals to both males and females. And it is not always clear which gender is the target. Macho means tough, sexy, and mean, and those qualities can attract men and women with equal power. As Vance Packard noted in *The Hidden Persuaders:*

The discovery was made that the grunt-and-groan spectacles of professional wrestling, supposedly a sweaty he-man sport, survive only because of the feminine fans. A Nielsen check of TV fans watching wrestling matches revealed that ladies outnumbered men two to one. The promoters of the matches, shrewdly calculating the triggers that produced the most squeals from feminine fans, stepped up the sadism (men writhing in torture), the all-powerful male symbolism (chest beating and muscle flexing), and fashion interest (more and more elegant costumes for the performers).

"Not every man can handle Metaxa," snorts an ad for the Greek liqueur, described in accompanying text as "not one of your kid glove drinks." Masculine fantasies were triggered by an accompanying photo of the beverage clenched in a steel-spiked glove reminiscent of the handgear worn for the Pankration,* one of history's most savage forms of boxing. "The

---

* A brutal combination of boxing and wrestling. Combatants sometimes killed each other and often suffered serious injury—eyes were gouged out of sockets, and necks, arms, and legs were broken.

Greeks drink Metaxa straight, concludes the copy appropriately, "by the fistful."

In a television spot for the Miller Brewing Company, football player Deacon Jones saunters into a bar, recites a few squibs of poetry, then warns everyone in earshot to drink his brand of beer or "I'll break your nose." Everybody in the bistro clears out, and small wonder—Jones was so convincing that Miller received letters from viewers who thought he was threatening them personally. In another spot, Bubba Smith tells how he ripped opposing offensive players away from ball carriers and quarterbacks, then tears the top off one of Miller's new easy-open cans. And when the Ideal Toy Company wanted to demonstrate the toughness of its toy trucks, who should it turn to for a foot-stomping squash test but Mean Joe Greene, known for slugging opposing players and threatening game officials.

There is, of course, nothing especially unique about the merchandising of athletic violence. Since Hollywood discovered optically enhanced savagery in *Bonnie and Clyde,* movie and television producers have been capitalizing on every imaginable freeze frame, slow motion, trick angle, and soft-focus rendering of cinematic viciousness. The themes of at least five recent films, however, explicitly combine violence and athletics: *Roller Ball, Two-Minute Warning, Slap Shot, Black Sunday,* and a 1978 epic entitled *Bloodsport. Two-Minute Warning,* made without National Football League cooperation and strongly condemned by police and league security officials, postulated a sniper attack against fans at a professional football game. Since then, at least two patrons at professional sports stadiums have been shot by snipers. "I think we're a violent country, and I think we like it," responded respected veteran actor John Cassavetes when asked to explain his participation in the film.

"The average fan loves violence," echoed Dave Schultz, one of the National Hockey League's leading bullies when he was with the Philadelphia Flyers. "I know that they want me to fight. They love it." Clarence Campbell, former league president, put the matter even more succinctly. "We must put on a spectacle," he said, "that will attract people." The formula apparently worked: in 1978–79, the NHL consistently outdrew pro basketball in five of eight cities where the two winter-season sports shared home arenas. In Philadelphia, hockey's rough-tough Flyers filled 100 per cent of their seats, almost half again as many as the National Basketball Association's 76ers.

Crowd-pleasing violence is far from new. When Marcus Aurelius declared a law forbidding the killing of gladiators, outraged mobs protested so vehemently that the order was repealed. Instead, the emperor wound up budgeting millions more for gladiatorial upkeep, and the number of playing dates nearly tripled.

What do we know of the sports business during those ancient times? In the beginning, the Romans preserved the status of gladiatorial shows as a dignified part of sacred funeral rites, just as they had been originated by the Etruscans of the north. Indeed, the first exhibition of Roman gladiators was held at a funeral in 264 B.C., twenty years after Etruria* had been conquered. For a long time the exhibitions retained their respectability, but gradually the battles grew larger in scale. Twenty-two pairs of gladiators helped celebrate the funeral of Marcus Lepidus in 216 B.C., but more than six dozen gladiators battled in memory of Titus Flaminus in 174 B.C. By the time of Christ, Roman emperors were exhibiting thousands of gladiators, and it had become fashionable to include at least a hundred pairs of combatants at most aristocratic functions and parties.

The big money was in the horses. A top charioteer could earn as much as 7,500 to 15,000 denarii (roughly $11,000 to

* An ancient coastal nation north of Rome and roughly opposite the island of Corsica.

$22,000 in today's dollars) for a single performance and become a millionaire within a few years. Competing stables lured away drivers with offers of hundreds of thousands—sometimes millions—of sesterces. Everybody loved the races. As Walter Umminger notes in *Supermen, Heroes and Gods,* the Roman poet Martial died in A.D. 102, miserable that he had never become as famous as a winning race horse.

By the time the republic was making way for the Roman Empire, every aspect of the races was controlled by four corporations. The companies marked their property—jockeys, drivers, chariots, and halter ropes—either red, green, blue, or white. Among supporters, the colors came to identify their favorite teams. The corporations took plush headquarters in the business district and set up branch offices in the countryside. As many as 14,000 horses were maintained at a time on special stud–training farms.

Eventually, hippomania, as the Romans' madness for horses was called, forced expansion. The initial four corporate teams had soon quadrupled to sixteen. Expansion fees were charged and the racing schedule increased until two dozen contests were run a day, alternating between single horse and chariot events.

There were season-ticket holders and soothsayers who predicted the outcome of major races (the best guide to judging the condition of horses was by smelling their manure). Roman crowds, who from the beginning never shared the Greeks' love of legitimate athletics, screamed with pleasure as the jammed field of chariots became the scene of mass collisions and injuries. Inevitably, the jaded cynicism of the fans infected their favorite performers. "I do not care if I am exploited," said the ex-slave Diocles, a champion driver paid handsomely to switch stables. "I exploit the owners too."

Gold and violence, money and mayhem. Are we repeating the ancient spectacle cycle? Judge for yourself. During the

1960s, the National Hockey League grew from six to four-teen teams; the National Basketball Association increased its teams by 70 per cent, and a new American Basketball Association added eleven clubs to the professional boards; baseball grew by nine teams and split its leagues into east–west divisions; and the merger of the National and American football leagues created a baker's dozen of thirteen teams. The new leagues also played more. By the late 1970s, baseball had added 868 games to its season; basketball, 614; hockey, 510; football, 124. At the end of the 1970s, according to *Sports Illustrated,* the annual gross revenues of the four major professional sports totaled some $700 million and were rising.

Salaries, meantime, have gone through some historic convulsions of their own. "Pudge" Heffelfinger may have been an All-American guard at Yale, but he received only $500 cash to become America's first professional football player in 1892. Even that had to be paid under the table, since Heffelfinger was playing as a ringer for Pennsylvania's Allegheny Athletic Association. Jim Thorpe signed with the Canton Bulldogs in Ohio for $250 a game, considered an outrageous sum at the time despite Thorpe's ranking as the world's most celebrated athlete.

Sportswriters sometimes like to cite old-time boxing gates and baseball paychecks in arguing that today's athletic super-salaries are nothing new. But the great Babe Ruth earned only $35,000 during his last full season as a player in 1934. Eddie Shore, superstar defenseman for hockey's Boston Bruins for fifteen seasons until 1941, hit an owner-imposed pay ceiling of $12,000 a year and finally settled for his employer's agreeing to pay his rent.

By comparison, today's bucks are simply incredible. Some athletes, including golfer Arnold Palmer, carry million-dollar payrolls just for their own employees. The equivalent of six National Basketball Association teams—thirty players—are each paid $250,000 or more a year, better than $1.25 million per five-man squad. The $733,358 paid by the San Francisco 49ers for O.J. Simpson's services in 1978 worked out to $45,834.87 per game, or, based on his running gains, *well over $1,000 per yard.*

A few weeks before Christmas in 1978, Pete Rose signed an $800,000-per-year contract with the Philadelphia Phillies. For various reasons, Rose already had turned down proposed pay packages from three other teams which included: a beer distributorship (St. Louis Cardinals), $1 million a year in salary (Atlanta Braves), and a top thoroughbred brood mare (Pittsburgh Pirates). As if the prospect of all that loot weren't enough, Rose spent his summer selling 5,000 envelopes (at five dollars a copy) postmarked the day he got his three-thousandth hit.

Actually, Rose is just one member of baseball's rapidly expanding millionaires' club—other recent additions include Dave Parker, Rod Carew, Jim Rice, and Rose's former teammate on the Cincinnati Reds, George Foster. Meanwhile, the earnings of women athletes have been skyrocketing almost as fast. In 1978 tennis competition, Martina Navratilova won $501,500; Chris Evert, $443,540; and Virginia Wade, $293,296—not counting winnings in excess of $100,000 each in World Team Tennis and a healthy take from the Federation Cup.

Working-stiff professional athletes don't even come close to such figures, of course. Indeed, the wide variance in player salaries is thought by some experts to contribute to playing-field violence. The average NFL defensive back who brings down Tampa Bay's Ricky Bell ($1.2 million on a multiyear contract), makes $47,403 and has a career expectancy of something over four years, less than enough time to qualify for an NFL pension. In the National Basketball Association, $30,000-a-year drones can be understood, if not forgiven, when they jab an elbow at Houston's Rick Barry ($500,000 per season, a $250,000 home, and a guaranteed post-career public relations job at $100,000-plus annually).

In-team friction can be generated as well. San Diego's respected defensive tackle Louie Kelcher stomped out of training camp when he learned that Charger quarterback Dan Fouts was getting $225,000 a year. On the 1977 Washington Redskins, Gerard Williams and Jake Scott were separated by only a few yards at their respective defensive backfield positions, but Scott made $125,000 and Williams only $30,000. Even mighty Pete Rose confessed that keeping up with baseball's Joneses was important. "It took me a long time to get to the top of my profession," Rose said. "If other guys were getting it [big paychecks], I wanted it too."

To be sure, news accounts of player salaries often have been exaggerated, if only because estimates are usually obtained from press spokesmen with an interest in making the club look generous. And many highly paid players—the New York Yankees' Catfish Hunter, for example—have opted for lengthy deferred payment schemes because of tax considerations. Still, the salaries of big-league players with even ordinary skills have far outpaced inflation.

Average player pay in the four major American professional sports more than quadrupled in the 1967–77 decade, from $20,783 to $92,659. Taken separately, basketball paychecks soared 715 per cent; hockey, 502 per cent; baseball, 400 per cent; football, 221 per cent. To measure the change in human terms, one only has to recall Jim Bouton, in *Ball Four,* groveling before the New York Yankee brass over a salary increase in 1963. After he had played a key role in the pin-stripers' stretch pennant drive and World Series victory, the club that Ruth built offered Bouton a princely $9,000, and only after much haggling agreed to boost the figure to $10,500.

The big money, the money that started coming late in the 1960s, metamorphosed American sports. It was not just that professional sports themselves became perpetual profit machines—the Nader-affiliated FANS estimated a pretax take of $3.9 million per NFL team in 1978—it was that everything connected with athletics took on financial dimensions that were hitherto unknown. Sporting goods grew to a $13 billion-plus industry (better than 1200 times its size in 1947), dominated by high-flying chain stores capable of supplying a tennis buff with more than two hundred brands of racquets, sixty-five different kinds of balls, and hundreds of styles of shoes.

Sports and their superstars were marketed by a new breed of promotional genius who never missed a dollar and spoke in terms such as upscale marketing demographics. Corporations with names like Uni-Managers International would provide—for fees of up to $5,000 per athlete per day—personal sales meetings or conference appearances by top pros. *Sports Illustrated* aimed the hawking of its own photos at large corporate advertising and promotional clients and offered business leaders a choice of 2,000 star athletes available through its speakers' bureau, "to sparkle at sales meetings, award dinners, conventions, store openings or wherever else the color and excitement of sports can help you shine."

Even running, perhaps linked more closely than any sport to the movement emphasizing fitness and alternative, cooperative athletics in the early and mid-1970s, became increasingly commercialized. Indeed, if Hugh Hefner was the guru of the last decade's girlie generation, *Runner's World* publisher Bob Anderson stood at the helm of a new, equally impressive, multimillion-dollar empire, this one focused on a generation of mostly college-educated, affluent runners whom major advertisers were panting to reach. Marathon racing, almost exclusively an amateur sport a few years ago, suddenly was paying its world-class competitors up to $50,000 a year. Sponsorship by big-time advertisers raised controversies among some die-hard amateurs, but that didn't keep Manufacturers Hanover Bank from spending $125,000 to back the New York Marathon, nor shoe manufacturers from struggling to keep up with the faddy whims of their upwardly and especially mobile clients. Baseball star Reggie Jackson even managed to get in on the act, bagging $30,000 from one manufacturer just to wear—not promote—its shoes.

Money, money, hear it jingle. Resentment, resentment, feel it tingle. Ticket prices went crashing through the Super-dome. Admission to the Rose Bowl, once $1.50, zoomed past $17.50. Super Bowl tickets doubled from an original $10 each, then shot up another 50 per cent—that is, for those who could get them. Regular-season bleacher tickets sold in some professional football clubs rose above $12 by 1979, and some teams around the NFL were planning to raise prices even higher, in some cases by as much as 20 per cent.

Even if a fan can come up with the $250 for a pair of Oakland Raiders season tickets, he or she may have to fight for a chance to spend the money. Season tickets for many professional teams are considered valuable family assets, handed down—along with increasingly preferred seating locations—from one generation to the next. Ownership of the 55,031 Washington Redskin home-stadium tickets, for example, is concentrated in the hands of just over 14,000 persons, according to *Sports Illustrated.* And huge blocks of tickets go to company executives who care nothing about their rising cost—they simply write it off along with other escalating expenses. All told, business concerns are the buyers of an estimated one-third of all tickets for major pro-fessional sports.

Could it be that some fist-swinging, bottle-throwing fans are angry about being squeezed out? Or at what they are being forced to pay to stay in? It is not simply that getting into any American stadium has gotten awfully hard to do, or that the price of beer and hot dogs would make a boulder belch. No, the real bite is being felt much deeper down in the pocket, in an area most fans only now are beginning to notice—taxes. The question comes down to what the owners of sport don't

have to pay—such as large tax bills—and what they are getting for free—such as large buildings.

The answer in each case is plenty. Despite their limited
availability to the public, about 70 per cent of the major
professional football/baseball stadiums built since 1965 were
constructed with public funds. Their *average* cost exceeded
$43 million, almost always well above initial estimates. Since
most were built with revenue bonds, under the law the public
was stuck for the difference. At the Louisiana Superdome,
originally touted by promoters as a "good bargain" at a projected $35 million, the tab for overruns alone far exceeded
$100 million. Interest on bonds meant the world's largest
domed stadium eventually would cost more than $300 mil-
lion, according to a November 27, 1977, article in *Parade,*
and income from sports and entertainment events could not
begin to cover the facility's $56,000-a-day operating ex-
penses. And the Superdome was just part of the $6 billion—
$1 billion more counting extra roads, sewers, and ramps—
that *Parade* estimated taxpayers committed, often unknow-
ingly, for elaborate stadiums and arenas.

At the same time the public is being sold on bigger and
better sports monuments, it often is being asked to accept
steep cuts in social programs. On the same day Mayor John
Lindsay of New York announced a $24 million remodeling
program for Yankee Stadium (a figure which soared to $240
million counting interest), his city began the process of firing
more than 6,000 schoolteachers for lack of funds. Cincinnati
built a $45 million sports complex while it cut spending for
education by 20 per cent.

The teams, meanwhile, have managed to convince community leaders that their mere presence is an important municipal asset. After threatening to move unless Buffalo taxpayers
enlarged the city's ancient War Memorial Stadium, owners of
the Buffalo Bills then used the same club to force construction of its exclusive 80,020-seat Rich Stadium. Now the city

pays off bonds for renovated but abandoned War Memorial, noted Bill Surface in *Parade,* while the county struggles to make payments owed for the $41.1 million new facility. But, for sheer flimflam slickery, it would be hard to match the following example, recounted by Paul Hoch in *Rip Off the Big Game:*

Without a big enough arena, it was implied that Vancouver could not get a National Hockey League franchise. So Canadian taxpayers were encouraged to build the $6 million Pacific Coliseum. The government in Ottawa and the British provincial treasury each put up $2 million. The City of Vancouver added $1.75 million and the Pacific National Exposition (which owns the coliseum building) added the final quarter million. The Vancouver Canucks were 87 per cent American-owned. So, what you had was three levels of Canadian government forking out about $6 million so that American millionaires could sell a Canadian game to Canadians.

Free-to-the-owner construction funds aren't the only lure. Publicly owned stadiums are exempt from property taxes. And since they have only to threaten a move to throw local politicians into uncontrollable fright, team owners often can talk their way out of other taxes as well. The city of Oakland, in financial straits even before passage of California's Proposition 13, dropped the idea of an amusement tax after warnings that major league baseball and football might be driven away. Indeed, at the same time the city contemplated a 25-per-cent cut in services because of an anticipated $10 million revenue shortfall, it was soberly considering the addition, at public expense, of 15,000 seats to the Oakland Coliseum. The purpose: to head off a rumored Raider move to Los Angeles.

In case the public ever finds a cure for its sports-edifice complex, the courts and tax laws have made sure professional teams have plenty of ripoff write-offs to fall back on. Until recently, tax laws permitted purchasers of ball teams to allocate a ridiculously small amount, usually about $50,000, to the cost of their franchise and to charge all the rest to player expenses, to be depreciated as fast as the owner wished.

As one wise baseball hand has noted, purchasers in effect were buying an unlicensed right to depreciate, one that could and did enable owners to classify hundreds of thousands of profit dollars as yearly depreciation. As soon as the write-off was exhausted, the franchise could be sold and the process begun all over again. It is hardly surprising that corporate distilling, radio and television, and brewery interests found professional athletics irresistibly appealing—any depreciation allowance left over could be gobbled up by the rest of the corporate empire. As economist Benjamin A. Okner observed in the Brookings Institution report on *Government and the Sports Industry:*

These advantages stem from the fact that the amount of income that can be sheltered from tax by writing off the value of player contracts usually exceeds the operating profits that can be earned by the team even if it is exceptionally well managed. Consequently, the true profitability of a franchise can be much greater than the published, "bookkeeping" amount.

For millionaire sportsmen whose franchises take the form of small corporations or partnerships, the benefits can be equally enormous. As an example, Okner postulated a mythical team whose new owners allocate $1.5 million of a $2 million initial price to player contracts, depreciated over five years. Figuring an annual straight-line depreciation of $300,000 and a net, predepreciation income of $100,000, the club will "lose" $200,000. The owners are free to report the loss separately for income-tax purposes, where, assuming they are in the highest marginal tax brackets, every dollar of Uncle Sam's tax bite can be reduced by as much as 70 cents:

Thus, the owners will realize $100,000 in cash-flow profits and $140,000 in personal tax relief, for a total cash-flow return from the team of $240,000—the team, meanwhile, reporting a $200,000 bookkeeping loss.

Subsequent tax rulings have set limits on the depreciation game,* and it must be remembered that sports give as well as receive. New Orleans officials, for example, estimate that a single Super Bowl was worth $30 million to their city's economy. Nonetheless, compared with the rest of American enterprise, sports enjoy distinct tax and other financial advantages. Baseball still luxuriates under the protective shield of a 1922 Supreme Court dictum which grants the game perpetual immunity from antitrust laws. The 1961 Sports Broadcast Act permits the NFL to barter with the television industry as a group, vastly increasing football's ability to escalate its already leviathan video fees.

It may seem far-fetched to suggest that tax favoritism, sky-high player salaries, and spiraling ticket prices have contributed to acts of violence by athletes and fans; yet it is money alone, Publius Pliny tells us, which sets all the world in motion. And atop that pile of sports money, peering down like an electronic king of the mountain, stands television. Nothing—not the salaries, not the speakers' bureaus, certainly not the nickel–dime promotion shticks—comes even close to matching the financial impact of the one-eyed monster.

Television has changed American sports in ways that are still becoming known to us. As Joseph Durso writes in *The All-American Dollar,* the seventies were the "super" decade in sports—the superstar, the Superdome, the Super Bowl, the super-salary. Watching it all, feeding it all, was the unblinking eye. "The broadcasting of games," writes Durso, "which had started innocently enough as 'special events' along with parades, ship arrivals, and political speeches a generation earlier, now moved into the frenzied area of commercial programming, with separate departments of the networks handling sports and rushing wildly for headline events and the sponsors to pay for them."

---

* The Internal Revenue Service, in a basketball case, reduced the allowable allocation of player costs in the initial team price to 50 per cent.

In many major sports, television contracts have become the difference between profit and loss. The 1969 New York Jets, a thriving team led by Joe Namath at his peak, played every home game before a packed stadium but cleared just $135,000 at the gate. In 1979 the Jets are not nearly as exciting on the field, but their take from television alone comes to several million dollars, thanks to a $656 million contract negotiated by the NFL with the three commercial networks. The biggest lump of television swag in history, the agreement provides each of the league's twenty-eight clubs with $20 million over four years, more than the average franchise was worth when the deal was signed. Figures in other sports also are impressive. Television revenues added $3.4 million to major-league baseball coffers in 1950, but that was a mere thirtieth of today's $92.8 million. The most recent four-year contract between ABC and the National Collegiate Athletic Association calls for college football to get $118 million, a 64-per-cent hike over the previous agreement.

Senate testimony a few years ago made it clear that a major reason the Kansas City Athletics moved to Oakland was the promise of an extra $800,000 in broadcasting revenues; similar considerations—a boost in media revenues from $500,000 to $1 million a year—led the Braves to abandon Milwaukee. "There is no way we could survive without television," commented William C. Ford, former owner of the Detroit Lions. "We couldn't make it without the income and the exposure."

The National Football League's first prime-time broadcast was aired in 1970. Under the league's latest contract, prime-time contests will be screened on Sunday, Monday, Tuesday, and Thursday nights, providing pro football's sponsors with six additional *hours* of commercial time per season as compared with the previous arrangement. Excluding local, independent, and public broadcasts, the three networks were airing more than two dozen hours of sports each week, year-round, by the late 1970s.

It was hardly surprising when a *TV Guide* poll revealed most Americans actually preferred viewing sports on television to witnessing them in person (with the single exception of professional baseball). "I have seen the future. It measures 19 inches diagonally," wrote Roger Kahn in a 1975 issue of *Esquire*. The late Wells Twombly of the *San Francisco Examiner* was more pessimistic. "Ultimately," he observed in a 1977 column, "the time will come when athletic events will be conducted on gigantic sound stages with studio audiences who have waited months to get free tickets, the only live human beings in attendance." Twombly added:

There was still a nobility about athletic competition, before they [television sports] utterly debased it, twisted it and reshaped it to meet their high standards of greed. They had no reverence for anything that wouldn't play in Peoria and, slowly, they taught the rest of us to be irreverent. To our mortal shame, we went along.

More than any single event, pro football's annual Super Bowl illustrates the interplay between big money, television, and sports. Traditionally the year's highest-rated television program, Super Bowl 1979 reached an estimated eighty-five million American homes, plus another fifty-five million in other countries, including Canada, Mexico, Turkey, West Germany, and Taiwan. Press credentials were issued to more than 2,000 media representatives from newspapers, wire services, magazines, and radio and television stations.

Super Bowl hoopla, Super Bowl hiccups. A single minute of commercial time can cost a sponsor upward of $300,000. Pregame commentators a couple of years ago bragged that there were more motorized vehicles in one place than at any time since Patton; the bill for one NFL cocktail party came to $75,000—besides catering, that paid for 12,739 pounds of food. Though no one suggested smelling the players' manure, soothsayers, astrologers, and spiritualists clung to the fringes of 1979's Super Bowl XIII. "The visions, the vibrations, that's what they say," intoned Miami spiritualist Madame Mary in picking the Steelers to defeat Dallas. (Pittsburgh did win, 35–31, and also fulfilled Madame Mary's prediction of a "very exciting" game.)

In amateur athletics, television's huge stakes have shifted even greater emphasis onto video sports, especially football, and made the importance of recruiting and fielding a winning team greater than ever. According to the *Wall Street Journal,* Notre Dame alone took in $1.5 million from two nationally televised, regular-season games and a Cotton Bowl appearance. "Even more importantly," added the newspaper, "there's the enormous recruiting edge that goes to coaches of perennial 'top 10' football schools who can guarantee prospects that they'll be given the opportunity to strut their stuff on the tube."

At a school like Ohio State, football is a "revenue sport" counted on for the support of thirty other athletic programs. It should not be surprising, therefore, that OSU under Woody Hayes routinely spent $85,000 and more each year on football recruiting, as much as the total athletic budget for the average NCAA school in 1969. "This is a business, a multimillion-dollar-a-year business," said one athletic director of a major university. "I've got to run it like one."

Woody Hayes lodged his players in luxurious dormitories away from the campus and then logged as many as 3,000 miles a month in search of new talent to replace them. Working from a master list of carefully screened top prospects, Hayes thought nothing of making personal visits as far away as New York, West Virginia, and Washington, D.C., often returning for a second,"closing" pitch, much like a traveling salesman. "He's at his best in the living room of a recruit," an admiring former assistant recalled in Jerry Brondfield's *Woody Hayes and the 100-yard War,* "with the boy's parents and maybe a younger brother hanging on every word, and almost struck dumb at the great man's presence." Hayes himself saw the recruiting operation in a strictly business sense: "These kids fill Ohio Stadium six times a year, 87,000 and more each Saturday. When you consider the total take, we're not investing much in the product, are we?"

Getting the star players means winning, and winning is crucial to filling those big stadiums—and keeping the television money flowing. Playing .500 ball simply isn't good enough. Given the pressure, the temptation to cheat has proved overwhelming for more than a few schools. The NCAA concedes as many as one in five of its major member schools commits serious recruiting violations, and at least some observers put the figure higher. The bait can include phony jobs, falsified academic records, a suddenly paid-up mortgage for the prospect's parents, free cars, and lavish apartments. "You take alumni buying tickets from players for $1,500 or $1,800," said one insider describing another payoff scam. "That is done all over the place."

Cheating in and of itself does not create violence and brutality in games, of course. But it is part of a sports-business philosophy which condones the subjugation of sportsmanship to achievement. The rewards of winning—specifically, money—give winning more importance. Money from the tube accelerates the process. Television nourishes the relationship between an increasingly elite, highly specialized athlete and a less selective, ever larger, audience.

In all of America's four major professional sports there are something less than 3,000 competing participants. Yet minor league baseball alone once employed thousands of players and steadily outdrew the majors almost two to one. At their height in 1949, the minors were attracting more than 40 million fans a year. With television, however, teams like the Hollywood Stars and the Oakland Oaks were doomed, even though years would elapse before big-league clubs actually moved into their towns. By 1976, the same year the majors were raking in $50.8 million in radio and television gold, minor league teams had shrunk by 70 per cent.

Television's Friday night fights gave boxing unprecedented national exposure at the same time that it dried up the small clubs and gyms which were the real strength of the sport. Sports became big business alright, but of the assembly-line variety, designed to satisfy cruder appetites. If television enlarged the audience for athletics, it also fed the craving for violence. As Christopher Lasch observed in the *New York Review of Books* for April 28, 1977:

As spectators become less knowledgeable about the games they watch, they become more sensation-minded and bloodthirsty . . . what corrupts an athletic performance [is] the presence of an unappreciative, ignorant audience and the need to divert it with sensations extrinsic to the performance.

In *Hockey in Canada: The Way It Is,* author Brian Conacher observed that the increased mayhem in that game could be explained by television's need to attract the masses, specifically "the violence-oriented American hockey fan."

The large numbers of people that are being exposed to the game now are often not aware of the skills and finesse that give the game its real appeal. But brawling is something they do understand, so as far as the games, television acceptance, and crowd appeal is concerned, it probably doesn't hurt to have a few brawls. If there is a little blood, so much the better for people with color sets.

In the 1950s and 1960s, Yankee pitcher Whitey Ford made a habit of secretly flashing his pick-off sign so television directors could catch his move to first or second base. Today, however, entire "athletic" events are staged specifically for the tube; one writer has labeled these phony contests "trashsports." Call them what you will, they are popular spectacles—a program known as the "Battle of the Network Stars" consistently ranks among the top-rated shows each year. Violence often is an element in the appeal of these trashsport shows. On one recent broadcast, billed as a "sports spectacular," a Hollywood stunt man flipped a bomb-wired car from a ramp. The camera probed and zoomed and replayed the explosion, while the announcer whipped up his audience by wondering whether the driver would survive.

Beat, belted, battered, mashed—those were the adjectives of victory and defeat employed during the brief sports segment of a local television news show.* The print media do little better. Watching star reporters, headline editors, and rewrite men hype up violent antagonisms is almost a spectator sport of its own. One writer celebrates a star basketball player's "finest moment" as landing a right cross on the jaw of an opponent. Another comments that a "benches-emptying battle would have improved" a dull football game in Cleveland. Headlines blare out countless declarations of sports "wars" between players, teams, and rival athletic associations. The 1978 American Football Conference playoff is gleefully tabbed the "Brutality Bowl" because thirteen participants had suffered injuries in the teams' previous meeting in the regular season.

The verbal muskets of sports talk fire on, spinning our stadium turnstiles and slamming into our sensibilities like dumdum bullets. "We got a letter from headquarters," begins a college cheer. "What'd he say? What'd he say?" comes the reply. To cheers: "He say, 'Hit to kill, boys, hit to kill!' "

- A boxer: "I don't want to knock him out. I want to hit him, step away, and watch him hurt. I want his heart."

- A hockey player: "I speared him, I pole-axed him, and I cut him close to the eye. Things like that happen in the heat of the game."

- A football player: "A defensive lineman can do just about anything. He can damn near haul an axe out of his jock and slash around with it before he'll be called for anything."

These are not the phrases of a civilized people at play; they are the catchwords of a sports business whose bottom line is

* ABC-TV affiliate Channel 7 in San Francisco, April 13, 1979.

maiming to win. It has become fashionable to suggest that by paying our amateur athletes we would avoid the hypocrisy of the present system. And, indeed, the concept of amateurism goes back to a time when sports were the plaything of the aristocracy; the idea of competing for money, with its intensified emphasis on success, was abhorrent. Now the tide runs hard the other way. Collegiate authorities worry less about the proprieties of professionalism and more about how to create a positive-cash-flowing Super Bowl of their own.

Those who love amateur athletics, however, should be deeply wary of the dangers of professionalism. Once a sport has locked onto the spectator cycle it is difficult to get off. Tolerance of mayhem evolves into a taste for it. Much like the old economic proverb that bad money drives out good, athletic corruption is difficult to contain, almost impossible to reverse. Afraid of losing the fans they have attracted by vulgar display, the sports establishment grows increasingly reluctant to cut back the ante. Violence peripheral to the natural roughness of a game becomes violence central to redefining sport as show business. That is the final valley of the spectator cycle, one we already have seen engulf at least two sports—wrestling and roller derby.

We cannot return to the past, yet the future is unappealing. "Of all the foul growths current in the world," wrote Sophocles, "the worst is money. Money drives men from home, plunders proud cities, and perverts honest minds to shameful practice." In athletics, the love of money erodes our standards and, eventually, serves as a primary feedstock in the brutalizing of our games. As Ray Kennedy and Nancy Williamson noted in a 1978 *Sports Illustrated* series on money in athletics, "There persists the uneasy feeling that, for all the ballyhooing of a new golden age of sports, neither the game nor any of its participants, not even the instant-millionaire jock, is the richer for it."

⑥ **Origins**

The only lasting answer to our contemporary taste for violence is to uncover the roots of hatred and rage and, through self-knowledge, move toward self-control.

—Arthur Schlesinger, Jr. in
Violence: America in the Sixties

Violence in sports may be more pervasive and, for complex reasons, more harmful than in the past, but it is hardly new. Since the sacrificial and funeral games of earliest recorded history, savagery and athletics have been teamed in mankind's religious, cultural, and recreational lives. The American Indians, for example, played an early version of lacrosse called baggataway, in which hundreds of players chased a grass-stuffed deerskin ball—the skull of an enemy reportedly was used by some tribes—between goals often miles apart. Baggataway players were free to foul, trip, and stomp one another. Their women—early cheerleaders, perhaps—chased along the sidelines after them, exhorting their favorites and beating the opponents with cudgels.

Among the ancient Mayans and Aztecs, the sacred ball-court game ended with the beheading of the losing side's

126

captain. Little is known about the rules of the game, though a match apparently involved two teams of seven men each, most of them members of the aristocracy. The game was played with a solid rubber ball which could be struck with virtually any part of the body save the hands, but it went over to the other side immediately upon touching the ground. The object: to drive the ball through one of two stone rings, carved with the figure of a plumed serpent and placed vertically on walls at either end of the court.

Based on mythological astronomy, the game was believed to reenact the struggle between light and dark in the heavens; the symbolic play was thought necessary to ensure the presence of the sun and the moon. According to legend, the first humans, twin brothers born in heaven, were beheaded after being enticed to Hades for a game of football. The head of one brother, which had been placed in a tree beside a road, was visited by the virgin daughter of one of the gods. She became pregnant when the skull spat a stream of seeds into her palm and later gave birth to Hunahpu and Xbalanque, who grew up to become young gods. The god-sons challenged the rulers of Hades to another game of ball and won. They exhumed the bodies of their father and uncle, whose heads rose in the sky to become the sun and moon.

While many details of the Mayan and Aztec games remain obscure, the reality of their existence can be documented in nearly fifty ball courts discovered in an area stretching through northern Mexico to Guatemala and Honduras. One of the courts at Chichen-Itza on Mexico's Yucatán Peninsula, for example, contains a playing field measuring 480 feet by 120 feet, about a third longer and a quarter narrower than an American football field. Players wore leather pads and sometimes helmetlike headgear to protect themselves from the force of the ball. Spectators fled immediately at game's end—the winning side was entitled to the clothes and jewelry of all those present.

There is little doubt that thousands died in the sacrificial ceremonies accompanying these games, whose courts almost always were located within a temple pyramid complex. In 1519, the conquistadors under Cortez estimated that the ball-court tzompantli—or skull rack—in the Aztec capital contained 136,000 human specimens. As Walter Umminger writes in *Supermen, Heroes and Gods:*

The emperor Moctezuma personally conducted the Spanish conquerors around these holy precincts, unaware of the horror the sight was inspiring in them. On the altar before the image of Huitzilopochtli they saw three human hearts still pounding and steaming in a golden "eagle vase," freshly cut from living victims. The walls and stairway of the pyramid were crusted with blood. "The stench," remarked Bernal Diaz, was "harder to bear than in a Castilian slaughterhouse."

The Mayans and Aztecs were not the only sophisticated ancients with a taste for brutality. For all the Greeks' reputed reverence for physical grace and harmony, the games of classical antiquity contained far higher levels of violence than is generally realized. If the Greeks are to be credited with the first efforts at organized athletics (the Olympic games of 800 B.C.), they also should be noted for spotting, early on, the vicious potential in bare-handed combat sports. Borrowing from Egypt and Mesopotamia, they evolved the Pankration (meaning "all powerful"), a mixture of boxing and wrestling so savage that it was steadfastly avoided by Milon of Croton, who lived in the sixth century B.C. and was the most famous of all ancient Greek wrestlers. Opponents fought with every part of their bodies and were free to kick, trample, and use strangleholds; they could legally dislocate and break the bones of opponents. Though officially banned, eye-gouging frequently is depicted in wall paintings and pottery fragments of the period.

Greek boxing was no more delicate. Like the Pankration,

matches continued without interruption, ending only when an opponent yielded or was killed. The increasing professionalism of Greek boxing can be traced through the protection fighters wore on their hands. From the time of Homer to the close of the fifth century B.C., Greek boxers wore only thongs, looped around the fingers and wrists and often wrapped around the forearms. The thongs were made of pliable oxhide and were rubbed with fat to keep them soft. As the spectacle—and the prize money—increased, however, hand protection underwent significant changes. "Sharp thongs," made of hard leather with sharp ridges and reminiscent of modern brass knuckles, came into use. Easily capable of breaking bones, the sharp thongs eventually were replaced by an even more gruesome weapon—the Roman cestus, weighted with pieces of iron and containing metal spikes fixed over the knuckles. These changes in hand covering brought predictable results: as the purpose of the glove increasingly shifted from protection to attack, boxing decreased in skill and finesse. The sport became more brutal.

It took centuries for Greek sports to deteriorate. In the beginning, athletics reflected both the Greeks' love of competition and the preservation by nobility of the aristocratic virtues of strength, courage, wit, wisdom, and liberality. "The Greeks," as Edith Hamilton has written in *The Greek Way,* "were the first people in the world to play, and they played on a great scale."

All over Greece there were games, all sorts of games; athletic contests of every description: races—horse-, boat-, foot-, torch-races; contests in music, where one side outsung the other; in dancing—on greased skins sometimes to display a nice skill of foot and balance of body; games where men leaped in and out of flying chariots; games so many one grows weary with the list of them. They are embodied in the statues familiar to all, the disc thrower, the charioteer, the wrestling boys, the dancing flute players. The great games—there were four that came at stated seasons—were so important, when one was held, a truce of God was proclaimed so that all Greece might come in safety without fear. There "glorious-limbed youth"—the phrase is Pindar's, the athlete's poet—strove for an honor so coveted as hardly anything else in Greece. An Olympic victor—triumphing generals would give place to him.

As enunciated by Pindar, the athletic ideal incorporated courage and endurance with modesty, dignity, and fair-mindedness, those elusive qualities the Greeks called *Aidos*. As Victor Hugo wrote of the Greek philosophy: "Far from proposing, as Christianity does, to separate the spirit from the body, it ascribes form and features to everything, even to impalpable essences, even to the intelligence."

By the middle of the fifth century B.C., however, classic athletics already were yielding to the demands of professionalism. "The very popularity of athletics was their undoing," wrote E. Norman Gardiner in *Athletics of the Ancient World*. Within one hundred years, sports were inundated with special privileges, escalating prizes, and tax exemptions for successful athletes. Some athletes were worshipped as religious heroes; others received honors formerly reserved for intellectuals and civic leaders. Professional athletes called "pot-hunters" wandered from city to city collecting prize money. "The real evil was over-competition," Gardiner observed, "and it was a danger not only to the state but to the athlete. The multiplication of competitions and of prizes was making sport a source of profit."

As athletics became specialized, the general populace increasingly withdrew into spectatorship. Training soon became more regimented. Greek athletes cast aside their former vegetarian diets for huge portions of weight-inducing meat. Even Aristotle spoke out against the extreme training being undertaken by young boys, noting that in most cases their future athletic careers were furthered little if at all, "for not more than two or three of them have gained a prize both as boys and as men."

The new athletics sacrificed the former ideals of beauty and strength. The gracefully proportioned, long-muscled gymnasts of an earlier era gave way to a thick-bodied, small-headed race of athletes bred for combat sports, their brutish expressions and physiques pictured on vases and mosaics of the time. The physician and critic Galen wrote of professional athletes:

They spend their lives in over-exercising, in over-eating . . . They have not health nor have they beauty. Even those who are naturally well-proportioned become fat and bloated: their faces are often shapeless and unsightly owing to the wounds received in boxing and the Pankration. They lose their eyes and their teeth and their limbs are strained.

Increasingly marred by corruption and bribes, Greek sports nonetheless flourished in an era which witnessed the rapid expansion of stadiums and arenas under the Roman Empire. The Greeks played themselves; the Romans watched others play. Seeing in athletics only a spectacle, the Romans perverted the gladiatorial combats they borrowed from the funeral games of the Etruscans. As Gardiner notes, professionalism emphasized strength over finesse, and the fruits of competition increasingly fell into the same hands. Elaborate athletic unions, comparable to our modern-day player associations, were built in cities all across Rome, many with their own gymnasiums and meeting and dining rooms.

The citizens of Rome demanded a good show in return. In *I, Claudius,* Robert Graves's protagonist recalls his grandmother Livia, the empress, expressing her anger after a series of slow matches:

This time Livia had got the heads of the Gladiatorial Guild together and told them that she wanted her money's worth. Unless every bout was a real one she would have the guild broken up: there had been too many managed fights in the previous summer. So the fighters were warned by the guild-masters that this time they were not to play kiss-in-the-ring or they would be dismissed from the guild.

In the first six combats one man was killed, one so seriously wounded that he died the same day, and a third had his shield-arm lopped off close to the shoulder, which caused roars of laughter. In each of the other three combats one of the men disarmed the other, but not before he had given such a good account of himself that Germanicus and I, when appealed to, were able to confirm the approval of the audience by raising our thumbs in token that his life should be spared. . . . The seventh combat was between a man armed with a regulation army sword and an old-fashioned round brass-bound shield and a man armed with a three-pronged trout-spear and a short net. The sword-man or 'chaser' was a soldier of the Guards who had recently been condemned to death for getting drunk and striking his captain. His sentence had been commuted to a fight against this net-and-trident man—a professional from Thes-saly, very highly paid, who had killed more than twenty opponents in the previous five years, so Germanicus told me.

Livia was paying him [Thessalian] 1,000 gold pieces for the after-noon and 500 more if he killed his man after a good fight. They came together in front of the Box and saluted first Augustus and Livia and then Germanicus and me as joint-presidents, with the usual formula: 'Greetings, Sirs. We salute you in Death's shadow!' We returned the greetings with a formal gesture, but Germanicus said to Augustus: 'Why, sir, that chaser's one of my father's veter-ans. I know him well. He won a crown for Germany for being the first man over an enemy stockade.' Augustus was interested. 'Good,' he said, 'this should be a good fight, then. But in that case the netman must be ten years younger, and years count in this game.' Then Germanicus signalled for the trumpets to sound and the fight began.

. . . The net whistled round Roach's [soldier's nickname] head and the trident jabbed here and there; but Roach was still undis-mayed, and once made a snatch at the trident and nearly got posses-sion of it. The Thessalian had now worked him toward our Box to make a spectacular killing.

'That's enough!' said Livia in a matter-of-fact voice, 'he's done enough playing about. He ought to finish him now.' The Thessalian needed no prompting. He made a simultaneous sweep of his net round Roach's head and a stab at his belly with the trident. And then what a roar went up! Roach had caught the net with his right hand and, flinging his body back, kicked with all his strength at the shaft of the trident a foot or two from his enemy's hand. The weapon flew up and over the Thessalian's head, turned in the air and stuck quivering into the wooden barrier. The Thessalian stood astonished for a moment, then left the net in Roach's hands and dashed past him to recover the trident. Roach threw himself forward and sideways and caught him in the ribs, as he ran, with the spiked boss of his shield. The Thessalian fell, gasping, on all-fours. Roach recovered himself quickly and with a sharp downward swing of the shield caught him on the back of the neck.

'The rabbit-blow!' said Augustus. 'I've never seen that done in an arena before, have you, my dear Livia? Eh? Killed him too, I swear.'

The Thessalian was dead. I expected Livia to be greatly displeased but all she said was: 'And served him right. That's what comes of underrating one's opponent. I'm disappointed in that netman. Still, it has saved me that five hundred in gold, so I can't complain, I suppose.'

Far from idealizing athletics, the Romans denigrated them, substituting mob entertainment for the old Greek idea of competition for the participants. By the first century B.C., fifty Roman cities could boast their own gladiatorial arenas. Augustus claimed that more than ten thousand men had fought each other during his reign. Pandering to the increasing lust of the crowds, the spectacles took a kinky turn. In Nero's reign, aristocratic women were thrown into the arena as combatants and, in A.D. 90, the emperor Domitian arranged a battle between women and dwarfs. The emperor Commodus, who proclaimed himself the Roman Hercules, fought as a gladiator on more than seven hundred occasions.

Usually gladiators were slaves or convicts who fought to the death. The ranks of free professional athletes, on the other hand, included Greek boxers, who, if they were lucky enough to survive the rigors of the cesti, might retire on a pension provided by their athletic union. Successful charioteers did far better. Stars of the 2,083-foot-long Circus Maximus could become millionaires within a few years. Even in decline, the Romans exhibited a rabid enthusiasm for racing. As Edward Gibbon notes in *Decline and Fall of the Roman Empire:*

The Roman people still considered the Circus as their home, their temple and the seat of the Republic. The impatient crowd rushed at the dawn of day to secure their places, and there were many who passed a sleepless and anxious night in the adjacent porticos. From the morning to the evening, careless of the sun or of the rain, the spectators, who sometimes amounted to the number of 400,000, remained in eager attention; their eyes fixed on the horses and charioteers, their minds agitated with hope and fear for the success of the colours which they espoused; and the happiness of Rome appeared to hang on the event of a race.

Mass spectator events virtually disappeared with the fall of Rome in the fourth century A.D., but that hardly brought an end to symbolic conflict and competition. Combat sports— tournament jousting, archery, and sword fighting—were formalized as aristocratic military entertainments. And the Coliseum tradition of publicly attended animal bloodsports— hunts as well as fights between wild animals were favored by the Romans—survived in the medieval fairs of England and Europe. More than one Stuart monarch banned "foteball" out of fear his archers' skills would go rusty. But few could find anything wrong with a bit of bull or bear baiting.

The tormenting of chained bears, running bulls, and even monkeys, donkeys, and rats with yapping, biting dogs was a staple of nearly every medieval country fair. Usually a pack of four or five dogs was unleashed on a single bear, chained with its back to the wall. Typically, the first of the attackers were ripped to pieces within minutes, but the fight went on until the bear proved its mastery of the others or its own wounds were too severe for it to continue. Actually, the wounds of the bear were carefully tended by its keeper, known as a bearward. Not so lucky was the common feline—in at least some locales a popular Guy Fawkes Day pastime called for burning cats alive in a basket.

Battles between humans continued the tradition of savagery. Pugilists fought with bare hands and little mercy. Their wildly popular bouts could end in severe injuries, blindness, and death. Not until the Queensbury Rules in 1866 would gloves be worn, and then only in England, the naked fist remaining a part of American prize fighting for thirty more years.* On the rough-and-tumble American frontier, such fights were still terminating in brutal gouging matches as late as the nineteenth century. In this *Travels in America,* Irish writer Thomas Ashe described such an encounter between a Virginian and a Kentuckian near the Ohio River:

Very few rounds had taken place before the Virginian contracted his whole form and, summoning up all his energy for one act of desperation, pitched himself into the bosom of his opponent . . . the shock received by the Kentuckian, and the want of breath, brought him instantly to the ground. The Virginian never lost his hold, and, fixing his claws in his hair and his thumbs on his eyes, gave them an instantaneous start from their sockets. The sufferer roared aloud . . .

Americans preserved more than one Old-World athletic tradition. At about the same time England finally was turning away from animal baiting, the Colonies were discovering it. And the ancient Aztec and Mayan memories weren't entirely dead either: in 1841 Horace Greeley's *New York Tribune* re-

---

* The last reported bare-knuckle fight took place in 1899 between John L. Sullivan and Jake Kilrain. Some 3,000 fans showed up at the secret ringside for the bout, which lasted seventy-five rounds and ended with both men soaked in blood.

ported that a ball game between two Indian tribes ended with
the winning team collecting the losers' clothing.

It should be added that violence in athletics is scarcely a
purely occidental tradition. The ancient Chinese were fond of
a nasty game known as "butting." Combatants slipped ox
horns over their heads and went skull to skull, leading, says
Gardiner, to "smashed heads, broken arms and blood running
in the palace yard." For all the roughness of their games,
however, the Chinese developed a code of sportsmanship
more refined than even that of the Greeks, whose obsession
with victory made them poor losers with slight regard for
their foes—Homer had said, "Always to be the best and to
excel others." The Chinese concept of *Iang*—to yield to another in honor—found little reflection in the culture of Western athletics. As the poet Lu Yu (A.D. 50–130) wrote about
football, "There must be no partiality, but there must be
determination and coolness, without the slightest irritation at
failure. And if all this is necessary for football, how much
more for the business of life."

Early kicking games deserve close scrutiny because of their
importance in the development of the great spectator sports,
such as modern football, which would follow. Indeed, the
Chinese practiced a game similar to football as long ago as
three centuries before Christ, though, like the British, they
considered the sport undignified for those of noble birth. The
game was played with a round ball made from eight strips of
leather and filled with hair. A silk cord or net was strung
between a single set of bamboo goal posts, and the object,
depending on which was used, was to kick the ball over the
cord or through a round hole in the center of the net.

By contrast, early football in medieval Europe lacked any
evidence of specialization and often combined elements of
what later became boxing, soccer, wrestling, polo, and hockey in a single sport. Little effort was made to develop special

positions or roles for players, and there was no separation between players and spectators.

As early as the tenth century, the English played a game called (perhaps not entirely symbolically) the Dane's head, in which teams of peasant villagers kicked a cow's bladder between towns, which themselves sometimes served as goals. No formal rules existed, and, in the swarming free-for-all, women and children dashed in to kick the ball—almost any means was fair. Nobody knows how many goals or points were needed to win, but as sociologist Eric Dunning points out in his excellent football history of the period, there was plenty of action. The ball sailed over meadows and streams, down village streets and over walls, followed by a mob of wildly scuffling players. Dunning records the impressions of Richard Carew in his seventeenth-century history of Cornwall. Carew commented on a primitive tackle game called "Hurlinge to the countrie,"* in which players scrambled over "hilles, dales, hedges, mires, plashes [puddles] and ditches" in pursuit of the ball carrier, who would be "layd flat on god's deare earth" when caught.

You shall sometimes see 20 or 30 lie tugging together in the water, scrambling and scratching for the ball . . . I cannot well resolve, whether I should more commend this game, for the manhood and exercise, or condemne it for the boysterousness and harmes which it begetteth: for as on the one side it makes their bodies strong, hard, and nimble, and puts courage into their hearts . . . So on the other part, it is accompanied with many dangers, some of which do ever fall to the players share. For proofe whereof, when the hurling is ended, you shall see them retyring home, as from a pitched battaile, with bloody pates, bones broken and out of joynt, and such bruises as serve to shorten their daies . . .

Football became part of the ritual brawls on saints' days and other religious holidays. Shrove Tuesday (the Tuesday before

---

* Hurling survives today as a Gaelic field game, a kind of combination soccer and lacrosse in which a ball resembling an American softball is used.

Ash Wednesday) finally was completely taken over by football and eventually became known as "football-day." Denounced by moralists and a military nobility who feared able-bodied football players would neglect their archery and hence the national defense, the game was subject to royal bans as early as 1314 and perhaps before. Dunning and colleague Norbert Elias have counted twenty-seven royal edicts against football between 1314 and 1615. Indeed, James I barred football from his court, as a sport "meeter for maiming than for making able the users thereof."

Even so, by the early 1800s the game was being played by upper- and middle-class youth in public schools. To the Greeks, athletics served the social purpose of strengthening the defenses of the state against outside attack. The Romans found games useful in promoting internal security because they diverted the attention of the populace. As Dunning notes, however, Englishmen were the first to see games, particularly soccer, as important to the economic well-being of their country.

In England, soccer proved closely analagous to working-class life in factories and assembly plants, emphasizing the qualities of strength, endurance, and the ability to bear pain, illness, and boredom. With the rise of an industrial middle class, and with the emphasis on science and quantification that accompanied it, the rules of soccer were committed to written form for the first time. The game that had been the property of village peasants was appropriated by the upper classes and then given back to the simple folk who had first enjoyed it.

Soccer's newly formalized rules were spread throughout the countryside, often by ministers or headmasters impressed by the game's ability to instill character training. "The cricket and football fields . . . are not merely places of exercise and amusement," noted the Royal Commission on Public Schools, "they help to form some of the most valuable social qualities and manly virtues."

Late on a brisk November afternoon in 1823, William Webb Ellis, a student at Rugby School in Warwickshire, scooped up the ball during a dull interclass soccer game and spurted down the field to score a goal. Ellis was severely criticized for breaking the rules, but within twenty years rugby had been recognized as a game in its own right. And by the last quarter of the century, rugby's influence was being felt well beyond the shores of England.

On Wednesday and Thursday, May 14 and 15, 1874, Canada's McGill University played soccer at Harvard University. The Wednesday meeting, which Harvard won, 3-0, was the first college contest in which admission (50 cents) was charged. But even more propitious was the game the following day, when the Canadians introduced their American hosts to rugby. That match ended in a scoreless tie, but it seemed faster and more spontaneous to the Harvard players, who soon indoctrinated their rivals at Columbia, Yale, and Princeton. In 1876, the four schools officially adopted rugby rules as the basis of American football.

Due, perhaps, to difficulties in adjusting to a game few thoroughly understood, the early days of football were violent indeed. Paintings of the period are reminiscent of the Civil War, with bandage-swathed players (they wore no helmets) sprawled across the field calling for help. A description of the Yale–Princeton game of 1884 in the *New York Evening Post* described the struggle witnessed by reporters as "real fighting, savage blows that drew blood, and falls that seemed as if they must crack all the bones and drive the life from those who sustain them."

Americans overcame the ambiguities of British rugby with a scrimmage line, by creating the role of center and reducing the number of players from fifteen to eleven, and by imposing a framework of yardage and downs. Soon, however, the game which had seemed so open began to slow down. Emphasis shifted from kicking to ball carrying and mass tactics—the flying and revolving "turtle-back" wedges, tackle tandems, and vicious hurdle plays. In the famous wedge, linemen protecting a runner often clung to special grips sewn into their pants—as they escorted the ball carrier downfield, they simply mowed down everybody in their path. The gridiron grind grew even more agonizing in 1888, when, at the urging of Walter Camp, schools agreed to permit below-the-waist tackling, vastly strengthening the hand of the defense.

In England, the teamwork they learned in such games as soccer and rugby eventually helped working-class men improve conditions in factories and industrial plants with collective action. Even before that, the lessons of cooperative masculine toughness, of playing by a set of rules, aided Britain in meeting the grueling physical demands of the early Machine Age. In the United States, however, football was chopping up the flower of America's collegiate aristocracy. By the dawn of the twentieth century, the game's problems with "tramp athletes"—players who wore the school uniform but often were not even registered for classes—and the slow, brutal style of play were drawing heavy criticism.

In a 1905 game between Pennsylvania and Swarthmore, the Penn players swore they would "get" Bob Maxwell, one of the great linemen of the time. Maxwell played the entire game, but when he left the field, a photographer snapped a picture of his battered face. The photo brought the building crisis over football brutality to a head: President Theodore Roosevelt summoned representatives from Harvard, Yale, and Princeton to the White House. If the viciousness and foul play were not cleaned up, the president said, he would abolish football by executive edict.

As it turned out, White House intervention triggered a series of reforms which—though their full implementation took more time than expected—culminated in the development of the forward pass and the permanent banning of mass plays in 1910. As Reuel Denney and David Riesman point out, the president's action was important for two other reasons. For one thing, it had been prompted by the relatively new phenomenon of photographic sports coverage. For another, Roosevelt's outrage was that of the first American president who was also an unflagging patron of sport. "To him, football was the great moral force capable of preparing its devotees to become aggressive and intelligent civic leaders," wrote John Allen Krout in his *Annals of American Sport*. "No one can estimate how mightily the leaven of his speeches and writings worked in convincing his fellow countrymen of the merits of the Gridiron game."

Denney and Reisman suggest that Roosevelt reacted to the brutality scandals of 1905* primarily because they were evidence of a bad sportsmanship which could only undermine the competitive ethic, an ethic viewed as central to industrial progress. As Denney reiterated in *The Astonished Muse*:

By contrast with the British, the Americans demonstrated a high degree of interest in winning games and winning one's way to high production goals. The Americans, as in so many other matters, were clearly concerned with the competitive spirit . . . (British sports, like British industry, seemed to take it more for granted that competition will exist even if one does not set up an ideology for it.)

---

* Criticism of football violence surfaced again in the early 1930s, when fatalities exhibited an alarming jump. In supporting a proposal that the regular season be limited to six games per school, Yale's Dr. James R. Angell commented: "I do not believe there is any obligation on the part of the college to furnish the general public nor even the alumni with substitutes for the circus, the prize fight, and the gladiatorial combat." As George Gip observes in *The Great American Sports Book*: "One of the most prominent critics was Dr. Beverly R. Tucker, a Richmond neurologist, who petitioned President Herbert Hoover to appoint a commission that would study ways of reducing the football mortality rate. The flurry of interest in Tucker's petition soon died down, of course, and little was heard of it as the year came to a close. Some attention was given to eliminating the kickoff play, which even then was recognized as perhaps the most violent of the game, but coaches and players across the nation were lukewarm to suggestions that the ball be given to a team on its 20-yard line. And so the petition that football become a less violent game faded into obscurity. The sportsminded public had other things to think about, such as whether Connie Mack should break up his Philadelphia Athletics 'for the good of the game . . . '"

Much of this seems to rest in the paradoxical belief of Americans that competition is natural—but only if it is constantly recreated by artificial systems of social rules that direct energies into it.

The idea that human competition and aggression is natural underlies the entire debate over violence in our games today. "Dancing is a contact sport," said Vince Lombardi. "Football is a collision sport"—and coaches as distant in philosophy as George Allen and Don Shula have agreed.

We accept the instinctuality of conflict as readily as we do the law of supply and demand. We are told that sports, like some form of sociological ejaculation, are especially important to the masculine members of our society as, in the words of psychiatrist Arnold Beisser, a "bridge across childhood, adolescence and adulthood." American males live in a world in which automation and changing laws and customs have all but negated their physical advantages over women. Sports, Beisser notes, is still an area in which a male's biological strength remains important, where the separateness of masculine sexuality may be reinforced. In his classic *On Aggression*, Konrad Lorenz expresses the belief that sport had its origins in highly hostile fighting between males, probably as part of sexual selection, and that "the main function of sport today lies in the cathartic discharge of the aggressive urge."

As appealing as such notions may seem, much evidence suggests their fallibility. "Anybody who argues for in-built aggression in homo sapiens must see aggression as a universal instinct in the animal kingdom," wrote anthropologist Richard Leakey and Roger Lewin, editor of the British journal *New Scientist*. "It is no such thing."

Leakey, Lewin, philosopher–anthropologist Ashley Montagu, and others do not maintain that man's nature is idyllic. But they argue strongly that his behavior constitutes an adaptation to environmental circumstances. "Aggression," says Roderick Gorney, who holds similar views as author of *The*

Human Agenda, "is like all human behavior. It is primarily learned."

Among lower animals, such as fighting fish and combative waterfowl, Gorney points out, instinctual combat does, in fact, exist. But higher mammals exhibit little or no innate inclination to destroy members of their own species. A dominant male baboon, for example, cannot ignore his instincts to eat, drink, copulate, and eliminate; yet no evidence suggests "a spontaneously arising urge to aggress that will damage the organism if ignored."

According to Gorney, "The evidence is that for most of our two–four million years, most human beings and behavior were consonant with the basic law of cooperation between members of the same species. Stone-age humans travelled continuously in pursuit of food, the women gathering plant foods while the men hunted for animals . . . they had neither the motivation nor the resources for much conflict." More than once, our own national survival has depended almost entirely upon our ability to work with others toward common goals. Indeed, America's most important historical triumphs—the colonists' successful settlement, the westward movement, our total mobilization during World War II—represent victories of cooperation, which in some cases required the complete suspension of "normal" competitive activities.

The games of many so-called primitives—the Tassaday, the desert Bushmen of the Kalahari, the Eskimos, the Pueblo Indians—show little evidence of built-in hostility. On the other hand, an instinct is by definition highly predictable, usually a specific response to a predetermined signal. As Leakey and Lewin point out, even territoriality varies widely among species and in some cases does not exist at all, depending almost entirely on the availability of food resources and sufficient space for the rearing of young.

In *Is Man Innately Aggressive?* Ashley Montagu dismisses

the territoriality theories of Robert Ardrey and others: "Is it not strange that, if man carries within him the animal heritage of group territoriality, his closest living relations, the great apes (gorilla, chimpanzee and orangutan) do not exhibit the slightest evidence of such territoriality?"

It was mothering, not instinct, which stimulated aggression among rats and mice in a study cited by Montagu. Experimenters found that when newborn mice were given to a rat mother, she nursed and cared for them but did not pass on the aggressive training they would have received from a natural parent. The rat-reared mice appeared plumper and exhibited less anxiety than the mouse-reared mice; they preferred the company of rats over mice. Montagu noted that "the most dramatic finding was that rat-reared mice would *not* fight when put in a standard fighting-box situation. This is in contrast to the increase of 44 per cent in fights among control mice [raised] by mice mothers."

The researchers decided to find out whether aggression also could be reduced in rats reared by their filial parents. At weaning, they kept twenty rat–mouse pairs together for thirty-six days, then returned the rats and mice to their separate colonies. When the experimental rats were ninety days old, they were tested for mouse-killing, along with a control group of rats never exposed to mice. Whereas nearly half (45 per cent) of the control rats killed mice, none of the experimental animals did. "Obviously, we must therefore reject any hypothesis that states that aggression is a genetically determined, instinctive response that cannot be modified by experience," Montagu quoted researchers Victor H. Dennenberg and M. X. Zarrow. "The social context within which the animal develops is critically important in determining his later aggressive behavior."

The instinctualists argue that athletics serve as a release for man's inherent hostility. But anthropologist Richard G. Sipes found the reverse was true:

I randomly selected ten warlike and ten peaceful societies throughout the world and ethnographically coded them for the presence or
absence of combative type sports. A combative type sport was de-
fined as one involving the acquisition of disputed territory, generally symbolized by the placing of an object in a guarded location (a
hockey puck in the cage, a basketball through the ring, or a football
at the opponent's end of the field), the subduing of an opponent (as
in some—but not all—forms of wrestling), or patently combat situations (fencing, dodging thrown spears, karate). Of the ten warlike
societies, nine had combative sports and one did not. Of the ten
peaceful societies, only two had combative sports and eight lacked
them. This indicates that warlikeness and combative sports tend to
occur together.

According to Sipes, a statistical check of his results indicates the probability of their occurring by chance as about
three in a thousand. Studies by other scientists of conflict
among Choctaw Indians and "anglo" societies, he adds, support "my findings that sports, especially combative team
sports, do not serve as functional alternatives to other forms
of aggression, such as warfare . . . if indifference to suffering,
zero-sum games, bravery, aggressiveness or other generalized
characteristics are found strongly present in one activity, they
most likely will be found throughout the culture."

The claim of a special masculine need to release tensions in
aggressive sports also must be subject to close scrutiny.
Women now participate in highly competitive, combative
games in record numbers. They have demanded the right to
play on interscholastic football, basketball, and track teams,
have formed professional tackle football leagues of their
own, and are featured in such spectator contests as wrestling
and roller derby. In 1978 three females won a court battle
granting women their boxing licenses in New York, despite
the opposition of athletic-commission members, including
former heavyweight boxing champion Floyd Patterson. A magazine devoted to female participation in martial arts, self-

defense, and combative sports is appropriately named *Fighting Woman News*. If the discharge of bottled up aggression is unique to the male hormones, why are women flocking to combative sports in such numbers?

The answer is more likely to be found in our culture than in our genes. As Thomas Tutko and William Bruns observe in *Winning Is Everything and Other American Myths,* we live in a society which places a high premium on competition and success: "The assumption is that somehow the winner does everything right and the loser does everything wrong." Victory is obsessive; being a winner becomes the only basis for individual worth. When Richard Nixon lost the race for the California governorship in 1962—only the second electoral defeat he ever suffered at the polls—his entire personality disintegrated in a bitter outburst against those he believed responsible for the loss. It may be less than coincidental that Vince Lombardi's line, "Winning is everything," would serve later as the slogan for Watergate's infamous Committee to Re-Elect the President. When Gerald Ford selected an acronym for his anti-inflation program, he chose WIN (Whip Inflation Now). "We have been asked to swallow a lot of home-cooked psychology in recent years that winning isn't all that important anymore," Ford wrote as vice-president, "whether on the athletic field or any other field, national or international, I don't buy that for a minute. It is not enough to just compete. Winning is very important. Maybe more important than ever."

Assertiveness training has become part of university and college catalogues, and best-selling books carry titles such as *Looking Out For No. 1.* In listing his most successful techniques in *Winning Through Intimidation,* Robert J. Ringer could not resist using football imagery: "Using Posture Power To Get the Ball," "Advancing to Midfield Is Relatively Easy," "I Reached the Opponent's 20-yard Line Through Proper Execution," etc. At the book's conclusion, Ringer defends his no-holds-barred approach to business success: "The techniques I used were not 'brutal' . . . I merely fought fire with fire: the techniques were no more brutal than the realities they were intended to reckon with."

America is far from being alone in her obsession with winning. In East Germany athletes are channeled into rigid, victory-obsessive, athletic training programs at an early age. Even before puberty, promising youngsters are herded into special sports schools intended to produce state champions. Successful young athletes get better living quarters, preferred positions on waiting lists for cars, and better jobs when their careers are over. "The presumably egalitarian East Germans breathe competition into everything," observed one journalist, "constantly seeking to identify the swiftest, the strongest, the ablest." The approach has been haunted by persistent reports of drug abuse by German athletes, but it has paid off with a string of victories in recent Olympic competition.

In Western societies, competitive contact games always have been rough, but aggression in the past was tempered by an insistence that playing hard, playing to win, did not countenance playing to cheat and to hurt. Did painful Christian memories of excesses at the hands of sportive Romans lie behind this doctrine? Who can say—but athletics were closely tied to religion nonetheless. As *Alumnus Football* memorialized the words of Grantland Rice:

> When the One Great Scorer comes to write
> Against your name—
> He marks—not that you won or lost—
> But how you played the game.

Sometime in the 1960s that synergism exploded. Football led America across the line between playing fair and playing to win. Within a few short years Rice's words, which had helped to caution and cool our sports temperament for more than half a century, were all but forgotten. The ethics of Lombardi and other coaches—Ohio State's Woody Hayes and George ("When you lose, you die a little") Allen—flattened everything in their path. Instinctualists might argue otherwise, but there was no way the philosophies of Grantland Rice and Vince Lombardi could coexist. The name of the new game was win at all costs and the hell with who got hurt.

The question, of course, is not whether winning suddenly became more important but, rather, why it did. "What is 'winning', and what is 'won'?" wondered Johan Huizinga in *Homo Ludens,* his classic study of play. "Winning means showing oneself superior in the outcome of a game." But why had that become so crucial in an era in which, ostensibly at least, we already were all-affluent, all-powerful, all-achieving?

The answer lies partly in the cynicism which followed the first Kennedy assassination: people no longer believed in anything. The decade which pronounced the death of God could hardly expect to peddle the rewards of good sportsmanship into a Great Beyond. As Arnold Beisser observed in *The Madness in Sports:*

With no hereafter for which we must prepare by living a moral life, winning becomes a new god incarnate on earth. Since we need no longer answer to a higher power, winning is placed as an idol before us. According to this belief, each of us must get whatever we can on earth, and to the victors go the spoils . . . Only those who fail to win are condemned. The strong and ruthless shall survive—and the meek shall inherit what is left over.

It may be too much to say that sport became religion. But everywhere one looked the Almighty and athletics seemed to be wrapped up together. The tombstone of a Roman patrician read: "Here is the body of Manilus Regulus, a good man, a fine father, a loyal husband and a devoted supporter of the Reds." More than a millenium later, in 1979 to be precise, Dodger baseball great Jim Gilliam would be buried with his uniform after suffering a fatal stroke. The year before, a special papal prize for sports was announced by Pope Paul VI just prior to his death, and, in the United States, the first nationally televised college bowl game was scheduled on the day of Christ's birth. When the Puritans came to power in England, they had King James's *Book of Sports* burned by the common hangman, but for millions of mid-twentieth-century Americans, the only Sabbath on which they shared and exchanged common goals and values as a community was that provided by professional athletics. "If Jesus were alive today," said Norman Vincent Peale, one of the nation's most prominent churchmen in the 1950s and 1960s, "he would be at the Super Bowl."

Meanwhile, the standards which governed just about every other form of human conduct, including aggression, seemed to be toppling. In the decade following the mid-1960s, the American murder rate more than doubled, reaching its highest level in history, according to Stanford University psychiatrist Donald T. Lunde. Today it is not at all uncommon for cities of even moderate size to experience a killing every other day. In Weymouth, Massachusetts, a graduating high school senior whipped out a gun and shot himself during commencement ceremonies. "I saw it on television," he said. "It's the American way."

As early as 1964 Barry Goldwater was basing a national political campaign on his assessment, naive but sensitive nonetheless, that something was wrong in the country. We had stumbled into an open ditch of doubt, and a generation of student activists stood ready to throw the dirt in after us. Suddenly our sports held special appeal. They offered certainty at a time when little certainty existed. Prevented from seeking total victory in Vietnam, we searched for it in our games. In real life, we were afraid; we preferred the echo to the choice. But in our hearts we knew what we really wanted, and fire-bombing an opposing professional football squad

back to the Stone Age was still okay. Like a drowning swimmer, we clutched at sports in a desperate grab for security. It
is among the chief ironies of our time that we strangled our
sense of fair play in the process.

Sports became part of a decade which expressed a peculiar
kind of national schizophrenia. As Arthur Schlesinger, Jr.
wrote in *Violence: America in the Sixties,* "the sadness of America has been that our worst qualities have so often been the
other face of our best." It was a time in which the deliberate
use of violence achieved perhaps the broadest-based political
support in our history. Legal but immoral violence was
sanctioned by the right in Vietnam; moral but illegal violence
was sanctioned by the left in our cities.

As our fervor for sports escalated ever closer to a religious
devotion—indeed, perhaps because of it—our athletics increasingly sacrificed their sense of moderation and proportion. Gone was the quality of play. Sport, as Huizinga said,
had become profane. Today we see our games consumed in
the same "over-competition and multiplicity of contests and
prizes" that overtook the men of Hellas. Perhaps we made
the mistake of assuming that sports, by definition, were good.

The issues become as basic as the kind of society we want
and will be able to provide. "Our sports lives manifest and
condition us for our lives in general," notes Gorney. "Athletics today may on a superficial level function well in an av-
aricious, competitive society which measures its state of
health by how many cars it sells." But if recent fuel crises
have taught us anything, it is that we face a future in which we
must learn to share.

In sports, as in other aspects of our lives, the problem is not
so much that we have lost respect for authority—Americans
have never respected authority. What we have lost is respect
for each other. Says Gorney: "Our culture is going to become
more cooperative or it is going to become extinct. In the
former case, sports will likely move away from a simple em-

phasis on winning toward a zestful enjoyment of the activity itself." Montagu's words are worth remembering:

No matter who or what was responsible for making us into what we have become, that does not for a moment relieve us of the responsibility of endeavoring to make ourselves over into what we ought to be . . . To suggest that man is born ineradicably aggressive, warlike and violent is to do violence to the facts. To maintain that he is innately already "wired" or "programmed" for aggression is to render confusion worse confounded, to exhibit a failure to understand the pivotally most consequential fact about the nature of man. That fact is not that man becomes what he is predetermined to become, but that he becomes, as a human being, whatever—within his genetic limitations—he learns to be . . .

7 Victims

After the game we were in the locker room and he looked awful. . . . I can still hear the sound of his metal chair scraping on the cement floor as he fell. He had collapsed. By the time we got on the plane to come home, we found out he had died.

—Artist and ex-pro football
player Ernie Barnes describing
the death of a teammate*

Johnny Bright, a Drake University running back in 1951, recalls being slugged by Oklahoma A&M defensive tackle Wilbanks Smith. Then the nation's leading collegiate ground gainer, Bright was hit while standing in the backfield after he had handed off the ball. Thanks partly to a sequence of Pulitzer-winning photographs by the Des Moines Register–Tribune, *the October 21*

* Former New York Titan guard Howard Glenn kept saying, "I can't make it, I can't make it," Barnes told the *New York Times*'s Dave Anderson in a May 6, 1979, column. The playing field was sweltering in 100-degree heat, and Glenn was noticeably shaky on his legs. Even so, Barnes recalled, Glenn obeyed his coach's signals to stay in the game. "His body was giving off a terrible odor," Barnes recalled, ". . . they said he died of a broken neck, but I think he died of heat exhaustion and improper care."

incident became the most celebrated example of sports violence of its time. Today Johnny Bright is a school principal in Canada, but he still has powerful memories of the incident:

He hit me on the first play of the game. I had just made a hand-off to the fullback, and he hit me as I was looking away. But I stayed in, and he came back at me four or five times.* I was wired up in the dressing room by a dental surgeon and given a pair of wire cutters to use if I got sick and threw up; then I went into the hospital when we got back to Des Moines. I missed the following game but played two weeks later.

I got a most impressive letter from the mother of Bob Mathias, the Olympic decathalon champ who was playing at Stanford and also had been slugged. You know, a lot of that was going on—they got to Frank Gifford at USC and Dick Kazmaier at Princeton. With me it was just the first time there was any direct evidence of intentional violence, documentation—it couldn't be camouflaged by game action.

For years after, I would look at a copy of that game film before I started each football season and I'd say, "John, don't trust anybody and look out for yourself at all times." I went to Canada and played twelve years in the Canadian Football League, I was so bitter at the situation in the United States. I was at Calgary first, then spent eleven years at Edmonton.

I think what's called violence now may not be due to meaner players so much as to an enormous increase in size and skills. When I played, linebackers might go to 190 pounds; now they're 240. There's also the coaching influence. Kids mature earlier as players, learn to hit earlier, in the little

---

* Despite his broken jaw, Bright threw a touchdown pass on the next play and managed to stay in the game for about half a dozen plays before being forced to leave. Smith denied his actions were intentional. "If I overcharged Johnny, I regret it. I am sorry he was injured," he told reporters at the time.

leagues. When I played you might have two or three guys on a team who were really good; now they're all good, they all know how to hit, so there is a higher mathematical chance of getting hurt.

But I would kick players off my team for slugging; I just couldn't condone it. We have to start changing attitudes at an early age. In Canada we have the super Bantam Hockey League, and the kids often fight because they see that in the National Hockey League. They get the idea that hockey players fight. I think the greatest thing in the last decade was the Canada–Russia series last year, when they played super hockey with no fighting. I believe kids have to see more of this.

Strange as it may sound, I think the greatest teaching device for boys would be to make them watch girls' games. The girls play just as hard, but they don't fight or carry grudges, even though they might cry a little. But it would show the boys that sports don't necessarily mean violence.

Frank Lucchesi, manager of the Texas Rangers baseball team, was attacked by one of his own players during 1977 spring training in Orlando, Florida. The forty-eight-year-old Lucchesi suffered a triple fracture of his right cheekbone as well as back injuries in the assault by infielder Lenny Randle, who was angry over losing his second-base job to rookie Bump Wills. In addition to losing his starting job, Randle contended Lucchesi called him an "$86,000-a-year punk," a charge Lucchesi denies. Originally slapped with a felony battery charge, which could have carried a 15-year maximum prison term, Randle pleaded no contest to a simple battery count and was given a suspended sentence. A $200,000 civil suit filed by Lucchesi was settled out of court in December 1977 for a reported figure of under $30,000. Randle subsequently left the Texas team for a better job with the New York

Mets.* Lucchesi returned to baseball in 1979 as a coach with the Rangers.

March 28, 1977—that's a day you don't forget. I was talking with a Minnesota sportswriter and I left him and started walking to the clubhouse. And I was stopped by Lenny Randle. He said to me, "I want to talk to you!" And I said, "Fine, Lenny, what is it about?" He said, "Well, I don't think I'm getting a fair shot. The other guy is playing more than I am, and I don't like some of the things that are said in the paper." I said, "Lenny, just a couple of days ago I talked to you and your wife about this situation, and we went over this thing." Then I said, "Now, if you wanna talk some more, let's go in the clubhouse so we can be alone." And he says, "No, I wanna talk here." Now, when he said that, I pointed—said, "Let's talk back there behind home plate near the screen. So I had my left hand up, started to take it back and put my right hand in my pocket, and that's the last thing I remember.

Now, of course, his story is different. He claims the day of the incident that I called him a punk, and that is absolutely not true. I was willing to take a lie detector test on that. From what the witnesses say, I was hit three times. I went down, and then I guess when I went down, he was on top of me somehow or I was laying on my back or my side, and that's when I was being pounded. And then I guess they grabbed him, and that was it. Of course, I don't remember that. I was out of it.

The last year and a half probably has been worse, the most negative time in baseball that I've had. Physically, I'm still feeling it. The right side of my cheek still bothers me, I had

---

* Lucchesi also lost his job as manager that season, though he does not claim the two incidents are related.

plastic surgery, and two or three ribs were broken in my back . . . I had over $2,000 worth of dental work. Plus there was the mental anguish on myself and my family. So you put it all together it was a pretty tough situation. It's something that I just hope never happens to anyone else in baseball, or in any sport for that matter. I guess it comes to a point where the inmates are running the asylum.

You hate to see violence in any sport, whether it's a ballplayer assaulting his coach or manager, or a ballplayer assaulting another ballplayer. It's different if there's a fight. What happened to me was not a fight. It was an assault. There's a difference there. Even if I had my hands up, I don't think I would have had a chance, because Lenny's very quick, and twenty years younger.

When the trial started, there was a quote of mine in the paper, with me saying, "What am I doing here and why?" And often I thought about that—why did something like this happen?

I just don't know. I'm not Lenny Randle, and I don't know if it was pride with Randle, or some of the things that were said, or what. I just don't know. Maybe players—some are egomaniacs, some are complacent—maybe their pride gets hurt, they can't handle it. I don't know.

For a while after it happened, I couldn't bite on an apple. It was hurting. And then I had to take pain pills because I couldn't sleep at night. Then I had to get on tranquilizers because I couldn't sleep on my right side. In fact, right now, it's still tender. So I had to sleep on my left side or my back.

I think I was on pain pills for, oh, four or five weeks, and then the tranquilizers for a couple of weeks. The second day after it happened, I had the plastic surgery. I had my teeth repaired too, but the bone on the right side under my eye still is not normal. My eyes are not as sound as they were two years ago, but there's no way for sure of knowing whether what happened caused that.

I don't want to knock the commissioner, but I think that sterner action should have been taken—not just because I was involved, but in case this ever happens again. I can't name any names, but a few people in the baseball establishment would like to have seen me settle out of court, before we went to trial. They may have worried the suit was going to hurt baseball's public image, but I looked at it the other way. If people get away with something like this, and no suit was filed, then some other ballplayer who's maybe a little disgusted with management, or not playing, will say, "Hey, wait a minute. Maybe I could punch him out and then be traded." I think the commissioner was quoted as saying that this was a club matter. I don't buy that because I think the integrity of baseball was involved.

The ironic thing about it is that he [Randle] ended up like a rose. He was making about eighty with the Rangers and went to New York and got a four-year contract—something over ninety or a hundred thousand dollars.

The main thing I wanted was justice done, so something like this would never, never happen again. To anyone in any sport. When we finally did settle, the monetary end was secondary—it was nothing.*

The first lesson I would say to kids is they should remember one thing. That whoever the superior is, has the last say. If a player feels he's not getting a fair shot, well, that's a manager's or coach's prerogative. There's got to be more respect for superiors.

I don't think what happened spoiled the game for me. I thank God for baseball. It has been good to Frank Lucchesi, and now I'm back on the field again. Basically, what happened is over, and I want to forget about it. I'm not a vindictive person—I wanted justice done, and I believe it was done. There's a big column in yesterday's paper here; it read: "FRANK LUCCHESI FINALLY HAS PEACE OF MIND." That's

* The out-of-court settlement in the case was reported to be less than $30,000.

how it is. With the incident over, I'm trying to concentrate on the game again.

Mark Miller, a San Francisco writer whose work appears in National Geographic *and other national publications, recalls a memorable experience with an obsessive football fan.*

In the autumn of 1967 I was a senior in college. I began to date the daughter of one of the university's leading professors, a man esteemed among his fellows. He loved football games, particularly professional football, and sat on the edge of a couch and watched the screen, mesmerized. When the Saturday and Sunday games were broadcast, he would sit in front of the set for hours on end, nervously twitching—almost mildly spastic. I thought perhaps he was suffering from some debilitating nervous disorder like Parkinson's disease. His wife would disappear to her sewing room during these episodes, distressed. The professor had a bad heart and high blood pressure and was forbidden to attend the university games. Besides the danger to himself, he became something of a menace to others, for when he watched football, he became uncontrollable. He had been known to elbow people violently, without intent, or to grab them—total strangers sitting beside him in the stadium.

The first time I saw him like that was a Saturday afternoon. He was sitting in his den watching television. Two professional football teams were having at it. From the living room, I observed the professor begin to twitch violently when the ball was snapped. Rising from his sofa in a half-crouch, he began to squeak and growl, twisting his body and stabbing his elbows into the air. Then he began to snarl—if the play went on long enough—things like "Get 'em!" and "Kill 'em!" When the runner was brought down, the professor would let out a strange cry of regret, pain, and pleasure and then collapse into his seat. During those moments, which I regarded as seizures, he was utterly oblivious to everything around him. This would go on throughout the game, his reactions filling the house with squeals, snorts, grunts, growls, and occasional shouts. He did this St. Vitus' dance every few minutes, the veins on his forehead swollen, his face flushed, his fists clenched until his knuckles were white. I found it difficult to watch television football with him, although politeness occasionally required it.

His daughters tried to deter him from this addiction. His wife had given up and brooded angrily, with the frustrated remorse of an alcoholic's wife, in her room. When his gyrations got so violent that they threatened his survival, she would rush out from her sewing room and switch off the television. The professor would collapse into his sofa like a puppet whose strings had been all cut at once—limp, as if the electricity in the set powered him as well. He would docilely accept her rescue and would then turn to his papers or to the refrigerator for food. But before long he would have the set on again, at low volume or without sound, in order not to alert her. But still he would be gripped by that weird hysterical excitement and rise up spastically with every running play. Broken field running propelled him to the heights of his excitement. Long passes elicited only mild reactions until caught and the receiver commenced his ball carrying; then he went wild again.

At all other times the professor was a gentle, almost ineffectual sort, with the jolly benignity of a good-hearted grandmother who knows nothing at all about the baser aspects of the human psyche, and doesn't want to know.

For seventeen years Joseph E. Naunchik was a coach in Pennsylvania, including sixteen years as a high school coach and one year at a small college. For nine years he was head football coach at Plum High School outside Pittsburgh. At the end of the 1978 season, Naunchik resigned, troubled and depressed. Part of the

*reason was what happened to Jeff Boynton, seventeen, perhaps the
best football player the school had ever had.*

Jeff was an outstanding player, highly recruited as a high
school athlete. He visited Arizona State University and was
recruited by Miami, Florida; Pitt; West Virginia; so that
should give you some kind of idea of the caliber of athlete he
was.

He had chosen West Virginia University, but he was playing a post-season game before he started, a kind of transition
game between high school and going to college. Actually, it
was the first Shrine-sponsored high-school all-star football
game in western Pennsylvania; it was a benefit for the
Shrine's Children's Hospital. The date was July 21, 1978, and
it was played at Mt. Lebanon High School Stadium, located in
a suburb of Pittsburgh.

Jeff actually had ended his high school career in November
1977, and, even when that game ended, he was taken to a
hospital with a slight concussion. We aren't really sure what
happened that time; we think it happened while he was a ball
carrier and being tackled. Anyhow, it was nothing serious,
although for precautionary reasons he was taken from that
game. So that had been his last high school game before this
all-star game, which was played at night. I was one of the
assistant coaches.

Jeff was a running back on offense, but in this particular
game he was being used as a wide receiver, offensively, and a
defensive back. He was playing in the third quarter, playing
safety on defense, and a pass was thrown, and Jeff came up
and made the tackle. It was really a very ordinary situation, a
very ordinary play. He came up and made the tackle and,
unfortunately, the first part of his body to make contact was
the top of his head. He made contact with the top of his head
against the receiver's hip. It wasn't a violent collision; it was
just a one-on-one play. And the pass catcher went down and
immediately got right back up, and Jeff just lay there.

My initial reaction was, I thought maybe he'd gotten the wind knocked out of him. And then we went out—I was out on the field immediately—when he didn't get right up. He was able to talk, fully conscious, and there were trainers there and doctors there, and they asked him what it was. He just had this sharp pain through his arm and down his legs. And even then I thought maybe it was, hopefully, just a pinched nerve or something.

But he wasn't able to move at all. No one touched him. No one. I guess the doctors were aware of what the results might be, so all they did at first was question him there. Then he started to move his arms a little bit. And, I thought, well, the worst is over. Because after I found out that it wasn't the wind that was knocked out of him, then I thought the worst would be that it is a broken neck or something. When I saw him moving his arms a little bit, why, then I told him, "Well, gee, that's good."

He's still on the field, laying on the field, we're talking to him. And I was trying to reassure him, and he said that his neck—there was this burning sensation in his neck and down his arms. Then after he started to move his arms a little bit, we tried to reassure him that everything was going to be all right. I really thought it would be, and the doctors who were present, they took all the precautionary measures and never removed his helmet from his head. They called for the backboard. What seemed like an eternity out on the field was probably—maybe from the time the injury took place until he left in an ambulance—oh, maybe fifteen or twenty minutes.

I guess a lot of people that were there feared for the worst but hoped for the best. Even the players were trying to tell him, "Get up, Jeff. Let's go," that kind of thing. But I think even Jeff may have been aware of what his problem was because he mentioned, "I think I broke my neck." Whether he said it realizing that that's actually what happened, or just because that's where the pain was, I don't know.

Anyhow, Jeff's parents were at the game, and they went with him in the ambulance to the hospital. Immediately following the game I went to the hospital, and it was at the hospital that I was told by his parents that he had suffered a broken neck. I stayed right there in the hospital waiting room. There were his parents, some close friends of his, teammates, and a couple of the West Virginia coaches, where he was going to attend school. All we did was sit there, pray, and just wait. The mood in the waiting room was very solemn, very depressed, because even though we didn't know what the prognosis was, it was just the mere fact that we knew his neck had been broken. It was enough to let you think what the diagnosis might be.

Myself, I was just praying really and hoping for the best, because I had the misfortune in my first year of coaching of having a boy die. The boy had an aneurysm, but, you know, you're thinking about that, about the other boy dying. And then we had another similar situation, a case of quadriplegia, at a neighboring school. I knew the player personally. It happened a year before Jeff's injury. Jeff knew the boy. And I felt a great deal of sorrow for the boy, and his family, and the coach, but it just hadn't happened to me. When I say to me, I mean in terms of a coach who had experienced this. I probably wouldn't feel the way I do unless it actually happened to me. Otherwise, it makes you stop and think about it just momentarily and then you go on about your business. With Jeff, it's made me stop and think more than just momentarily.

Anyhow, at the time I just didn't know what Jeff's situation was. You just hoped he was going to live. I knew that all the things we taught him were technically correct. We taught all the correct fundamentals in terms of tackling. I never have been a win-at-all-costs type of coach. I have a great concern for my players' welfare. So I had no guilt feelings, I don't think anybody did, because there wasn't anyone to blame. You know, it wasn't a case of negligence on anybody's part.

My concern right then in that hospital waiting room was for Jeff Boynton and his family. Not for myself.

Well, the next morning they transferred Jeff to Presbyterian Hospital in Pittsburgh, where they were going to perform surgery. We left there I guess maybe around three in the morning, and the next morning I was at the hospital at eight. Jeff underwent a five-hour operation. They removed the fractured vertebrae and took a piece of bone from his leg and fused it to his neck—at least that's the best I understand it, medically.

Then the doctor, the neurosurgeon, came out and explained to Mr. and Mrs. Boynton—the part I overheard was—that the operation was a success. And what happened at that point, everybody just felt a great, tremendous feeling of relief. By hearing the doctor say the operation was a success, everybody felt everything was going to be all right. And later, well, I guess Mr. and Mrs. Boynton asked the doctors about his movement, his paralysis. And they wouldn't make any definite commitments at that time. They just said, well, at this point he doesn't have any movement; that's all we can say. So there was still a great deal of hope for a complete recovery on Jeff's part from just hearing the doctor say that the operation was a success, which it was, but we didn't know the details.

The next morning, Sunday, I went down to see Jeff again. It was about eight and he was in the recovery room, and I was the only one there, but he was sleeping. I was just standing by his bedside, and the doctor, the neurosurgeon, came in. He just checked Jeff out briefly, and I followed him down the hall and asked if I could speak with him. He said yes, and I asked him about Jeff's condition. And it was then he told me—I asked him if Jeff would ever be able to walk again, and he said he didn't think so. I said does this mean he's going to be confined to a wheelchair? He said, hopefully, a wheelchair. He told me then that Jeff was quadriplegic. It was the very first time I was exactly aware of Jeff's situation.

I don't know if I can describe my reaction. Dumbfounded, I guess. I just couldn't believe anything that tragic could happen. It was one of those things that you read about happening to other people in other parts of the country. Never something that you're involved in. I just couldn't believe what I was hearing. Even at this very minute, the only thing Jeff can do, he has some limited arm movement. He has no finger movement or hand control, and he has no movement in his legs. He's classified as quadriplegic, and his movement takes place in a wheelchair. He has to be catheterized and has no bowel control whatsoever.

Since Jeff got hurt, I've thought about the value of high school football, whether it was worth it. I have two young sons myself. What if this happened to them? Maybe high school players could play flag football, or touch football. That would help compensate for the physiological differences. I think there are more injuries now than five or ten years ago. Players are bigger, stronger, they have the capacity to inflict more damage. I think the equipment itself may lend itself to injuries.

This is one of the things that frightens me about football. We spend a great amount of time teaching proper tackling procedures—never making initial contact with the helmet or face mask. We teach tackling with the shoulder; we spend a lot of time on form tackling. But once that game starts, these kids, they make contact with whatever gets there first. Many times they aren't in a position to remember what they've been taught. They don't think, I've gotta get my head over here, get my shoulder here. They react and try to make a tackle.

Jeff certainly knew better, and he'll be the first to tell you how he was taught to tackle. Jeff's initial reaction when he was coming up to meet the ball carrier was to try for the interception. But the ball was caught, and then he had this immediate decision to make the tackle. And he had his body, he got his body in an awkward position and wasn't in good control of himself. This is why his head was the first thing to make contact.

I resigned my job here. I really enjoyed coaching, and I don't know that I want to get out of it totally, but maybe the best way of describing it is taking a leave of absence, at least from high school coaching. If I miss it badly enough, maybe I'll get back into it. But going through last season, with what happened to Jeff certainly on my mind and I'm sure on the minds of our players, I'm just not ready to go through something like that again. Jeff was in our program for four years, and I got very close to him. My wife, too, she got to know Jeff and was very sorry about what happened—now she's against our sons ever playing football.

I still believe a lot of good comes from high school football, but I'm not as enthusiastic about it as I once was. There was a time when I thought high school football taught a great many lessons to young boys that they could use later on in life. I know now that football isn't the only sport that can teach these lessons. I'm not so sure that you can't learn the same things in swimming or tennis or other non-contact sports.

Jeff asked if he was the reason I was getting out of coaching, and I told him no. It's the truth. I wouldn't want anyone to think that, because I enjoy coaching very much. But there are other factors—fan pressure, the pressure that's put on you as a coach to win, the pressure of parents, the hassles that you get from parents, the injuries. It's just getting to be too much. I've got some background in training in terms of prevention and care of athletic injuries, but I'm certainly not a doctor or even a trainer. And I feel the responsibility they're putting on coaches is just more than I want. You are the one that's held accountable. Too often I see situations where you're just standing out there all by yourself when something happens. All of a sudden you look around for some help, and there's nobody there. And I guess I've had enough of that at this point.

Jeff Boynton's injury isn't what made me resign my job, but I wouldn't want to be involved in coaching another kid where that happened to me. I just don't personally know how I could handle something like that again.

In 1978, baseball fan Lynne Atkins, then nineteen, was shot in the abdomen at San Francisco's Candlestick Park. Her assailant never has been found. Local news media mostly ignored the incident. The San Francisco Examiner *ran a front-page story, then never wrote a follow-up. The* San Francisco Chronicle *made no mention of the shooting, not even in a subsequent story about violence at the park published a few weeks later. Lynne is joined in her remarks by her father and mother. The family home is in Millbrae, California, a suburb of San Francisco.*

LYNNE: It was June 16, and my boyfriend and my girlfriend and I had been to Candlestick Park to see the Giants and the Mets. It was a really good game, and afterward they had fireworks. We were watching from inside, and we said, well, if we get out in the parking lot we can see them better. So I'm standing by the car, we were just about ready to get in, and all of a sudden I felt a weird thing on my side, and it made me drop to my knees. I don't know if I screamed or what.

It's hard to explain what it felt like because the only thing I could think of was impact. It just hit so hard and fast. At first I thought it was a rock. I had been hassled by these little punk kids that are always hanging around there, pushed around and shoved. They come in the bathrooms and try to look over the stalls, so I thought there were some kids throwing rocks. And my first reaction was I fell and screamed, because my girlfriend asked what happened, and I said, nothing, just get in the car. That was my first reaction—I just wanted to get out of there and get in the car. And I got in the car, and I looked at my hip. I had a hole in my coat. And then I looked and I had a hole in my pants, and then I opened it up and I had a hole in my side. And then I said, "I got shot." I said, "You guys, I think I got shot."

My girlfriend went into total hysterics, and I was trying to keep her calm. I was perfectly calm, I guess, because you automatically go into shock. I don't remember feeling pain until the last, when they were injecting dye into me and poking me at the hospital. Then it started hurting. When you get shot, you think blood is going to be all over. No blood. Just a little hole and a little blood coming out. The only thing that went through my mind was my boyfriend had seen a cop car. I said take me to the hospital; I'll be fine. So he pulled over to this police officer, and he said, "My girlfriend got shot." I remember the cop saying, "Can she walk?" And as soon as he said that, I was out of that car. I got into the cop car, and I was sitting in the front seat. My girlfriend was in the back seat.

I remember thinking, there's no blood coming out of here, any minute blood's going to come running out of my mouth, and I'm going to die of internal bleeding. That was my first thought—there's no blood outside, gotta be inside. So I was expecting to die on the way there. The cop was really nervous. He was crying and whimpering all the way. And here's me and my girlfriend, she's crying with her arms around me, saying, "Oh, my God!" She's crying hysterically. I'm just trying to keep everyone calm and telling the cop, "Don't worry. I'll be fine."

When I got to the hospital, the doctors and nurses and everyone were standing out there waiting for me with a stretcher. They took me in the operating room. I guess they did exploratory surgery; then they opened me up and did a double-barrel colostomy. The slug is still in there—they couldn't get it out. It's about a quarter-inch from my lower spine and they didn't want to fuss with that. They think it's either a .22 or .38, but there's no way of being sure.

Altogether, I was in the hospital a month. I got peritonitis, I got so infected. They pumped me with antibiotics. Tons of 'em. Intramuscular, IV, just every way—they pumped me with antibiotics for eighteen days. They brought two pieces of the intestines to my stomach, so that I was unhooked. They take the part that goes to your rectum and then the other part is from your stomach. This way your body can heal inside.

They give you a plastic bag. What a mess! It was just horrible; it was very embarrassing. All I can remember is being out someplace and you get, everyone gets, gas. But it came out through the bag. It was a terrible mess. You just let the bag fill up to a certain point—you have no control. It just goes when it goes, and you can't say when. Then you have to change it, and you have to irrigate it, which is like an enema, only you put the tube in through the hole and you hold it. You fill your insides up with water until you feel your stomach cramping and then, all of a sudden, it makes a big noise and everything comes out. The first time I did that I got really sick to my stomach. It was just so gross.

MOTHER: She used to cry.

LYNNE: Thinking about what happened, it seems like, God, there was so much pain, so much hassle. At first I was really conscious of the scars. The bullet wound is tiny, but I have five scars, and one of them is twelve inches long. So I'm thinking, what am I going to wear? I'm going to have to hide my stomach all my life. Now I don't care really. Everyone says, you could have plastic surgery. I just can't. I went through two operations in three months, and there's no way I'm going to go through one again. Maybe someday.

FATHER: I didn't want Lynne to go in the first place. I used to have season football tickets. It got so violent out there that for kicks people would take a full can or bottle of beer and throw it. A guy right in front of me got hit in the side of the head, crushed his skull. I thought, geez, that's terrible, but it's probably one in a million. Two games later, another guy throws one out at a referee, and it was the same thing—hit him in the head. There were fights all over, brawls. Then they raised the ticket prices three times, and it was getting to be fifteen dollars just to go there, and you have to fight the traffic in and fight the traffic out. That did it for me, and I said, I'm never going to another game. I didn't want her to go either. The Monday before it happened, I told her, I don't want you to go, period. But the following Friday she went before I came home from work.

LYNNE: Well, we wanted to go. We had our tickets—my boyfriend, my girlfriend, and I—and they picked me up after work. I'm not really a big baseball fan, but I like watching it, sitting up there and yelling. I played baseball; I was on the baseball team in high school. I guess I'd been to about five games at Candlestick already that summer.

FATHER: At first I was thinking, if she'd listened to me, this would never have happened. Those kind of things go through your mind—they don't accomplish anything, they don't make any sense, but you can't help thinking it. Because nobody— no parent—wants to bury their own kids. I was very worried with the outcome, not so much the incident, but the outcome. Everybody was talking to me about are they gonna catch them. I didn't care about the guys that shot her. I was worried about her and how she was going to come through this.

LYNNE: Would I go to Candlestick again? I don't think I would. Not because I'm paranoid, but because it's so violent. It's nothing in the baseball game, it's in the people. There have always been a lot of fights, a lot of violence out there, but more this year. The same night I was there, some guy got hit in the face with a brick. He was driving, he was leaving the stadium, and three guys opened up his car door and smashed in his face with a brick. Afterward we were in the same hospital.

Baseball players' wives—four of them—came in. I was mad

because I thought, I go out there and get shot, and I don't even get to meet any of the baseball players. They send their wives. Anyway, they come in with flowers or a plant, and they all say they're real sorry. They get me a baseball, and they're saying we're sorry that our husbands couldn't be here, but here's a baseball and some flowers. Then I saw there was another lady standing out in the hall waiting to go see the other guy that got hit with a brick. They had flowers for him too.

Something else that blew my mind is that Bob Lurie [owner of the Giants] called me up while I was in the hospital and said, I'm sorry to hear what happened, and I'd like to send you something. And I thought, well, I wonder, maybe he'll send me some season tickets or something. I get this little box in the mail, and I open it up and its another autographed baseball. They're signed by all the Giants. They must have a bin of them and they throw them out to people. That's all he sent me—no card or anything. Just a little ball that came in the mail.

I was out of work four months. I guess it cost me $2,000 or $3,000. I had to fill out all these papers, for victims of a violent crime. If you're a victim of a violent crime—meaning you didn't provoke anything; like you get mugged, or you get raped, or you get shot, or something—the state pays for your hospital expenses, up to $10,000; the work you've missed, up to $10,000; and they pay up to $10,000 in rehabilitation if you need training to go back to work. But it takes the state forever. I haven't heard from them since it happened.

FATHER: They say they have so many cases ahead of hers, they've got to evaluate those, and then they'll get to hers and evaluate it. There's no guarantee they'll pay it. Got to evaluate it.

LYNNE: This incident has made me more aware of things. It's made me more appreciative. Little things. Everyday things. Like being outside and saying, God, you know, you don't realize. You came pretty close.

There are other little weird things. Once in a while I flash on it. I don't like to say anything—people would think I'm strange. But I remember so much more in the last four months, since my last operation, than right after the shooting. At first I was blank, I didn't remember anything, and then slowly it fit back together. Driving up to the hospital, looking over and seeing four doctors and five nurses all standing there, and I thought, they were all there for me—they knew exactly when I was coming, and they were just waiting for me. Since it happened, I've felt more uncomfortable in crowds. I don't like being in the city. I've gone shopping at Macy's, and I didn't like it. I thought, let's hurry, let's leave. As soon as possible, I want to get out of this city.

MOTHER: That's a real fear—the crowds. Now more than ever. I wouldn't go to San Francisco for almost a year. Right after she got shot, this fellow, a tourist from Amsterdam, got shot by a sniper. He was on a cable car. It's crowds. You just never know.

LYNNE: I've been lucky, but if I'd have had to wear that bag permanently, I would have been really bitter. In a way I still feel cheated. You hear of these people who sue and get all this money. But it seems like I went through so much, and I haven't even gotten the money from the state. And in a way I feel like I should have gotten something, some compensation.

FATHER: I hold the system responsible more than I do the person who shot her. If they want to stop it, they know what can be done to stop it. A lot of the violence that is going on, most of it, is dollar oriented. Somebody's making a profit from it. And as long as people are making a profit from it, even if they know its creating violence, they won't stop it.

People go to a game in a violent mood. They start drinking. There's very little needed to start a fight. And when it's San Francisco and the Los Angeles Dodgers, I really believe a lot of people go down there just to fight. They sell beer. They say they don't want alcohol, but everybody there's got a bottle. But it's not just the idea of the beer sales; it's the idea of all the sales. Because they make a lot of money out there—it's a big business. And it's also an ego thing for the city. The city likes having the Giants. The mayor put up a hell of a stink when they were talking about moving. He didn't want them to take the Giants out of San Francisco.

The mood of the whole stadium is very much like a tinder-box. The city knows the violent situation that exists. They could do more about it than they've done—they don't be-cause it's an attractive thing to people. It's got an attrac-tion, even though it's a violent attraction. There's the cata-lyst and the resin, so to speak. And all it has to do is get together.

Actually, it goes even further than that, because the person that shot Lynne could have been a black person from Hunt-er's Point that had his own frustrations and maybe didn't have the price of a ticket. But he had a bullet and a gun. And shot into a crowd. Maybe this guy that shot my daughter, if he'd been working, maybe wouldn't have been so frustrated.

There are a lot of ways I think society can stop violence, and one of them is by lightening the pressures that people are dealing with today. I think through inflation and a lot of things these pressures are coming out and manifesting themselves. I think people are getting to the point where they can't deal with the pressures we have. They can't even deal with the price of feeding themselves. They can't deal with the pressure of finding a place to live if the landlord raises the rent 20 per cent. The people can't deal with the pressures, and then they go to the ball park to release their tensions, and there's this tinderbox. Everything's just exploding. San Fran-cisco knows what's going on there. And San Francisco is respon-sible for it just as much as the person who pulled the trigger.

In September 1973, Dale Hackbart, a Denver Bronco linebacker, was seriously injured in the opening game of the National Football League season. Hackbart subsequently filed a $1 million lawsuit against the Cincinnati Bengals and their running back Boobie Clark, who Hackbart claimed caused the injury by the "malicious and wanton" use of his forearm. The Bengals called the entire incident "a mystery" to Clark and said their star running back "never intentionally injured Hackbart." While the trial court dismissed the action, the Tenth Circuit Court of Appeals did not agree that "professional football is a species of warfare," so that even intentional injuries were beyond legal redress, and ordered a new trial.

I guess the best way to describe it was that the ball was thrown in the end zone and Billy Thompson and I were both going for the ball. Billy intercepted and started downfield, and I threw a block at Boobie Clark. We were in the zone defense, so Billy was playing strong safety, he had the deep outside, and I had the middle. And the ball kinda split the zone. Billy just jumped in front of both of us and picked it off.

I attempted to block Boobie Clark. I hit him above the waist or into the midsection and rolled over, and I was about to get up. I had done a kind of somersault, and I was facing the other direction, looking toward the field. I didn't know what happened at the time, but as the film showed, Boobie started down the field toward the sideline, and then he just walked up behind me and hit me in the back of the head with a forearm.

It drove us both to the ground. I went down on the ground and he went on top of me. He didn't say anything. He just got up and started down the sideline. I really didn't understand what happened at the time. Being hit like that, he did knock me kind of silly or goofy. I was dazed. I got up and just looked at him. I said something. I don't recall what the heck I said to the guy. My left arm was numb, just went numb. I started back across the field to the sideline—the play was over by then. By the time I got over to the sideline, the feeling came back in my hand. I think that was the end of the half.

I didn't have any bad feeling toward him until I looked at the game film the next day. It was kind of a turnabout, the whole thing. I didn't even realize that my neck had been broken—the fifth, sixth, and seventh vertebrae.

I played two more games—against the San Francisco 49ers and the Chicago Bears—after that. I had a great deal of pain. The next day I put an ice pack on my neck—I couldn't even describe to you how I felt. When I woke up in the morning, I still had the ice pack on my neck, and I had to slide my pillow back and forth in order to move my neck. Then I kinda rolled out of bed, got my feet on the floor, and then lifted up my head. I was going to play golf with a friend of mine in the morning, and I couldn't do that. I went right to the training room and told them I really was in a lot of pain, and they treated it with ice.

In practice, nobody could even touch me or brush up against me. As a matter of fact, I couldn't dry my hair off for about a week and a half. It hurt to put a towel on my head. My neck was very stiff; I lost a lot of agility. I can recall running down on several kickoffs and making some tackles, and when I would hit people, my arm would just go numb on me. Then it would come back, in a few seconds or so.

I tried to avoid hitting people. I just, I didn't want to stick my head in there. Coach Ralston said I wasn't performing up to my abilities, and I didn't think I was either. But I didn't know why. I had played thirteen years, and I had played in pain before; so I just considered it part of the game. But this was more—I just thought there was something more that was wrong with me, but I didn't know what it was.

John Ralston told me he was going to put me on waivers after the second or third game, so I decided to go down and have X-rays taken on my own. I went to a friend and he looked at the X-rays and he said there was something strange about them, but he really didn't pick it out. So he sent them to the University of Colorado Medical Center. The doctor there said I think there's something wrong and we'd like to take some more sophisticated X-rays. So I went down there and spent about two-and-a-half hours. And that's really when they discovered the fractures were there.

I can remember very vividly sitting there when they were taking all these X-rays, and the guy was saying, well, what happens, Dale, when you turn your head to the left? And I said, I get some pain and I get dizzy. And they were looking at these X-rays, so finally I said, what's the problem? The guy said, well, you've got a broken neck. We don't want you to move; we don't want you to twist your neck. Stay where you're at. I said, what do you mean, stay where I'm at? He said, don't move. We're going to put you in immediate traction, and we're going to put a brace on you. These two radiologists couldn't believe it. They said, this is a miracle this guy is walking around.

Since then, in about 1975, I had to have an operation on my neck. The muscles began to atrophy in my back, and I started to lose strength in my left arm. They told me if I didn't have an operation there was a possibility I could lose the use of my left arm. They did a laminectomy. They went in and cut out about one-third of the sixth vertebra and decompressed the nerve.

Up until then, the injury really slowed me down. I had a body cast on. Not one of those plastic casts—it was one that I wore around my neck, and it fit over my shoulders. It was made out of soft collars; then it had steel that fit over my shoulders. Even after the operation, I'd say it took me another full year to recover. I was never confined to a wheelchair; I just wore the brace. But I'd say for about a year and a half I had the total brace on.

It's a situation I have had to live with. I feel very fortunate that I wasn't confined to a wheelchair, or ended up like Darryl

Stingley. I still have pain that comes and goes. I'm in the tire business and I do a lot of driving, and sometimes the physical part of the job—I do a lot of lifting—bothers me to a degree. I try and do everything I possibly can, I'm thoroughly active, but I get tired very quickly.

What happened ended my career. I was thirty-five or thirty-six at the time, and I might have played another year, maybe two years, I don't know. Either with Denver or somebody else. That was just the end of it. But, like I say, I was very fortunate.

The thing that really upset me was the incident, the foul. There was no penalty called on the play. But whether it had been called or not, I just didn't think as flagrant as it was, that it should go unnoticed. That nobody should call attention to it.

I have dealt with this, emotionally, but I guess the thing that disturbed me most was the judgment, when the judge said if you walk out on a football field, you're going to have to anticipate or assume that somebody's going to do this to you, at one time or another. That's the single thing that bothers me the most.

I don't think the game should be that way. I think players have to respect one another. It's a rough game, and players have to—you have to be in shape. You gotta take those hits. You have to play in pain. But I think what Boobie did to me was completely out of the context of the game. It never should have happened.

Everybody is trying to make a living at the game, and when I say you have to respect a player, it's like a defensive back making a tackle, an end catching a ball, or the quarterback throwing—that's what they do, and if you have a certain thing you do, and it's something you do well, going out of your way to intentionally injure a player is just not part of the game. Never has been. That's the thing I've really had to adjust to, looking at that doggone film, when I got injured, seeing it over and over again, asking, why did it happen?

Like I explained, he did stun me when he hit me, but I knew who he was because I saw the number "36." When I got over to the sideline, I was standing there, thinking, wow, that guy really whacked me. And one thought occurred when I was sitting in the locker room at half time. I thought, I'm going to get even with this guy because he really whacked me, even though I didn't know the seriousness of the injury. Then I thought to myself, what the hell's wrong with you? Here you are playing a game. He's trying to do his job; I'm trying to do mine. Had I really felt that way, I probably could have really gone after Boobie during the game, and I could have seriously injured him.

When I was playing, I always said, when it became work, I'd quit. And I always had a lot of fun when I played. When I go back and look at some of the things I did, and some of the physical contact I had, I just can't believe I got involved like that. There were some violent collisions.

When I started professional football in 1960 with the Packers, there were mean guys and bad guys and players you would look at on film and, say, hey, you gotta watch out for this guy. Now I would say the game is more sophisticated, but my impression is that players have begun to express their physical opinion more. I guess that's the way to put it. Players have gotten, to a certain degree, out of control.

As I've seen the game progress, since 1960, I would say that happens more now. Also you've got more coverage of the game. You've got instant replay. Some of the same things happened back in 1960, but nobody called attention to it.

And none of the players really took a stand on it. It was the feeling of a man is a man, and if you're going to play a man's game, you gotta get in there and keep your mouth shut and play the game. When I filed the suit, I just felt as though something had happened to me during the course of the game that never should have happened. I felt the incident just went completely above and beyond the call. I was probably a lot more emotional than I am now, but I thought somebody's gotta put an end to it.

It was kind of strange the first time I met Boobie. It was here in Denver, when we took the depositions. We kinda walked up eyeball to eyeball and looked at each other, and I didn't know what to say to him. I don't think really that Boobie knew what the heck to say to me. We sat down at the table and took the depositions and just kinda stared at each other trying to figure out what to say.

Then we had the case, which was tried about two years later. And nothing was said. I think he felt bad about it, at least that was my impression. When we were sitting in the trial I looked at him, and they showed the incident on film. Two or three times. When he looked at the film he put his head down, put his hand on his forehead, and it was like he didn't want to see it again.

In the heat of the game I think players get carried away. The judge said there are no rules and regulations to govern the conduct of professional football players. You can't govern their conduct. That's the thing that's hard to deal with. I've got two boys, eighteen and fifteen. I directed them out of sports as much as I could. My boy is a senior at Boulder High, and he hadn't played football since he was in eighth grade. This year he decided to play football. I just kind of cringed and said, "Oh, no."

But, you know, I really enjoyed watching him play. I think it's helped me a great deal to have my boys involved in athletics, to kind of cope with this, with the violence end of it. When you ask, is this a violent sport? you look at it and you have to say, well, yes, it is. Professional football in particular. There's nothing really you can do about it, I guess.

He, my son, got a shoulder separation, and they thought he

had broken his arm. They took him down for X-rays. I told him, that's what you have to expect of it; that's part of the game. You play, you have to be a rough-tough kid."

But I'm glad he played because I think it helped me to go out there and watch. I was upset with the game of football because of what had happened to me. But then, watching my older boy, I said, well, you know, I guess that's the way of life, and you're going to have to roll with the punches, to learn to live with something like that. You've got to be realistic. Football is part of the American culture.

While South American soccer referees have been known to carry guns for self-protection, so far such extreme measures have been thought unnecessary in the United States. That is, until umpire R.B. Williams pulled a pistol to defend himself against an angry crowd at a softball game in Mississippi. The local sheriff's office joked that Williams may have been the first umpire who threatened to kill the crowd. The words of the man himself, however, reveal a serious incident with painful memories.

This was a softball game in Kings, Mississippi. It was a community softball game, part of a regular summer league, and I was the chief umpire. They had passed this rule that if the batter comes up out of the batter's box and makes contact with the ball in front of the plate, he's automatically out. So that's the way this incident started. One of the players got up, hit the ball, and made a triple out of it. But we made this rule, and I called him out. Then the same thing happened to the other side. One of their boys hit the ball, and he got up and jumped up in front of the plate, and I called him out. It was in the bottom of the sixth, so the game was almost over.

The spectators, they just had a fit. All the players were arguing, and then they started charging me. The fans stood up and were yelling and making a lot of noise, saying a lot of things. Then all the players started charging. There was about fifteen of 'em—some came off the bench. And they all started yelling what we ought to do to this so-and-so. One said, "Let's do away with him, let's get him! Let's get this son-of-a-bitch! "

It was time to do something. That's the first thing that went through my mind, that they were just going to do me up. That's what went through my mind. So I had a little gun in my pocket, and I pulled it out and told them to stop, don't come any further.

Well, they stopped. And we had a third team there, Big Mama's team, and those boys live in the same neighborhood. And two of my friends, Joe King and Dave Blue, they came up and caught me and said, "Let's go, let's go. Don't do nothing violent."

I didn't pull a gun to hurt nobody—nothing like that. I pulled the gun in self-defense because some of them dudes had bats. And they said let's do this so-and-so, he's cheating on us. That's when I pulled out the gun and told 'em not to come no further. I figured they were just gonna try whooping me up, you know, with the bats. I really was carrying this gun to protect my family and my car. I didn't have the gun for this purpose. I never would have figured this would happen. It wasn't my intention to do nothing like that. I wouldn't hurt nobody.

I was picked up and placed in the county jail. Bond was set at $750, and I made bond the same day. I was charged with carrying a concealed weapon, pointing it, and aiming it. I had to get a lawyer. The lawyer got the case thrown out.

It really makes me feel bad, what happened. Sometimes I lay back and think if I hadn't had that gun, I might not be around. But no, it really makes me feel bad. A lot of my friends were sitting around watching the game, and my children too. And it didn't make me feel too good. But I guess getting frightened and getting scared, you might say, that's one of the reasons I pulled it out. I got scared, and then I thought about having this gun.

That was the last game I umpired. My mother, my wife, children, and friends, they told me to let it go. Because the money I paid the lawyer, $650, I could have had that to help my family along.

Sometimes I see some of the other players, the same ones I had to pull the gun on. Some never say anything to me. Some of those boys, we're really close. Some of them have come up to me and told me that they were sorry that it had to happen, that it happened like it did. But some of 'em—they look at me like I'm a pig. It's something that I did, and I'm sorry.

There was another argument about two Sundays before, in a game between Big Mama's team and another team. The game rained out, and they had played five innings. Seven innings is a game in softball, but the rule is that if you complete the fifth inning and rain comes up, whoever's in the lead wins. So Big Mama's team was in the lead this Sunday, but the other team just wouldn't give up. I was calling the game. They argued and argued. I said, well, you all know this is the rules, it's in the contract; so there's nothing to do but give up the money. I hold the money the two teams bet; they just put up this little pot, twenty-five dollars. They said, well, we're not going to give up the money. Those guys, they lose hard.

Anyhow, I still like it—no, I still love it. Maybe, in the next few years, I might umpire a few more games. Maybe, maybe not. Every time I think about this, I just, I feel sad. A lot of fellows say I was a good umpire, which I tried to be. But I don't know. I might try it again and I might not. Never know.

On November 21, 1977, Virginia Tech University football player Bob Vorhies was found dead in his dormitory room. Earlier that day Vorhies had been subjected to after-practice "punishment drills" for alleged misbehavior following his first running play as a collegian. A special grand jury exonerated the Tech coaching staff a few months later. Following is the transcript of a report entitled

"Death of a Football Player," produced by ABC-TV's Sports Magazine and narrated by Howard Cosell.

COSELL: This is Virginia Tech University, established in 1872, with a student body of 20,000. It has modern facilities like Lane Stadium, Tech's 40,000-seat football stadium that is filled with Saturday-afternoon madness during the fall. Only now, there is sadness. Because on November 19, 1977, a freshman fullback named Bob Vorhies carried for the only time of his college career. He was eighteen, six-foot-two, 242, one of the most widely recruited athletes in this nation.* But two days after the Wake Forest game, Bob Vorhies died, and no one knows why.

It was Bob Vorhies's only play. Good for twelve yards, and how proud he was of it. That night back at the athletic dorm, Bob demonstrated to his teammates just how he had gained those yards. He lined up in a three-point stance, barreled into a storage closet at the end of the corridor, smashing it loose. The assistant coaches told him he would be disciplined; but months later the door is still broken, the splinters are still on the floor. At the field house just two days after he broke the door, Bob Vorhies was put through a disciplinary drill. It was muggy in there that November afternoon, because nearly a hundred Tech players had just completed a workout with ten 100-yard sprints. Marvin Baker, thirty-two-year-old graduate assistant, administered the drill. He would not speak with us, but his attorney, Roberts Moore, provided this account.

MOORE: It is my understanding that the drill which Robert Vorhies was requested to complete, and the drill which had been completed by a number of other student athletes at Virginia Tech, consisted of ten 50-yard dashes, ten 100-yard

---

* Considered a superb blocker, Vorhies also was the eastern states' shot-put champion and the second best indoor shot-putter in the United States in 1977. He was considered one of the best entering freshman college athletes in the country.

dashes—each dash having to be completed within a 30-second time period—two 100-yard bear crawls, fifty pushups, fifty situps, and four additional drills over a 100-yard distance.

COSELL: Let's reexamine that disciplinary drill Bob Vorhies had to do. Ten 50-yard dashes, each to be completed and begun again with fifteen seconds; ten 100-yard dashes, each to be completed and begun again within thirty seconds. Two 100-yard bear crawls. Fifty pushups and then fifty situps, and he had to do four other 100-yard drills—all this just minutes after the regular practice had ended.

MOORE: I can tell you that one sprint took approximately thirty-one or thirty-two seconds, and Coach Baker requested Robert Vorhies to do the drill again.

COSELL: There were three witnesses to the punishment drill; two of them, a Virginia Tech professor and his wife, were jogging in the field house that night. Jim and Cathy Richardson supplied authorities with this one testimony in a confidential police report obtained by ABC Sports: "The coach stood in the middle of the field house with a stopwatch and had the player running successive 50-yard wind sprints with no rest between each sprint except the jog back to the start. This continued until the player was extremely fatigued, as evidenced by sluggish movement and hard breathing. We could hear heavy breathing for a distance of over seventy yards. The coach then had the player run the entire field. The player was run both ways of the field in this manner at least twice. However, the apparent exhaustion at this time had the player reduced to a slow pace. It appeared he could hardly lift his feet. No abusive language or gestures were used by the coach. He did encourage more effort with statements like, 'Push 'em.' Once the coach said something to the effect, after looking at his stopwatch, 'Eleven seconds late. Let's go again.'"

The other witness to the punishment drill was Robert Wingo, a janitor. He was working at the time, in the field house, and didn't see the entire exercise. But Wingo did tell ABC Sports he saw Bob Vorhies doing the bear crawls. Wingo recalls: "He was crawling and he dropped down, and the coach made him get back up. He said, 'Get back up.' He made him get back up!"

Marvin Baker maintains through his attorney that when the drill was over, he and Bob Vorhies jogged from the field house to the coliseum, where the football locker room is, but when Vorhies got there, he was too tired to shower, too weak to cut the tape off his ankles. Eventually he walked back to Hillcrest Dorm. He wasn't feeling well. Went straight to his room. Skipping dinner. He had planned on going to the movies with his friends, Steve Wirt and Jeff Bowling. But now he didn't have the strength for that either. Still too weak to shower. Still too weak to cut the tape off his ankles. So he went to his room.

FRIEND [identity unclear on author's tape]: He's sitting in the toilet, and we asked him how he felt, and he said he didn't feel too good, was tired, real tired, and he had diarrhea. Then we asked him what was running like, and all he told us was he got double duty. I spoke to him a little bit, and I asked him if he puked any. And he said, yeah, that he'd puked some blood. He didn't say any more after this, and I said, well, have you eaten any dinner? And he said, no, I'm tired; I'm going to lay down.

COSELL: When Jeff Bowling returned from the movies that night, he went to the room where Bob Vorhies lived by himself. His teammate was lying on the floor; an alarm clock was ringing. It had been set for 9:45—only now it was 11:04. And Bob Vorhies had been dead for hours. A special grand jury of seven agreed with the autopsy report: probable sudden cardiac arrythmia. Irregular beating of the heart. But they couldn't say what caused that. Dr. David Oxeley, who performed the autopsy, gave the testimony. Jim Lampley spoke with him.

DR. OXELEY: Well, as we stated in our report, the temporal relationship [limited time] between the drills and the time of death suggests there may be some relationship between the drills and Mr. Vorhies's death. However, there is no anatomic connection, and the physiological connection remains obscure. We don't know—probably never will know—if indeed it exists.

LAMPLEY: So while it may be easy for the layman to look at this situation and say, this guy had to undergo a very strenuous set of exercises after football practice that maybe had something to do with the fact that he dropped dead, from a scientific standpoint, the bottom line is that a young, very healthy athlete dropped dead and you don't know why.

DR. OXELEY: That's correct.

COSELL: John Lowe, the Vorhieses' attorney, disagrees. He believes there is a link between the punishment drills and Bob Vorhies's death.

LOWE: Well, I think certainly the obvious connection between the extraordinarily strenuous punishment drill that Bob Vorhies went through and his death a short time later is a connection that we believe is medically sound. We believe that the exercise certainly at least was a strong contributing factor to the death.

JEROME VORHIES, BOB'S FATHER: What I would like to do is to get enough information to have criminal charges pressed against anyone who caused Bob's death and also anyone who covered up the circumstances of Bob's death.

COSELL: It's not money you want then? It's criminal prosecution?

VORHIES: Yeah, I mainly want information why he died. Because right now, the only thing the grand jury said . . . is they don't know medically why he died and they don't know why he died . . . We would like to find out. Because a boy like him, you just don't die.

LOWE: The case certainly is not closed. Anybody who thinks the case is closed is seriously mistaken. We are still in the process of doing a very careful, deliberate fact-finding job. We're talking to many people. We are trying to be as thorough as we can so that we can get a true picture of what took place.

COSELL: Mr. and Mrs. Vorhies sit upstairs in the apartment building behind me and they still cry a lot. And they probably always will, over the loss of their eighteen-year-old son. Perhaps it would help them if they could find out how and why their boy died, if the punishment drills were the real cause, but instead they face a potential legal and medical maze. Maybe they'll never know. We felt this subject important because every parent in the nation has to have a vital concern. We draw no conclusions, but we do believe this, and have one conclusion. It is time, forever more, to eliminate punishment drills for athletes in this nation. And maybe, by our exposure of the circumstances in this case, we can help in that process. This is Howard Cosell for the ABC Sports Magazine.*

---

*Note: As this book was going to press in the fall of 1979, Vorhies's father announced that he was filing a major lawsuit against Virginia Tech alleging negligence by the school and its officials. The suit charged that young Vorhies died as a result of the punishment drills and because the system of disciplining football team members failed to adequately protect the health of players. A Virginia Tech spokesperson expressed the institution's deep regret at the youth's death but withheld specific comment on the charges pending litigation.

⑧ Kids

The game of hockey is a game and if we don't be careful something drastick [*sic*] is going to happen.

> —Letter from ten-year-old elementary
> student to Canada's Royal Commission
> on Violence in the Communications Industry

"COME ON, ROBERT! KICK IT, KICK IT, GOD-DAMNIT!" yells the attractive young brunette in the wine-red blouse.

"MOVE UP, JOEY, MOVE UP!" shouts the thirtyish man next to her.

The screaming parents line the playing field like a row of screeching geese. The ball, a white globe splotched with black pentagons, hop-skips between twenty-two small players.

"HUSTLE, HUSTLE, HUSTLE! COME ON, ROBERT, BEAT HIM OUT! BEAT HIM OUT! KICK IT, KICK IT!" . . . "KILL THEM, JASON, KILL THEM! JASON! JASON!" . . . "YEA-A-A-A-Y!" In a frenzy as the ball sails downfield for a goal, the attractive young woman grabs the blonde next to her, and the two begin an ecstatic, circular twirl.

On a grassy field in Livermore, California, two groups of wobbly-legged little boys are playing soccer, the sport that was going to save us from the childhood excesses of junior hockey, Pop Warner football, and Little League baseball. Most of the youngsters are between seven and eight. They are divided into two eleven-member squads—a white shirt–green shorts team and a green-on-green club. About fifteen parents face each other on either side of the field. All are white suburbanites, in their late twenties or early thirties. Right now at least, they are yelling their lungs out.

To their left, the green-on-green coach, a muscular young man with an imitation afro, screams and waves his arms. His team is losing, and at half time he angrily motions the players off the field, pausing as he spots a straggling, seven-year-old goalie. "Dammit!" he shouts, jerking a thumb toward the other squad members. "Get the hell up there right now!"

Once surrounded by his band of woebegone players, the curly-haired Apollo glares down sternly at their upturned faces. "Okay, you guys," he growls, "do you want Slurpees or water after the game? You're sure playing like you want water." Heads hang, soccer shoes scuff against the turf, fifty-pound bodies shift in discomfort.

Somewhere, far from this softly rolling valley which juxtaposes old California towns with a spreading sea of modern, frame-and-stucco tract homes, seven-year-old boys tug against a straining kite string, drop their baseball gloves at a sand-lot game to stare at a passing train, dissolve into jive talk when pals interrupt a three-on-three inner-city basketball contest. But that is play. This is discipline.

Deep in the concrete and linoleum belly of a Livermore government research laboratory, a sophisticated computer whirs through hundreds of microsecond calculations. Rather than logging the vital statistics of space-age weaponry, however, these coded, keypunched cards pigeonhole the athletic hopes of thousands of school-age youngsters. The data is precise: speed in the forty-yard dash; time in the "box" run; scores for kicking distance, accuracy, and dribbling skills; classification by age, weight, height, and sex.

Held in late spring, the Livermore Soccer Club (LSC) player draft is a miniature version of the same system that sorts out college talent for the National Football League. The kids wind up on a print-out, ranked by ability in six age groups, from eight through nineteen. Youngsters with the highest computer scores are eligible for drafting by coaches who lead Livermore in "high competition" contests against neighboring towns. The others, a vast majority, wind up in the LSC "house" league, where the computer again selects the young competitors by ability, and the draft is repeated in each age group. The final segregation is a color ranking into nine best-to-worst divisions—blue, red, green, yellow, and so on—with gold serving as the badge of soccer ignominy.

Whatever the effect on their egos, however, one thing seems certain: Livermore's young soccer players learn early about how large organizations work. Honoré de Balzac compared bureacracy to a giant mechanism operated by pygmies. But in the LSC, the giants operate the mechanism and the pygmies are nearly outnumbered. Players provide the foundation for an elaborate hierarchy of adult commissioners, coordinators, and committee members. Indeed, there is one grownup for every four children in the soccer club. Each team has a head coach, assistant coach, and something called a teamparent coordinator— 420 big folks in all, not counting kibitzers—and the league itself is served by six equipment managers, half a dozen or more registration officials, and 150 referees. And it doesn't stop there.

Consider the LSC's twenty-member governing board, four times larger than Livermore's city council and nearly triple the size of the local school board. Besides eight coach representatives, called "age group coordinators," eight members represent "administrative offices": the assistant director, finance officer, house-league commissioner, publicity officer, separate appointees for referees and team-parent coordinators, and the LSC registrar. A club secretary, equipment officer, and treasurer also hold seats on the board but do not vote; the LSC director votes only in case of a tie. Yet another member serves as the club's regular delegate to meetings of the region's district board, itself a subgroup of the California Youth Soccer Association, which maintains separate boards for northern and southern California.

If you liked the *Mikado,* you'll love Livermore soccer. Making punishment fit the crime is the job of a separate administrative body. A seven-member disciplinary committee is appointed by the house-league commissioner and is composed of parents and other local residents familiar with the game. Unfortunately, finding knowledgeable adults isn't always easy. In fact, since few learned soccer as youngsters, even many LSC coaches themselves do not know how to play the game.

To some extent, the Livermore Soccer Club's overly complex human structure may merely reflect soccer's rampant growth. Little League baseball, Pop Warner football, and other junior sports greatly increased in popularity following World War II. But there never has been anything like the phenomenal growth of youth soccer in California.*

If Pete Rozelle were to drive around Livermore any Saturday morning in the fall, he would witness a chilling sight for the billion-dollar NFL. On literally every community playground and schoolyard, pro football's affable commissioner would find thousands of boys—and girls—playing soccer.

Soccer pervades Livermore. LSC officials boast that half of

---

* At 70,000-plus, the California Youth Soccer Association's projected 1978–79 north-state enrollment had jumped more than 2,000 per cent in less than a decade. Including the 32,000 CYSA players in southern California, the 135,000-plus rival American Youth Soccer Organization, as well as independent, Police Athletic League, and YMCA clubs, more than 250,000 California youngsters are playing soccer today who didn't know a corner kick from a throw-in a few years ago.

all male children between grades two and four take part in their program. The twenty-mile-long "Tri-Valley" area, which includes Livermore and a handful of similar suburban communities at the southern end of San Francisco Bay, is close to being an American youth-soccer capital. Indeed, nearly 15,000 Tri-Valley youngsters competed under the CYSA banner in 1978, around 15 per cent of the association's total membership.

In Livermore and just about every surrounding town, parents have turned to soccer because they believe it is a healthier game for children. Kids who play soccer don't wear heavy pads and headgear, experience less body contact, and have fewer injuries than they would in football. So far there has been no evidence that soccer endangers bone growth, as throwing a hardball can. Doctors love the way the game helps to develop young chest cavities and to improve cardiovascular conditioning. Soccer also has psychological advantages: because the ball is constantly moving, no one youngster stays under prolonged pressure to perform. Most important, kids get to play. In 1978, Livermore's Pop Warner team held tryouts attended by some 150 boys. About 30 made the team. In soccer, more than 2,000 boys showed up for spring trials, and—as guaranteed by youth soccer rules—every one was assured of a playing berth. At least as significant: more than 800 girls had a league of their own.

Unfortunately, zooming growth and domination by families with ties to nearby government research facilities have brought jealousy and resentment to the Livermore Soccer Club, causing painful exclusions, hurt feelings, and the needless denial of some boys' and girls' chances to play.

At least one group, parents of an under-eight boys' team called the Green Hornets, believe the politics of Livermore soccer have worked to discriminate against themselves and their children. They charge the LSC board with favoring "in-group" members in handing out choice coaching assignments and tournament travel and entry-fee expenses, and with controlling the player-selection process so that desirable athletes remain on their teams.

When the Hornets chose to become affiliated with the CYSA's rival, the American Youth Soccer Organization, the LSC soccer board responded by banning its teams from even practicing with the club. With virtually every inch of playground space in enemy hands, the Hornets were forced to lease a field from a nearby community college. Even then it has proved difficult for many out-of-town teams to travel in for games. The result: the Hornets have spent more than a few Saturdays just sitting around.

The Livermore soccer establishment insists that its written policy statements prove most of the Hornets claims are exaggerated or untrue. Even so, troubling questions remain. Is the LSC so overorganized that it stifles the playfulness of youngsters? For whom does the organization really exist? "The whole direction of youth sports is that they are scaled-down versions of professional games," says Kenneth Dolan, soft-spoken former LSC director. "When you structure the game with adult supervision, you start placing adult values on kids. It is not always pleasant, but this is part of growing up." Too much competition, too much pressure too soon, often accompany adult leadership, admits Dolan, a physicist at nearby Sandia Laboratories. "I see it in our own program," he says, "and it grinds on me."

Livermore's soccer parents are decent human beings, but the games of their children may have become too important. They spend huge sums of hard-earned dollars on uniforms, the "right" soccer shoes, special post-season tournaments and bowl games,* and expensive clinics to professionalize their offspring's skills. If the history of junior football and baseball

* The Hornet families spent $6,000 to send their sons to a prestigious invitational tournament in Las Vegas—busfare alone topped $1,200. When the families were rejected by the LSC board in an appeal for financial help, they raised the money on their own by holding garage sales.

programs is any teacher, their efforts may ensure that soccer, among the most physically and psychologically healthy of organized children's sports, will be spoiled.

In their comfortable living rooms, the parents talk of the valuable lessons of self-discipline and self-confidence that can come to a young girl or boy from soccer. But only they can explain why adults have created such an enormous role for themselves. Soccer has only seventeen basic rules (compared to more than 120 official strictures in American professional football), and children would play the game with or without supervision. "Soccer is a great game," says Karen Tootle, one of the Green Hornet moms. "It's the parents that screw it up."

University of Illinois psychologist Douglas A. Kleiber contends that when adults take charge of children's recreation, the kids may lose an important opportunity to make decisions themselves. "When children play games unsupervised by adults, they argue over rules and fairness," says Kleiber. "If children spend most of their time in activities supervised by adults, when are they going to learn how to develop and apply rules instead of simply obeying instructions?" A specialist in leisure behavior, Kleiber believes some good can come from grownups taking part in sports supervision. But, he contends, when adults make all decisions, "it is they who are playing the game and not the youngsters."

Who is responsible for viciousness in children's sports? Parents in Virginia Beach, Virginia, were bullied with physical threats and pressure—most of it coming from other parents—to get them to falsify birth certificates that would keep their kids eligible for junior football. "Nobody likes anything like this," says Needham Cheely, Jr., a Virginia Beach recreation official whose investigation helped confirm the charges. The scandal blew open after complaints by the mother of a twelve-year-old player for the Courthouse Knights, undefeated champs of the league for ten- and eleven-year-olds. Mrs. J. A. Cox said she had been asked by another player's parent to alter her son's birth certificate so he could participate in a post-season bowl game. When Mrs. Cox refused, she received ugly comments and hostile stares from other parents of Courthouse Knights players. The night after the bowl game a gang of youths, including team members, marched on her home and threatened her son. Later that same evening five anonymous telephone callers cursed at the Cox family and told them their lives were in danger.

The investigation prompted by Mrs. Cox's complaints confirmed that falsified birth certificates and registration cards had allowed otherwise ineligible players to compete. One member of the Courthouse Knights was thirteen years old, and another lived in Norfolk, several miles outside the legal registration area. As it turned out, the league was riddled with rules violators, and the practice of cheating and faking records, encouraged and often aided by the league's upstanding citizen–parents, had gone on for years. The scandal ended with the Knights being stripped of their city championship, their thirteen regular and post-season victories, and the opportunity to compete in the Mayor's Cup.

Why had it happened? "Winning is all," commented one saddened father of a Knights player. "They [grownups] are pushing this like professionals. They lose track of what they are doing and that the sport is to help the boys. . . . All of this was adult generated, and now the kids have to suffer." Cheely believes the punishment and subsequent rules changes will prevent a recurrence of the scandal, but he concedes it may take much longer for the players to forget their shame and again learn to appreciate their joy in the game. "It is not the kind of thing," he admits, "that you get over in a day."

In *Sports in America,* James Michener recounts how the importance of winning dictated the response of Little League officials to the growing success of Asian youth baseball programs in the 1960s. After years of domination by American clubs, the Little League World Series was won twice in succession by Japanese teams and then by Taiwan from 1969 to 1974. In nine games over three years, the lean young athletes from the land of Chiang Kai-shek outscored their Yankee opposition, 120–2. Unable to prove, despite a secret investigation, that the Taiwanese had cheated to beat American boys at their own game, American officials did the next best thing: they excluded all but American squads from "World" Series competition. "If you can't beat 'em, ban 'em," was one waggish comment Michener recorded about the incident.

Another apple-pie institution, the soap-box derby, was disgraced by scandal in 1973. By then, as Michener points out, the race—which once had been run by boys using orange crates and peach-basket rims—had become a battle between adult engineers using liquid plastics to build sleek-bodied cars costing thousands of dollars. A fourteen-year-old boy was caught using a hidden electromagnet, designed by his engineer uncle, to give the car an extra thrust at the start. In statements after the incident, the uncle, implicated in alleged derby cheating by his own son a year earlier, said it was "common knowledge that eleven-year-olds cannot build winning racers. That was why there were adult professional builders." Other evidence suggested that doctored tires and bearings, illegal axles, and extra weight had become commonplace at the derby.

Michener's book includes an interview with Jonathan Brower, a California sociologist. The following remarks by Brower were based on an extensive study of youth baseball games, but just as easily could have been about soccer or the soap-box derby.

Laws exist to protect children at work and school but their 'play' as governed by adults goes unchecked. Playground ball is a pressure-packed thing for boys. For good athletes it may be fun. At least they can tolerate it, but for boys who are not good athletes and who try to please their managers and parents, it's a matter of tension.

Parents get too caught up in the win ethic. One father proudly told a friend, 'My kid doesn't care about sportsmanship. He says winning is what's important.' *This thirst for victory and its accompanying competitiveness was far stronger among managers and coaches than players* [emphasis added]. The kids would offer help to other teams. Adult leaders frowned on this interteam cooperation because they did not want assistance given to those whom they might later be fighting for the championship.

Anybody with a good memory or someone who has watched kids play knows that youngsters and adults approach games from entirely different directions. For one thing, kids handicap each other to offset natural differences and make games fair. When kids get up a game of baseball, for example, if one youngster is thirty pounds heavier and three years older, he bats from the wrong side. To adults, most kids are lousy when it comes to athletic concentration. An otherwise able outfielder who also happens to be a nine-year-old boy may drop his glove and stare straight up at the sky if an airplane passes overhead. "Let a fire truck go by and it's looney tunes," Dickie Maegle, the former Rice running back and a Little League coach in Houston, once said. "I've seen 'em so excited at kickoff, with the crowds yelling and bands playing, that the kicker completely missed the ball. I've seen 'em running for a touchdown when their pants fell down to their knees." And kids who play without adult supervision have an easy way of handling games that aren't fun—they quit. No youngster left to his own devices would have wasted his time, as American Little Leaguers did in 1973 and 1974, in a series of contests in which the combined score, in favor of Taiwan, was 84–0. They would have picked up and gone home.

"Children do not instinctively believe that winning is everything in sport," concluded Canada's official investigation into violence in youth hockey. "If one has any reason to doubt the truth of that statement you need only recall your own experiences of shinny [sand-lot hockey] as a boy," wrote

William R. McMurtry, the report's author. "There were endless permutations and combinations of sides. No one kept score . . . you measured youself, by yourself, taking pride in any new move learned or developed . . . when coaches and parents hysterically *demand* victory at any price they seldom realize just how great the cost is."

Youth sports programs exist primarily to acquaint youngsters with a pyramid-shaped economic system in which they will have little chance of being full-fledged adult participants, another expert told the Canadian investigators. "Introduced after people have developed positive self-reliant images of physical self, freely-chosen competitive sport may well provide self-fulfillment," testified University of Alberta professor Harvey Scott. "However, before the person loves and is sure of his body and his physical self, it functions primarily as a destroyer of self and eliminator of participants."

In other words, overcompetition becomes a convenience for the system. In children, it eases their adjustment to a hierarchical structure of winners and losers. The impact is not to free them for open and creative competition, for the full experience of athletic laissez faire, but rather to condition them to accept their station in life.

"In both school and games the spirit of the experience has been distorted beyond recognition," educator David N. Campbell has written. "A parade of frustrated fathers [is] determined that their son will be a winner and make up for their own personal failure. All over the country little league and school coaches deliver Knute Rockne half-time speeches, but the emphasis now is more exaggerated, an anxiety ridden command to win: *all that matters is winning.*"

Campbell believes too much emphasis on winning has helped create systemwide mistrust. "In school the assumption is that no one learns without threats of grades, failure, being less than first . . . sorting, ranking and labeling . . . winning and losing are what our schools are all about, not education."

Psychologists Linden L. Nelson and Spencer Kagan compared cooperation and competition among children five to ten years of age and from different cultures. The researchers, from California's Polytechnic State University at San Luis Obispo and the University of California at Riverside, respectively, used specially designed games in which the youngsters had to cooperate to "win." Organized in pairs, they tried to place a pointer suspended by four equidistant strings into a target hole, pull two strings of blocks through a single hole, and manipulate a marble holder designed to come apart if both members of the pair tugged at once. There were other games as well, but the idea behind each was the same: the kids had to work together to "win." Prizes, including rings, whistles, badges, and popguns, were offered to the three groups of children, who came from distinctly different white middle-class, rural Mexican, and Mexican-American backgrounds.

The Nelson–Kagan results offer an insightful if somewhat disheartening glimpse of the American character. The Anglo children displayed excessively competitive behavior, even when doing so meant they would wind up "losers." The Mexican children teamed up and got the prizes. Among the seven-to-nine-year-olds, Mexican children cooperated in more than half, and the Mexican-Americans in a third, of the trials; the middle-class Anglo kids cooperated an average of only 10 per cent of the time. Put another way, the Anglos showed themselves to be five times as competitive as the Mexican kids and three times as concerned with winning as the Mexican-Americans. Given a choice, they tried to take toys away from their own partners in 78 per cent of the trials, *even when it meant "losing" the toys for themselves.* "The American competitive spirit may be alive and well," said Nelson and Kagan in reporting their findings in *Psychology Today.* "But it has produced a culture whose children are systematically irrational."

Like urban youngsters in Canada, Holland, Israel, and Korea (who reportedly exhibit similar tendencies), the American kids demonstrated an absence of sharing so profound as to suggest "the environment we provide for these children is barren of experiences that would sensitize them to the possibility of cooperation." For the most part, that environment conforms to what game theorists describe as a "negative sum game"—i.e., the number of losers exceeds the number of winners—or at best a "zero sum game," in which for every winner one competitor must fail. In an elementary classroom, a student stumbles and hesitates over an answer while hands sway and an impatient instructor finally turns to a little girl who always knows the right answer. On an athletic field, young Pop Warner players sit in clean uniforms on the bench, training for a lifetime as spectators.

"One of the main implications of our research," says psychologist Nelson, "was that there ought to be other than purely competitive kinds of games that can be used with children." Nelson emphasizes the experiments clearly showed that cooperation can be learned—that is, children "sensitized" with a prior cooperative experience exhibited far less destructively competitive behavior. "But the general orientation in our society," Nelson notes, "is toward winning, toward getting more than the other person, toward being better than others. We're so competitive it often blinds us to cooperative possibilities."

Utah psychologists Donna M. Gelfand and Donald P. Hartman exposed separate pairs of five- and six-year-old children to aggressive or non-aggressive adult role models,* then asked the youngsters to compete in games involving hand strength and bowling accuracy. "Our results clearly supported the view that competition promotes aggression,

---

* The "aggressive" adult repeatedly assaulted a large inflated doll with a mallet; the "non-aggressive" adult joined the youngsters in playing with clay.

even above the heightened aggression ordinarily caused by exposure to an aggressive model," the researchers concluded.

Competitive tendencies were much stronger with adult support, a follow-up Gelfand–Hartman study showed. "Adult models, whatever their behavior, play a major role in determining the nature of boys' [the second study did not include girls] responses to frustration induced by competition," the psychologists said, noting other research indicating "the children's comments about their own failure in games are powerfully influenced by verbal models provided by adults. If the adult model engages in self-criticism or self-blame, the child observers will do so also . . ." *San Francisco Chronicle* columnist Herb Caen recalled a scene some years ago when Jimmy Connors, then about thirteen, and his mother, Gloria, arrived in the Bay Area for a National Juniors tennis tournament in Burlingame, a plush suburb of San Francisco. Connors, weary from a late flight, lost his 9 A.M. match. As the future champion sat down in exhausted despair, his mother took the tuna sandwich she was munching and smeared it all over his face. "And you wonder," wrote Caen, "why he [Connors] is a bit—ah—odd?"

Parents scream into the faces of coaches and referees, hand out diet pills and plastic suits to their overweight kids, sock it out over close calls, and yell about whether their offspring should play shortstop or second base. In Livermore, abusive remarks and threats from parents and fans prompted so many referees to quit that Jerry Landrum, president of the local referees' association, warned that the entire program was endangered. After a fan slugged and chased a referee in an under-twelve game, Landrum wrote an open letter to soccer players' parents and spectators, calling fan conduct toward LSC referees "outrageous" and warning that the association would file criminal charges against future violators. "I am appalled and disgusted that this could happen in our community," wrote Landrum.

From one part of the country to another, youngsters have
been learning about another thing grownups do a lot—go to
court. In Miami, angry parents hauled the Optimist Youth
Conference before a judge a few years ago after the OYC
ousted an entire 250-player group for brawls and vicious
fighting incidents that included post-game rock throwing,
slugfests, and car theft. Indiana's state athletic association has
been the target of some three dozen parent lawsuits challeng-
ing rules against high school youngsters "red shirting" (staying
back a year to gain an extra season of football eligibility). And
in West Springfield, Massachusetts, parents hired attorneys
and threatened court action in a complicated dispute over
which of their eight-to-ten-year-olds should have made the
West Springfield Hockey Association's first string. "I've gotten phone threats about how the parents were going to get
even with me," coach Richard Girard told the *New York Times*
in 1978. Besides rattling their ever-present swords of threatened litigation, some grownups actually came to blows over
Girard's "A" and "B" team selections. "They told me to be-
ware," the coach said. "My wife's been verbally abused at
games . . . Everything on our level seems to be a miniature
version of the big time."

Including violence, it would seem. In aping the pros, junior
hockey teams around the country have sacrificed the finesse of
set-up plays and skilled, open-ice checking in favor of poorly
controlled, straight-for-the-goal slap shots and wholesale
fighting. Good young skaters find themselves dominated by
bullies and roughnecks whose sole talent lies in their fists.
"The coaches are encouraging the kids to fight," says Andy
Bathgate, former star forward with the New York Rangers.
Bathgate recently walked out on a junior hockey game in
Toronto after watching three hours of fights. "They specialize
in intimidation," he adds. "A coach sends out a ten-cent kid to
beat up a dollar player."

Is it surprising that anger, fights, and rejection add up to a loss of joy? "It's very painful to think of all the youngsters who love sport, but who are being eliminated at every stage," says San Jose State University sports psychologist Thomas Tutko. "The genuine benefits of athletics—health, sociability, and developing personal growth, cooperation, loyalty, and pride—are being undermined . . ."

Several years ago, Ohio State basketball player Luke Witte and two teammates were beaten for a full ninety-five seconds before a national television audience during a fist fight between OSU and the University of Minnesota. Afterward, the respected coach of a championship public school team reported the reaction of his team, all witnesses to the bloody incident, to the *Milwaukee Journal.* "My kids were upset. They came to me and asked me about it. I told them that this was not the way it was supposed to be. A lot of high school kids who saw that may have turned sour. They may have said, 'Is this what basketball is all about? Is this worth working hard for?' "

Actually, the lesson may be even more powerful than that. Exposure to sports violence can have at least two "educational" consequences, York University sociologist Michael D. Smith, perhaps the foremost authority on hockey violence, told Canada's McMurtry investigators. First, such acts expand the boundaries of acceptable conduct, legitimatizing behavior that once would have been considered well outside normal play. Second, the "climate of approval" of sports violence can encourage collective outbursts by fans.

Researchers like Smith are among the thoughtful observers of sports who are clearly concerned about the violent, winning-is-everything trend in our games—and its impact upon children. But they also admit to having difficulty explaining why conditions seem worse today than even a few years ago. "Any single answer," says psychologist John J. McCarthy, a hockey coach at the University of Cincinnati, "is bound to be too simplistic."

McCarthy believes people engage in aggressive impulses at different times and for different reasons. "If you look at our culture, it is clear we are going through a period when behavioral boundaries are loose. When this happens you are going to find more acting out of aggression, with the effect being more pronounced in sports." McCarthy found in his own research that highly penalized players also were the most successful. The lesson is clear, according to McCarthy: "The aggressive player is recognized and reinforced by his actions."

Many youngsters have been badly confused by negative athletic role models precisely at a time when positive influences were needed most. So concludes psychiatrist Roy M. Whitman of the University of Cincinnati's College of Medicine. "I think athletics have been disappointing to kids," says Dr. Whitman. "Adults can relegate athletics to a secondary position, they can keep their perspective; but to kids sports are primary." What can be the lesson, for example, for junior marathoners whose parents push them into training habits which may spoil their enthusiasm for running later in life? "You wouldn't believe the horror stories I've been told," says author–columnist Dr. George Sheehan. "Kids of nine or ten running eighteen or twenty miles, with their parents riding behind them on bikes, not allowing them to quit and screaming at them if they ask to drop out. I've seen children flown in from California [to the East Coast] to compete in age-group races."

Worse still, what message do kids get when they see members of the Washington Redskins yelling ethnic obscenities at a field-goal kicker for the Philadelphia Eagles? What of the lessons provided by that powerful master of fun and games, the Pittsburgh Steelers' "Mean" Joe Greene? When judgments by game officials were going against him and his team in 1977, Mean Joe studded the airwaves and newspaper columns with gentle thoughts, such as:

"If they get in the way, I'll cleat 'em in the spine."

"I wish a bolt of lightning would come down and strike one of their hearts out."

"If I get half a chance, I'll punch one of them out."

"I'll call them the dirtiest name I can think of. I'll talk about their momma."

It is important to distinguish between the impact of Greene's words upon adults—who may prefer to dismiss his comments as ritual taunts uttered for effect—and upon children, who make such distinctions far less easily, if at all. Especially after Greene's nationally televised double-barreled assaults a few weeks later, when he punched, in succession, Denver Bronco offensive guard Paul Howard and center Mike Montler. Millions of children were part of the television audience that witnessed—*and then saw replayed dozens of times*—what would have been interpreted on most American streets as back-to-back instances of common assault. Greene and his team never were penalized on the field for the incidents, and more than a week passed before a fine was levied by pro football's front office.

Can anyone say with certainty that the message was lost on a sixteen-year-old girl—a television violence junkie, according to her friends—who poked a rifle muzzle across her window sill in San Diego, California, and opened fire on an elementary school across the street? Put another way, can sports be isolated from the epidemic of viciousness and fear among American youngsters? A Ford Foundation study reported that juvenile arrests for violent crime tripled between 1960 and 1975, with thirteen-year-olds committing the most serious offenses in the under-eighteen group. By 1978, close to half (41 per cent) of youngsters entering California's youth correctional facilities had committed violent crimes—assault, murder, armed robbery, and rape.

While the fathers and older brothers of American youngsters may well have shrugged off the mesmerizing replays of Woody Hayes's right to the chops of Clemson's Charlie Bauman, there is every reason to believe that younger kids were scared by what they saw. One national survey found that one quarter of American children between the ages of seven and eleven are afraid someone will hurt them if they go outside to play. Such fears were twice as high among kids who watched large amounts of television and higher still if they had seen fights and gunplay on the tube. Until the advent of television, the odds were high that a child would grow to maturity without ever having seen a murder. Today, the average fifteen-year-old has seen the fictional destruction, mostly by homicide, of 18,000 human beings, according to a report by Dr. Michael B. Rothenberg in the *Journal of the American Medical Association.*

American audiences are exposed to more television violence than are the citizens of any other nation, according to an exhaustive 1977 *Public Opinion Quarterly* review of two decades of television-violence studies involving more than 30,000 subjects. Three-fourths of all television characters were touched by violence in some form, and nine out of ten shows contained some type of mayhem in a prime-time and weekend programming "violence profile" by George Gerbner, dean of the University of Pennsylvania's Annenberg School of Communications.

Unlike the bigger-than-life fantasy worlds of Hollywood motion pictures and the legitimate theater, television pushes its way into our homes as a diminutive friend. It assumes the authenticity of our own living rooms. More important, as community medicine specialist Anne R. Somers noted in an April 8, 1976, *New England Journal of Medicine* article, it shares an unfortunate propensity to show violence in "the context of ordinary life and routine problem-solving." When a Detroit schoolteacher was shot to death in front of her horrified first-grade class, at least one of the children immediately likened the experience to watching a television show. When an ex-GI who helped liberate Dachau was invited to a northern California high school class to discuss the television special "Holocaust," he was surprised by the students' reactions. "I discovered," Ben Langella wrote in a June 2, 1978, letter to *San Francisco Examiner* television critic Bill Mandel, "that 'Holocaust' was popular *only* because of the violence. The kids told me they liked the series because it was like 'Kojak', only with more killing. Nowhere did they talk about man's relationship to other men."

Available research almost uniformly suggests that violence which conforms to realistic life situations carries more instructional power than that which does not. The Rand Corporation's George Comstock listed some of the major factors contributing to imitative aggression among children after television viewing: ". . . the suggestion that aggression is justified, socially acceptable, motivated by malice, or pays off; a realistic depiction; highly exciting material . . . conditions similar to those experienced by the young viewer . . . circumstances like those of his environment . . ."

Ronald Slaby, in research at the University of Washington, compiled some of the lessons kids learn from television mayhem:

Violence is rampant.

Violence works.

Violence frequently is rewarded.

Violence often is justifiable.

Violence often is fun.

Violence is clean.

Violence sometimes is done in unusual ways.

Violence is more appropriate for males than females.

Violence is something to be watched, tolerated, and even entertained by.

While scores of studies have probed dramatized violence and its effect on the young, researchers, especially in the United States, have shied away from investigating televised sports savagery. "It's a super-difficult area," complains an expert at the Annenberg School of Communications. "The hard part is separating out just exactly what constitutes violence."

Can we assume, then, that violence in video sports has no impact? To the contrary, it requires a leap of imagination to believe sports does not meet at least some of the criteria outlined by Comstock, does not teach, perhaps far more convincingly, some of the same lessons as fictional violence. Indeed, three physicians writing in the medical journal *Pediatrics* singled out television sports for its strong tendency to foster an "Evel Knievel" syndrome in kids. "Televised violence," they noted, "especially during sporting events and news reporting, is increasingly implicated in imitative and aggressive behavior by children."

The pioneering studies of Stanford University's Albert Bandura showed conclusively that watching filmed aggression heightened hostility levels in youngsters. Today, Bandura believes, the prestige and recognition of star athletes may give them far more power to influence the young than the anonymous adult aggression models used in psychological experiments. "It conveys permissiveness," he says. "The intimidating player is depicted positively, as a good intimidator, and that puts a positive stamp on using aggression."

At least as important: the absence of swift and unambiguous justice. Even in the case of Woody Hayes, who was fired almost immediately after his final outburst in Jacksonville, the electronic media were crowded with self-serving apologies and testimonials to a "great" career. Somebody proclaimed a Woody Hayes Day in Ohio, and by early 1979 Woody was in

Hollywood, negotiating film rights for his life story. Baseball player Len Randle, who rearranged the face of his manager in Texas, wound up with a better job with the New York Mets. And the fining of Joe Greene took place so long after the incident that many kids probably missed it altogether. "The child," says Bandura, "learns that aggression is prevalent as a pattern of behavior. If violence in sports is seen as justified aggression, as part of the nature of the activity, that serves to further legitimatize its use and can be expected to have a greater instigative effect."

One myth about television violence—that its effects are short-lived—may have been unmasked by University of Illinois researchers L. Rowell Huesmann and Leonard D. Eron. In a technically sophisticated study conducted over a ten-year period and involving more than four hundred student subjects in upstate New York, the two psychologists found that "a boy's aggressiveness at age nineteen was directly and significantly related to the amount of violent television he watched at age eight, regardless of his initial level of aggressiveness, social status, intellectual ability or parent's behavior. Through imitation, the child appeared to learn aggressive habits that persisted at least ten years." Girls escaped relatively unaffected, for reasons including the absence of aggressive female role models on television when the study began in 1960.

Televised sports violence *per se* was analyzed by Ontario, Canada's Royal Commission on Violence in the Communications Industry. "The uniqueness of sports as a potential socializing agent of aggression becomes readily apparent," reported L.M. Leith, a University of Alberta psychologist investigating the effects of viewing aggressive sports on third-to-fifth-grade boys. "The more important, powerful, successful and liked the model is, the more a child will imitate them. Obviously, in the eyes of both children and adults alike, the professional athlete meets all these criteria . . . *it seems reasonable to assume that an internal vicarious reinforcement occurs as a result of viewing aggressive sports models. If a player acts in an aggressive manner, gets away with it, and is then rewarded for his actions, the viewer has learned that aggression pays"* (emphasis added).

The amount of sports programming broadcast on Canadian television, much of it beamed from the United States, increased by 200 per cent between 1960 and 1975, according to a commission study by Dick Moriarty of the University of Windsor. Moriarty and his colleagues at the Sports Institute for Research carefully scrutinized hundreds of hours of televised baseball, hockey, lacrosse, and other contests. "Antisocial sports behavior—that is, acts rated as "aggressive" or "very aggressive" according to a predetermined index— outweighed "pro-social" behavior by a ratio of 3 to 1 in prime time. Though unable to prove a scientific link between wrongful athletic conduct and antisocial acts in the non-video world, the researchers had seen enough to make a strong plea for further investigation. "Everyone has an opinion," complains Moriarty, "but there is very little in the data bank."

The Royal Commission itself was unequivocating in its critical assessment that athletic mayhem on television was responsible for hockey violence in younger age groups. Even in rural Ontario's icy northwest, an area noted for its hockey enthusiasm, civic, educational, and business leaders expressed deep concern over the impact of televised sports violence on the young. While the mostly Indian population in this area has a strong cultural tradition of non-violence, the kids mimicked the fist-swinging style of their video hockey heroes, noted the principal of a small school in remote Moosenee. "Before television," he testified, "the children did not throw down their gloves and fight."*

---

* Pressed to make their own views known to the commission, most kids came down on the side of athletic law and order. "Fighting is not part of the game, but some leagues think it is," wrote Lee Morita, a ten-year-old sixth grader at Elizabeth Simcoe Junior Public School. "Violence in amateur hockey has gone up every year and the referees aren't doing anything about it."

"It is bad enough that the rule breakers incapacitate one another," complained the president of Ontario's Fanshawe College, "it is worse that they exemplify an undesirable pattern of behavior to the next generation, and it is criminal that their influence in this respect is facilitated by the communications industry. . . . The message is often wrapped up in a parcel called toughness or heroism and is presented to our young people as a standard and acceptable mode of life. Essentially, however, it is destructive."

The McMurtry report, which culminated in an investigation by Ontario's Ministry of Community and Special Services, had its origins in a series of violent incidents in youth hockey during the early 1970s. In 1973 a boy was killed in a post-game fight.* The following year a vicious riot—joined in by many of the 750 attending fans—between two amateur teams in Ontario ended with five players and a game official being beaten. The report concluded that, at all levels of the sport, the use of violence as a tactical instrument was increasing. "This type of conduct is becoming more prevalent in the younger age groups. Violent games which were once unheard of at the Pee Wee [age twelve] and minor Bantam [age thirteen] level are now not uncommon." Later the McMurtry hearings pointed an accusing finger straight at the tube: ". . . the images presented by TV dwarf the effect of home and school in the minds of most sports conscious youngsters. If we are to improve the climate for amateur hockey it is important to appreciate the nature and extent of the influence of the professional model."

The Ontario Hockey Council (OHC) presented good news and bad news when it reported to the Royal Commission in 1976. The council had been successful, its chairman said, in

---

* Judge Barry Shapiro's charge to the jury: "The losing team used to call for three cheers for the winners, and the winning team reciprocated with three cheers for the losing team. How far have we traveled away from this concept? . . . " as quoted in a 1975 column by Red Smith of the *New York Times*.

proposing remedies for all the major ills besetting the game with one exception: "It is powerless to influence the on-ice conduct of professional hockey players, which, seen by youngsters mainly through the medium of television, is the single strongest determinant in shaping the attitudes prevalent in minor hockey."

Even those who believe that the problem of athletic violence has been overstated recognize its awesome power—bolstered by the electronic media—to instruct. "We're out there five days a week trying to teach high school kids to be good sports," a Pennsylvania assistant coach told *Time* in a November 20, 1978, article. "Then they go home and watch television, and what do they see? Pro players dancing in the end zone and spiking the ball to humiliate opponents, spearing, taking cheap shots."

It should be added that television sports have a teaching aid denied mere fictional savagery: the amazing machine brought to us by Ampex and known in the trade as the HS-100c, or, simply, instant replay. With its application limited almost exclusively to sports, the instructional potential of video replay can only be guessed. Like the best educational tools, instant replay selects an event from our environment, then repeats it until we know it by heart.

Consider the impact of what is perhaps college football's most historic single moment in 1978: Woody Hayes's punch-tossing swan song in the Gator Bowl. Well over a hundred ABC-affiliated television stations replayed the incident on evening and late-night Saturday news shows after the game, according to Donn R. Bernstein, ABC's media director for college athletics. Since other networks also had access to the tape, it was reshown by NBC, CBS, and independent stations as well. By the following day the clip was reappearing for another full cycle on national professional-football telecasts by NBC and CBS and during a Howard Cosell "Wide World of Sports" interview. The Associated Press snapped a still photo from a television screen and distributed the image to thousands of newspapers in the United States and abroad. Bernstein estimates the domestic television audience at approximately fifty million homes. Worldwide, well over a hundred million people may have witnessed the incident through the eye of ABC's single 50-yard-line camera. The coverage given the famous World War II punch thrown by Hayes's hero—General George Patton*—seems paltry by comparison.

Phone calls from outraged viewers flooded ABC's New York headquarters after the Hayes incident. But the fans weren't angry because an American college coach had belted an opposing player; a switchboard poll indicated that more than half were protesting the network's failure to provide immediate replays.** "The critics got on us for neglecting our journalistic duties," says Bernstein, "but that's not why the ordinary people called. They simply wanted to see it, see it, see it. They were like vultures."

Like most of his colleagues, Bernstein has learned to live with the violence inundating television sports. "I'm a gentle man and a devout coward. I personally hate it. But that's what people want to see. Violence is a National Football League trademark; they're proud of it. And why do you think people watch the Indiannapolis 500? I know. They want to see a crack-up, to see somebody get hurt."

Take the NFL highlight films sometimes loaned to kids'

---

* Patton lost his command after striking a shell-shocked GI he accused of cowardice.

** Because the event was missed by the broadcast team assigned to the Gator Bowl, replays had to be copied from a "history" tape master at ABC television in New York. It should be noted that, by its nature, instant replay tends to capture acts of violence and illegality which game officials fail to detect. A few instances: the Joe Greene uppercuts against Denver in the 1977 NFL playoffs, the striking of Lynn Swann by George Atkinson of the Oakland Raiders, and the famous fumbled-ball touchdown that won the 1979 Rose Bowl. In cases such as these, youngsters not only are being instructed in how to perform such acts, they are being given graphic proof that such acts can pay off. Nevertheless, in 1979 the NFL again rejected incorporation of instant-replay results in the penalty and fine process.

summer camps and televised by stations around the country. The films are choreographed to classical music such as "Afternoon of a Faun" or "Blue Danube." There's lots of percussion, and the films have catchy titles like *Search and Destroy* and *Eyeball-to-Eyeball.* What they show—for example, when Chicago running back Gayle Sayers gets nailed by Dick Butkus as the tempo reaches *allegretto*—is athletes kicking the hell out of each other, usually in slow motion.

How much opposition is there to cutting down on the mayhem? It took a nationwide advertising boycott by the 6.6 million-member Parent–Teachers Association to reduce violence in television dramas. Television marketing executives long have been aware of a phenomenon called "closure," a psychological buzz word for the natural tendency of viewers to try and organize what they see. At least some experts believe that to achieve closure the audience must pay better attention to the show and, ipso facto, to their commercials as well. Such considerations may help explain a headline in the industry publication *Advertising Age* at the height of the PTA's antiviolence campaign. Its bias blaring in Bodini Bold, *Advertising Age* proclaimed: "ANTI-TV VIOLENCE MOOD GETTING WORSE—JWT [advertising giant J. Walter Thompson] CONVINCED 'WE HAVE SOMETHING TO WORRY ABOUT.' "

Sports coverage is an integral part of prime-time television which regularly outdraws fictional programming in ratings. Yet athletic mayhem on television remains almost entirely unchecked. The dangers of ignorance and neglect may be far more profound than most of us guess. How many children, for example, have turned away from healthy, competitive games after seeing roughnecks like Billy Martin, Dave Schultz, and Mean Joe Greene?

The hyped-up, media-ballyhooed sports heroes who punch their way to the top and then use intimidation to stay there may have helped spawn another, less apparent tragedy among older youngsters. Literally thousands of ghetto teenagers have tossed away their chances at an education because they thought their street skills could carry them to the pinnacle of professional sports. What they overlooked were the immense athletic gifts which separated a Jack Tatum or Conrad Dobler from the general populace.

White Americans have assumed that sports, a la Frank Merriwell and Tom Brown, go hand in hand with character building, college diplomas, and salable job skills. But for many minority athletes, sports have gone hand in hand with the academics of sliding by and, eventually, with lives of crime and violence. "We have some outstanding athletes around here," complains the basketball coach at a mostly black high school in Oakland, California, "but how many of them can read and write? We train them to be the best on the field, yet no one is doing anything for them off the field."

"Because I saw sports as the primary avenue to black success, my education suffered," wrote Eric Monroe, a promising prep basketballer who went on to armed robbery and heroin addiction by the time he was twenty. "I was deeply engrossed in basketball while my classmates were equally engrossed in algebra." Monroe, writing to the *New York Times* from his prison cell in October 1977, noted that he was consistently pointed toward nonacademic subjects by administrators and counselors who correctly regarded him as a superb athlete. "I knew that scholastically I was not where I should be, but I also realized that sports and drugs pacify one's consciousness. So I passed my high school years basking in the glow of my athletic success or blowing my mind on dope . . . I did not relish the image of a brainless jock. Later in life, however, I was classified as something worse—a junkie."

In a multimillion-dollar lawsuit filed the day after Christmas 1978, seven black California State University at Los Angeles athletes charged they were cruelly deceived by recruiting offers to play football and basketball. CSULA coaches arranged for their entrance, it was alleged, not under the athletics program, but as special-admissions minority applicants.* Expensive cars the students thought were part of the deal were later repossessed. The "scholarship packages" the coaches had the youths and their parents sign turned out to be loans—not until they left school did the athletes learn they were obligated to repay the money, the suit charged.

The coaches had arranged for entrance grade requirements to be ignored and had provided third parties to take standardized admissions tests, said the suit. "Later," according to a twenty-three-page brief filed by attorneys for the Los Angeles–based Western Center on Law and Poverty, Inc., "instead of the substantive college education which they had promised, the same coaches deliberately steered the young student–athletes into educationally valueless curricula [mostly worthless physical education courses] designed solely to maintain their playing eligibility . . ."

CSULA coaches and school officials refused to confirm or deny the charges. But the plaintiffs' brief recalled the traditional formula whereby minority youngsters have played sports in exchange for a free education, aiding "numerous ghetto youths in escaping from the bonds of poverty." In the CSULA case, it maintained, "that formula is now working to further exploit and handicap these very people . . ."

Many white players, too, wind up with little to show for their athletic careers. Less than 1 per cent of college football players make it to the pros, but many more sacrifice their formal educations in trying. Of nineteen seniors on the 1976 Associated Press All-American team, only six held their diplomas a year later. Of the ten most recent Heisman Trophy winners at the time of an AP survey, half—Tony Dorsett, Johnny Rodgers, Steve Owens, O.J. Simpson, and Steve Spurrier—failed to graduate. "The top athlete, the one pre-

* The effect, according to the suit, was to deny other, more academically oriented minority students, an equal opportunity for scholarships.

paring for a pro career, graduates at a much lower rate than his less talented teammates," concluded the AP's Fred Rothenberg.

"The gifted athlete is often counselled on how not to gain a formal education, how to avoid any challenges in the classroom," says San Francisco 49er coach Bill Walsh, formerly head of the Stanford University football program. From Pop Warner and Little League on, promising players are led to believe that athletics will satisfy their every future need, Walsh told the *San Francisco Chronicle.* "We're not asking as much of our athletes educationally as we are of other students," he added, blaming much of the problem on lax academic standards of the National Collegiate Athletic Association.

Young athletes will remember what we teach them. If the emphasis is placed on excessive and irrational competition, the televised rewards of sports brutality, and the prizing of athletics above intellect, then we should not be surprised at the results.

One tackle in sixty minutes of football! What are you guys made of? From that pig farm where I live? Is that what you are—a bunch of stinking pigs? You go out there and show these people what you're made out of! I've just had it with you guys. Spend all this time with you guys and then you come out and pull something like this— catch you sitting around. Get out of here! Let's go play some football!

—Florida midget-football coach berating his team on a December 28, 1975, edition of CBS's "60 Minutes"

We believe sports are an important part of a boy's education here. A boy learns a lot out on the playing field. It's like life. You learn to kill or be killed out there. You know what I mean?

—Georgia schools superintendent explaining in an April 2, 1979, *Wall Street Journal* story why he chose to "red shirt" his two junior-high-school sons

There was something infinitely more sensible about that time long ago when adults did not meddle in the games of children. Perhaps it was simply that both parties had better things to do. The kids went off to the corner vacant lot, where they worked out informal handicaps so whichever team took Fat Harry or Mollie or Owen Scoville's skinny brother Tom got an extra player or another turn at bat. Without rules or adults to see to it, everybody—regardless of age or shape or sex—got to play. Parents worked at jobs which were hard and low paying but which their children understood. There weren't many uniforms or post-season bowl games for eight-year-olds, or screaming, win-happy moms.

We have forced our youngsters to accept violent, competitive athletic apprenticeships. Despite its guise of celebrating the spirit of American enterprise, such training, at last, becomes un-American, the antithesis of enterprise. At a ridiculously young age, children are taught to submit to an adult hierarchy, their spirit of individualism sacrificed to a blind belief in organization and rigid regulations.

The American dream always has been that anybody can win; but adult-supervised games have taught many more children to be losers than winners, for that is the negative sum game's nature, its bottom line. We must ask what we believe and want, not just for our offspring, but also for ourselves. The dream of youth is that any boy or girl can become whatever he or she chooses. It would be a national tragedy if that hope were to die between the yard markers of overorganized, adult-dominated sports. "Break up the Yankees!" used to be the cry when the Bronx Bombers dominated the baseball world. Perhaps today's slogan ought to be: "Give games back to the kids!"

On a grassy field in Livermore, California, a band of eight-year-olds runs toward a black-and-white-splotched ball, moving in ways that adults who may not know their game have taught them, learning early how to win and how to lose. Their parents' voices drift upward, rolling like an angry wave toward a cyclone fence a few yards away.

"KICK IT, YOU GUTLESS WONDER! KICK IT, KICK IT!" . . .

"POP IT, JASON! POP IT, POP IT, JASON! JASON!" . . .

"YEA-A-A-A-A-Y!"

⑨ Solutions

Violence ends by defeating itself. It creates bitterness in the survivors and brutality in the destroyers.

—Martin Luther King

If we hope to reduce the violence in our sports, changes must be initiated in four distinct areas: game rules and penalties, playing gear and equipment, the legal system, and, above all, our own attitudes and expectations. None of these changes are easy to accomplish; to some extent each requires a fundamental reassessment of our traditional relationship with sport and, in turn, its relationship with the law. Ultimately, all of us must become wiser consumers, both as spectators and as participants in athletics.

The conventional means of controlling violence in sports has been the imposition of fines, penalties, and suspensions. Although this system, if vigilantly employed, offers an effective method of curtailing sports brutality, it has proven less than successful in the past. In one recent season, for example, the National Hockey League fined sixty-two players more than $9,000 for brawling, but that did not stop the violence.

"Fines and suspensions are just like slapping a baby on the wrist," says one hockey player. During the first eight weeks of National Football League play in 1978, roughing-the-passer calls jumped 59 per cent, but that didn't halt a leaguewide massacre of quarterbacks. The National Basketball Association imposed a huge fine in the Tomjanovich incident (see Chapter 2) but it also has permitted greater physical contact than is found at amateur levels.

NBA officials are told to allow body contact, "to make certain the stars of the game, the men who earn the $300,000 salaries and draw the 15,000-seat crowds, do not spend the majority of the evening on the bench in foul trouble," maintains Art Spander of the *San Francisco Chronicle*. Players, notably Kareem Abdul-Jabbar, have complained bitterly of biased rules enforcement, but lesser-known hoopsters seem to be the worst victims. As Spander points out, such star players as Artis Gilmore and Walt Frazier sometimes take more steps than allowed before shooting but rarely are called; Wilt Chamberlain played fourteen years and 1,045 games without once fouling out.

In professional football the story is much the same. An NFL spotter counted twenty-three uncalled fouls, worth more than four hundred yards if penalties had been imposed, during the Pittsburgh–Oakland game in which Swann and Atkinson had their famous tangle. Game films show blockers holding on almost every play. "Holding goes on all the time," says one prominent defensive end, "but if you play by the rules on every down, you might as well join a women's league."

When officials do act aggressively, they are accused of spoiling the games they regulate. The NBA finally outlawed hand checking, but the move brought howls of protest from coaches and fans. The sports establishment has shown little sincere interest in strictly enforcing rules. The reasons are the same as those that have permitted trainers and coaches to follow nineteenth-century conditioning practices and to provide inadequate health care for amateur athletes. Most owners, managers, and coaches are consumed by the competitive nature of their endeavors.

Even if a player receives a stiff fine for brutal behavior, there is no way to be certain he is the one who actually pays it. NBA Commissioner O'Brien says he has personal assurances from all club officials that they will not reimburse players who are fined by the league. Nevertheless, O'Brien has conceded, he does not have access to the teams' books.

There are some signs that the leaders of professional sports are beginning to recognize the importance of enforcing game rules. At its winter conference in Honolulu in 1979, for example, the National Football League passed new strictures to protect its quarterbacks. The NFL also voted to instruct its referees to blow their whistles sooner to end plays, passed a rule making throwing even a missed punch illegal, and amended its roughness penalty to prohibit a tackler from open field butting, spearing, or ramming. A new management-players Joint Safety Committee initiated a series of injury probes, including frame-by-frame game-film analysis aimed at reducing the league's toll of mangled knees.

Broader reform measures seem necessary, however, if our sports are to become appreciably safer. To begin with, game officials must receive far greater support than has been the case recently. Football and baseball participants have been especially guilty of subjecting umpires and referees to unending criticism, mockery, and instant-replay second-guessing. Clearly, incompetent officials should be dismissed, but the rest deserve backing and respect. "Officials simply must have greater support," insists San Jose State sports psychologist Thomas Tutko. "They represent our final line of control. We need hard, firm, clear-cut lines at the core of every sport when acts of blatant violence occur." Tutko believes only fundamental penalty revisions can curb violence-caused athletic injuries. Some specific suggestions:

"Eye-for-an-eye" penalties. In other words, if Roger Staubach is knocked out of the game because of an illegal cheap shot, the opposing team would sacrifice its quarterback for an equal time period—which could mean a few minutes, a quarter, or the rest of the game. To help with such decisions, says Tutko, a "designated medical officer" could supplement the regular officiating staff.

Cumulative penalty records. This would relate a player's eligibility to his conduct for an entire season, not just a single game. Thus, in football, a player could be out of action for the year once he had drawn, say, ten personal fouls. Upon returning to competition, he would be subject to a "parole period" in which a single infraction could bring immediate expulsion.

Increased and modified penalties that reflect the severity of injuries, intentional or not. Thus, in baseball, striking a hitter with a pitch would automatically advance the batter to second rather than first base. If the ball strikes the batter's helmet, he would automatically take third.

Greater protection of officials. "Bumping or striking an official should bring an immediate and automatic suspension for at least one month," says Tutko, "regardless of the sport or the cause."

Tutko's suggestions represent an attempt to tie the rule structure to human hurt, to emphasize the reduction of injuries over yards lost or free throws awarded. In effect, they would hold professional players accountable—with their careers—for the physical damage they inflict. "It's a shame somebody has to get crippled like Darryl Stingley before something is done," says the psychologist. He remains deeply skeptical about prospects for immediate improvement. "Real reform will probably have to wait until the son of a congressman or senator is killed in sports."
Stiffer penalties "could virtually stop most of the illegal

violence in hockey, football, and other sports," agrees York University's Michael D. Smith, perhaps the foremost expert on hockey violence. "And I also think it would have an impact on crowd misbehavior, no question about it. Violence has paid off for players and teams for years," says Smith. "Creating a rule structure so it would not pay—that means really tough, tough penalties—could turn things around."

Sports Illustrated's lengthy series on football brutality concluded with a number of recommended changes for that game. Among the most noteworthy: that deliberate helmet-first hits be outlawed at *all* levels of the game—including "face to the numbers," "stick" tackling, and all other head blocking and tackling techniques by whatever name; that late and unnecessary hits be penalized more severely than they are now. Another suggested reform: sharp increases in yardage sacrificed for most personal foul penalties.

Sports other than football also can be made safer. As one New York surgeon has observed, some baseball injuries caused by shoe-high slides into baseman can be curbed by requiring that spikes be made of plastic or rubber. Canadian amateur hockey launched a cleanup by kicking out high-sticking players for a year at a time, by slapping Pee Wee hockey (for kids aged eight to twelve) coaches with day-long suspensions when their team's penalties exceeded twenty-six minutes in a match, and other changes. Game rules also can be used to reduce fan violence. In some European countries, the home team is held responsible for whatever happens on the soccer field or in the stadium to affect the game; a bottle tossed from the stands can cause cancellation of a match or even an automatic loss of the game.

The bullies must be expelled. The entire sports world is disgraced when a football player can openly slug two opponents in succession and return to competition without so much as an unsportsmanlike-conduct penalty. Such an act should have been good for at least a season's worth of bench warming. Basketball, hockey, and baseball, too, have had their share of undisguised—and unpunished—violence.

As we have seen, psychological and physiological evidence links drugs with increased violence in sports and with higher injury levels. Therefore, drug use—particularly the use of amphetamines and steroids—must end, and the only way to be certain this happens is to administer urine or saliva tests on a routine basis. It can be argued that drug tests represent an unwarranted intrusion into the private lives of athletes. In fact, such tests already are employed in most international contests, including the Olympics. The most pernicious aspect of drug use in a highly competitive environment is that if one athlete uses drugs, others will also. The only way to halt the escalation is by making sure *nobody* is a user, and that can be accomplished only by testing all participants. Sadly, it is clear that such tests must be administered at all levels of athletics, including major interscholastic contests in high school.

At least one major athletic institution—tackle football—stands in serious danger of extinction below the college level. It is becoming increasingly difficult to defend a game which injures nearly half a million youngsters a year, whose per capita injury rate, according to the Department of Health, Education, and Welfare, is four times higher than any other contact sport. There is nothing facetious in the statement that tackle football has become an unhealthy sport for growing boys. According to reliable estimates (see Notes for Chapter 1), the majority of its injuries take place during practice sessions, when qualified emergency help rarely is available. For thousands of youngsters, a high-school gridiron career will mean hobbling post-operative pain from knee surgery. In La Porte, Indiana, fifteen high-school lettermen had major injuries by mid-season 1978, including four broken backs, four broken legs, and a broken hand. Emergency shock treatment was needed to save one player, according to the *Michigan*

City News–Dispatch—the boy's heart failed after he had been hit in the chest.

Elimination of high school tackle football may sound extreme, but it would not be without precedent. Boxing, for example, has virtually disappeared as an interscholastic sport. Everyone finally agreed that the physical cost was simply too high. With football, the game need not be eliminated totally; it still could be played in its touch and "flag" forms.

The 1980s, however, offer hopeful indications that such drastic action will not be necessary. For the first time, authorities in both professional and amateur football seem to be taking the game's scandalous injury levels seriously. Though data from several seasons will be needed to verify the trend, shoulder-first tackling finally appears to have slowed the horrifying increase in spinal-cord mishaps at the high school level.

On the other hand, we should remember that such actions have come only after years of mounting injuries and were taken by officials worried about lawsuits and an outraged public. "If a few top drawing cards, mostly quarterbacks, hadn't gotten hurt, the safety steps would not have been taken," says one gridiron cynic. "My feeling—and so far I don't see it happening—is that you have to start by being sincerely concerned about the health of other humans; otherwise the whole thing is a façade."

The sports establishment has exhibited an almost built-in resistance to change. It took years to eliminate the wedge in football, despite the frightening formation's awesome toll on youthful bones and flesh. Clipping, first taught by Walter Camp in 1908, was not outlawed until 1949. Well into the 1970s high sticking still was considered a minor penalty in hockey.

Authorities have shown the same disregard for players' well-being when it comes to playing equipment. Stadium owners, convinced that synthetic turf would be cheaper and more photogenic than natural grass, helped the plastic-blade business become a $1 billion industry, despite persistent reports of higher injury rates. "Synthetic surfaces for football use cannot be justified on an injury prevention basis," concluded the Stanford Research Institute (SRI) in a "client private" report for pro football.

The National Football League Players Association unsuccessfully petitioned the Consumer Product Safety Commission to halt further installation of the artificial surfaces as long ago as 1973, then waited around for years of inconclusive rulings, bureaucratic waffling, and ultimate rejection. At last, some stadiums, including San Francisco's Candlestick Park, are switching back to good old-fashioned grass. Players claim the seams in artificial turf tend to buckle with wear, making playing more like stumbling over an aging, rumpled carpet. Only a thin pad separates the abrasive playing surface from its bone-cracking base, source of 33 per cent more concussions than natural turf, according to SRI.* Heat levels can be towering as well; players have been carried from the Orange Bowl's plastic turf because of temperatures which topped 120 degrees. Indeed, SRI found hot-weather injuries to be twice as prevalent on artificial turf as on grass.

Artificial turf has played a paradoxical role in football's epidemic knee injuries.** Several years ago a series of important studies at Temple University's Center for Sports Medicine and Science concluded that knee injuries could be reduced by switching from conventional football shoes with seven long, thin cleats to soccer shoes with their shorter and wider cleats. This finding presented players with a very real conflict between the desire to reduce injury risks and the desire to win, since conventional football shoes offer greater

---

* Pittsburgh quarterback Terry Bradshaw suffered a contused neck and spine in his well-publicized headfirst upending on Cleveland Stadium's natural grass a few seasons ago. What would have happened had he been jammed down on a synthetic surface? In 1976, Tom Pate, a Canadian player, died from a headfirst crunching on Calgary's artificial field.

** Knee injuries account for approximately 25 per cent of all gridiron mishaps.

traction, helping a running back make sharper cuts and a lineman to hold his ground longer when blocked. Eventually, players accepted the advantages of the new shoes, but just about the time they did, stadiums began switching to artificial turf. Whereas soccer shoes were clearly safer on grass, their greater number of short cleats virtually welded them to the plastic playing surfaces, especially on hot days. In most instances the problem can be overcome by using shoes with more conically shaped cleats, but the soccer shoe paradox illustrates the sometimes interrelated difficulties in attempting to reduce injuries by changes in equipment.

Similarly, the hard-shell plastic helmet reduced skull fractures in football, but only at the expense of increased spinal-cord injuries. In fact, hard-finish helmets and shoulder pads accounted for nearly one in four contact injuries of all types, including a surprising number of long-term mishaps (those which sidelined a player for fourteen games or more) and less serious "punishment" injuries, according to SRI's study for the NFL. The institute also reported that the potential solution to the problem—softer outer surfaces for helmets and pads—was rejected by equipment makers. "Helmets have already been developed with soft outer shells to protect the opponent as well as the head of the wearer," said SRI, "but no trend to wear them except in a few colleges is indicated." The reasons for rejecting the softer surfaces constitute a disturbing commentary on the game:

Conversations with equipment manufacturers revealed some of the complaints regarding soft helmets, such as "they cannot be painted with team logos" or that "teams do not wish to increase their equipment costs" . . . . a feeling [was] expressed to one manufacturer that a team "did not wish to protect the members of the opposition unless their team was also protected by others wearing soft-shelled helmets."

SRI found much the same attitude when it came to softer surfaces for shoulder pads. Arguments from manufacturers ranged from economic considerations to simply "we want to hear the crack of the pads to determine whether our [client's] players are hitting hard enough." Concluded SRI: "No substantive arguments against their use [soft pads], as they might be related to injuries, have yet emerged." Dr. Donald Cooper, team physician at Oklahoma State, told *Sports Illustrated* that coaches have resisted softer materials because they do not "give 'em that big *whack* when somebody gets hit . . . coaches want to hear noise. They *love* noise." They also seem fond of color. According to *Job Safety & Health,* a publication of the Occupational Safety and Health Administration, college coaches "have been known to count the number of different splotches of color on a defensive player's helmet [from collisions with opponents' helmets] as evidence of a player's drive to win."

New high-technology materials could supply a safe, soft outer surface for football helmets and pads. One such material, already successfully used in hospital mattresses and special shoes, relies on a system of tiny interlocking levers in which the resistance of the padding increases with the pressure applied to it. The material initially drew keen interest from one major manufacturer. However, the sporting-goods company insisted on putting the material *inside* the helmet, and the small firm that created the product decided against continuing the relationship. "We wanted to help get the brutality out of the game," said the president of the company that makes the cushioning, "but you've got to be out of your mind to get involved."

Equipment and rule changes alone, however, cannot totally eliminate violence and consequent bodily injury in sports. Athletic viciousness continues to flourish because we associate that viciousness with socially valuable qualities—with leadership and success. "When we see a youngster with athletic talent," says Dr. Tutko, "we begin right away telling him how good he is. We allow him—we encourage him—to make his perception of himself special. When he begins to express his feelings in dominant, violent behavior, we sanction that, too, because he is a winner." Distinguishing "acceptable" violence from the kind we denounce as illegal becomes even more difficult, largely because we ourselves remain uncomfortable about the distinction.

Athletic violence that clearly exceeds the normal rough-and-tumble of play, which would be illegal in a nonathletic setting, must be made a crime. As early as 1907, when Owen McCourt died the day after being savagely clubbed in a hockey game, there have been calls to bring the criminals of sports to the bar. "There was no justification or personal provocation for the blow," stated a court report of McCourt's death, which also recommended that "legislation be enacted whereby players or spectators encouraging or engaging in rough or foul play may be severely punished." Six decades later, as hockey writer Stan Fischler points out, we're still waiting.

Today's assaults on the athletic field are among the most widely witnessed crimes of violence in history. We need clear-cut laws to deal with them. Favoritism in the judicial system is widespread and widely acknowledged; the deferential treatment of recent, well-connected political criminals has fostered cynicism about the fairness of our laws. To see a coach who has struck a player in plain view of 100 million people escape with equanimity into a round of honorary banquets and commemorative holidays undermines not just the world of sport; it is a slap in the face of all justice.

The lack of sure, swift punishment for illegal acts can only encourage athletic goons to continue their ways. As Gary W. Flakne, the prosecutor in hockey's famous Forbes case (see Chapter 2), pointed out in *Trial* magazine:

A myriad of psychological and sociological pressures exist which are imbued at the earliest possible moment in the young athlete who engages in a body-contact sport. He is taught from the outset to intimidate his opponent and to precipitate physical altercations rather than to avoid them. With hockey players, the stick soon becomes a weapon rather than a means to score goals . . .

Flakne is convinced that only firm action by law enforcement authorities can curb the further spread of sports violence and its "pervasive ramifications on our society." He believes the pivotal issue is whether an incident takes place outside the realm of normal play and contact. For instance, if Terry Bradshaw is dumped on his head as part of a tackle, the action would be considered within the realm of play and hence not prosecutable. On the other hand, a clear case of assault exists when a player leaving the field is slugged or hit with a yard marker by an opponent.

Why have endless difficulties been predicted for the attempt to bring simple justice to the playing field? A typical case of sports violence has been seen by many, many times the number of witnesses needed to bring an everyday scofflaw to heel. The facts of such cases—the who hit whom first and why—are rarely disputable. In many instances the entire episode is preserved on videotape. Courts have held that athletes engaged in rough contact sports assume some inherent risk of injury, giving rise to what lawyers call a defense of consent. But Flakne and other members of his profession maintain that such a defense was never meant to exonerate a defendant who intended harm to an athletic opponent. "If one party license another to beat him, such license is void, because it is against the law," was the Massachusetts court ruling in *Commonwealth vs. Collberg,* an 1876 case involving an illegal boxing match.

The closer one looks, the more it becomes apparent that the real resistance to making sports violence a crime is based on our own reluctance to admit that law enforcement involvement is warranted or desirable. It is not necessary for umpires to become policemen, arresting players, writing citations, and assigning court appearances. Law officers, ordinary citizen witnesses, or county attorneys can make the complaints, just as they do in countless other assault cases. Flakne undertook the Forbes case, for example, at the behest of his county grand jury and was somewhat surprised when that group of fellow citizens voted to indict. Certainly it cannot be argued that there is a shortage of law officers on hand at sporting events. Most stadiums today swarm with cops; enforcement of legal game behavior would mean diverting only a small part of the officers' attention from the stands to the playing field.

There are indications of a shift in the way courts are viewing the issue of responsibility in sports.* In a State of Washington case, a high school wrestler's spinal cord was severed during a brief moment when a referee's attention was momentarily diverted to a separation in the floor mats. The court rejected a consent defense, finding that "one is never held 'to assume the risk' of another's negligence or incompetence," in effect distinguishing between injuries which are an integral part of the roughness of the game and those which can be blamed on inadequate performances by coaches and officials. "A participant may assume the risk of the former; he does not assume the latter," wrote Samuel Langerman and Noel Fidel in *Trial.* "He trusts his coach to send him out, adequately instructed and equipped, well-matched, and well-supervised, to meet whatever bruises, bangs or breaks chance brings his way." The same may be said of the great wave of product liability lawsuits sweeping many major sports. These actions, too, represent efforts to shift the burden of responsibility from teenage participants to those who oversee them. For it is adults who design and manufacture sports equipment and, to a large extent, determine the tone and character of the games others play.

* See Notes and Bibliography for a brief survey of articles dealing with the legal implications of sports violence.

For too long, grownups have gotten a free ride in kids' sports. Parents, coaches, and community recreation officials have forced youngsters to play adult games, conveniently ignoring some facts of childhood physiology along the way. Children are not just physically smaller than adults, they are physiologically different as well. One has only to recall Martin Ralbovsky's powerful vignettes in his book *Destiny's Darlings* to appreciate the painful scope of this distinction. Ralbovsky interviewed the members of the Schenectady Little League team twenty years after they won the world's championship in 1954. Bill Masucci, the winning pitcher, recalled he had played the entire series with an elbow that "hurt so bad I could hardly stand it." Ralbovsky then asked whether the sore arm healed after the club's great victory: "Bill Masucci glanced over at a window, which was covered by a white lace curtain. 'I can't throw a baseball from here to the street now.' "

Damage to the epiphysis (the soft bone ends, where growth takes place) became the shame of the Little League and led the American Academy of Pediatrics to oppose small-fry tackle football as well. But this is only one example of a young athlete's biological immaturity. Children up to age six can follow a ball visually only if it moves horizontally, according to experts. "Not until he or she is about nine years old can an average child visually follow a ball moving in an arc—say a fly in baseball—move to a point, and catch it," says Don Morris, a professor at California State Polytechnic University in Pomona. Ball color, speed, texture, and angle of trajection are factors which influence the ability of youngsters to catch and hit, according to Morris, a motor development expert. Despite these facts, most kids' games have been designed for adults, and suggestions that they be changed are enough to cast doubt on one's patriotism.

One of Morris's favorite examples is basketball. He points out that the only reason a basketball hoop stands ten feet off the floor—far too high for any preteenage youngsters to fully enjoy the game—was the insistence of a janitor at Springfield College, where the game was invented. When James Naismith wanted to nail up the peach-basket rim that launched the game in 1891, the custodian demanded that it be placed on an inside gymnasium wall well above the floor. "How many eight- and nine-year-olds," asks Morris, "quit the game because they could never put the ball in the hoop? . . . If Julius Erving gets a kick out of slam dunking, why shouldn't an eight-year-old? But how many eight-year-olds do you know who can leap high enough to stuff the ball?"

Morris believes adult games should be redesigned to suit the physical development and maturity of the children who play them. Youngsters should be provided with "lead-up" skills to prepare them for traditional games and with the opportunity to assume responsibility for their own actions. In his book *How to Change the Games Children Play*, Morris suggests using lowered, adjustable rims and larger, lighter balls in basketball. Another variation, useful whenever equipment can't be modified, is to hang a hula hoop from the basket—the player gets one point for a hula hoop goal and three points for making the traditional basket.

"Certain games can and do cause harm," observes Morris, "simply because their structure predisposes the youngsters to injury." By designing games to allow for children's age and developmental differences, athletic trauma—both physical and mental—can be sharply reduced. For example, a "softball" game introduced by Morris and modified by the ninth graders who experimented with it, took the differences among thirty-eight students into account. Each player could decide under what conditions he or she would bat. Thus, the best player chose a regulation bat and ball and a standard throw from the mound, while the least skilled used an oversized, light bat and opted for a large, rubber ball rolled on the ground.

Schools from Atlanta, Georgia, to Portland, Oregon, are using Morris's "games analysis" approach to match youngsters' true physical capabilities with the games they play. In one popular baseball–soccer hybrid game, a "pitcher" rolls a soccer ball to the plate, where a "batter" tries to kick it. The kids learn about softball at the same time they are getting practice in kicking, catching, throwing, and rolling.

Because of the potential harm of competing at too young an age, Morris does not recommend team games below the eight-to-nine-year-old, third-grade range. Even colors are important: Morris's research—which has been independently confirmed by several investigators—has shown that for most preteenagers white balls are harder to catch than those which are colored (see chart).

MORRIS'S GAMES ANALYSIS

ACTIVITY	EASY ──────────────────────────────→DIFFICULT
CATCHING	
ball color	blue yellow orange red green white
ball speed	10 mph 15 mph 20 mph 25 mph 30 mph
ball texture	soft (balloon, firm (playground ball, hard (softball, beach ball, rubber ball) baseball) Nerf ball)
trajection angle	horizontal vertical arc
KICKING	
position	stationary horizontally rolling bouncing roll in flight
type kick	toe kick instep kick punt outside-foot kick
ball texture	beach ball playground ball soccer ball football
location	no step and kick one step and kick three steps, run, and kick
JUMPING	
type jump	down horizontal vertical
body position	compact extended

For practical reasons, the sports played by older youngsters are less amenable to changes in basic structure. By the time a boy or girl reaches high school age, he or she either plays baseball or does not. Here the focus for those who wish to reduce sports carnage must be to improve playing gear, protective apparel, and general provisions for health care.

With annual athletic injuries to youngsters running well into the millions, parents simply must educate themselves about the risk of violence and injury faced by their offspring. Perhaps the simplest advice is to discourage a child from *ever* playing ice hockey or tackle football. However, since many youngsters want and need the physical testing of a rough contact sport, parents in this situation should do everything possible to ensure the well-being of their youngsters. Following is a comprehensive checklist, designed to help parents determine the quality of the sports programs offered to their kids. The list was compiled with the help of Lewis Crowl, an NATA-certified trainer in Sacramento, California.

Attitude of the coaching staff. This may well be the single most important determinant of a child's experience. A win-at-all-costs philosophy usually prompts a coach to overlook the inherent risks of his or her sport, to push kids too hard, and to encourage them to play when hurt. Is your youngster's coach an empire builder, who wants only to climb the career ladder? Ask around; talk to the coach. "We can with some accuracy infer coaches' motives by observing their behaviors," writes University of Illinois sports psychologist Rainer Martens. "When coaches play injured youngsters; when they leave players sitting on the bench the entire season; when they routinize practice so it becomes a complete bore . . . when in the frantic race to be first, the developmental objectives blur into the background, winning is out-of-bounds." But don't assume that just because a coach is successful, he or she is an unscrupulous little Lombardi. Many fine coaches also are successful on the field—Penn State's Joe

Paterno and UCLA's John Wooten are good examples. But if
your child plays for some gorilla who screams in kids' faces
and shoves them around—in other words, somebody who
emphasizes winning over having fun—get your youngster off
the team fast.

Training and preparation of the coaching staff. If your
youngster's coach is qualified by the National Athletic Trainers Association, consider yourself among the fortunate few. If
you happen to live in a state in which coaches must be certified as to their skills in sports medicine, that's almost as
good. Both situations are rare, however (see Chapter 3), and
more likely you'll have to ask whether the coaches have had
basic preparation in such areas as the care and prevention of
athletic injuries and advanced first aid. That may sound like
very basic stuff, but nonetheless is the case in many schools
where academic or non-school employees serve as coaches.

Availability of information. Does your local high school
offer "parents' night" sessions with coaches and trainers? Especially if held before the start of football season, such meetings can go a long way toward enlightening parents. "Most
mothers have never seen a pair of hip pads," says Lew Crowl.
"Even fewer know the way they are supposed to fit." These
meetings also can provide practical precautionary advice,
such as not leaving an athlete home alone after he or she has
complained of a minor head injury. "Parents' nights" held
specifically for sports activities are the exception rather than
the rule at most schools. If your school does not offer this
kind of meeting, volunteer to organize one yourself, in your
own home. Showing your interest and concern in itself can
help change attitudes and reduce injuries.

Type of instruction. If your child is being taught to elbow
under the basket, hit headfirst with a football helmet, or carry

his or her hockey stick above the waist, he or she is being schooled in practices which are illegal. Familiarize yourself with the rules of the games your children play. Particularly in tackle football, illegal techniques such as "stick" tackling and blocking and "chop blocking" (see Glossary) are more than simply examples of unclean play; they are techniques capable of permanently maiming your children or others. At least for the adolescent player, the only safe football tackle is one that comes shoulder first.

Conditioning. In general, coaches have put too much emphasis on upper-body (chest, arms, and shoulders) development. What is needed: more attention to knees and necks. Simple arch exercises, such as picking up a pencil or other object with the toes, can reduce "pronation" (turning in) of feet, a potential contributor to knee and hip injuries. Knee extension exercises, usually done with a weight bar, are worthwhile only if the athlete slowly raises and fully extends the leg, then gradually lowers it again; too many coaches, according to Crowl, allow their players to zip through the routine by "pumping," all but eliminating the exercise's benefits. Almost every high school weight room includes a bench press, but how many have a hydraulic neck exercise machine? Such machines can be a big help in strengthening neck muscles.

Equipment. If your child is playing football, be certain his or her helmet is of good quality and fits properly; an ill-fitting plastic helmet is hard to beat as an efficient skull cracker. Encourage (if it isn't required) the use of soccer shoes as a substitute for old-fashioned football shoes. If a youngster is playing ice hockey, insist that he or she wear a face protector at all times, including practice. In basketball, try to encourage the wearing of knee pads; a "T-brace" and wrapping can help save ankles. In baseball, make sure your child wears a batting helmet, preferably the more modern type with earflaps, even on the base paths.

Health-care provisions. These are the most important considerations of all. They may determine whether your child lives or dies following a serious injury. Some key facts you should know *before* allowing your child to participate: (1) Is a doctor present at *all* interscholastic contact-sports contests, including wrestling and basketball? If not, what steps have been taken to ensure immediate, on-the-spot availability of qualified help? (2) How available is medical assistance at practice sessions? How easy/difficult is it for a doctor to get to the scene? At one high school surveyed by the author for *The Physician and Sportsmedicine,* the closest contact with the outside world was a pay telephone booth near the practice field. Treatment of an injured athlete was significantly delayed when nobody at a scrimmage session had the necessary dime to call for help. (3) How far is the school from the nearest hospital emergency room? Is an emergency vehicle available for fast transportation? At another school questioned earlier by *The Physician and Sportsmedicine,* a player with a badly broken arm was hauled twenty-five miles in a bouncy station wagon because no local ambulance was available. (4) Are ambulances standing by at interscholastic football games? What about other emergency equipment? Does the school possess an airway passage device, resuscitation gear, modern splints, and a proper stretcher? The same injured player who jounced his way to help in the station wagon first suffered a painful fall on the playground when a rotted canvas stretcher split open.

As a guiding principle, especially with younger children, remember the following tenets of a young athlete's bill of rights, as it appears in *Youth Sports Guide for Coaches and Parents,* published in 1977 by the National Association for Sports and Physical Education. You might want to post a copy in your home or make the list available to other parents in your community.

1. Right of an opportunity to play regardless of ability level.
2. Right to participate at a level appropriate to the child's physical and psychological development.
3. Right to qualified adult leadership.
4. Right to play in a safe and healthy environment.
5. Right to share in decision-making in their sport.
6. Right to play as a child and not as an adult.
7. Right to proper preparation for participation.
8. Right to an equal opportunity to success.
9. Right to be treated with dignity by all involved.
10. Right to have fun.

In 1976 the Ontario Hockey Council and the Ontario Ministry of Culture and Recreation published *You and Your Child in Hockey,* a small booklet intended for parents of hockey players. Three of its key reminders apply to any sport:

- Kids imitate adults. They not only mimic the actions of their parents, they "absorb the attitudes that they think lie behind their parents' actions. Be a positive model for your children."

- It's their game! "It sometimes seems that kids' hockey is overrun by adults. They organize it, administer it, coach it, establish and enforce the rules, and do just about everybody else . . . The game is for those who *play* it, and everybody else should be as inconspicuous as possible. Let's help our youngsters establish and achieve their hockey goals, and be careful not to impose our own goals on them."

- Does your kid really appreciate or need your yelling? The answer, obviously, is no.

Lew Crowl adds a note of his own, specifically aimed at parents of pre-high-school children: "If a kid comes up and says he's not feeling good and wants to come out of the game, take him out. It's true that sometimes older kids get to be con artists—they'll tell you they don't feel good when they're just lazy and don't want to practice—but my experience has been that when a twelve- or thirteen-year-old tells you that, it's really because he's either sore or he sincerely doesn't want to play. Either way, he or she should come out at once."

Alternative games offer yet another approach to many of the problems plaguing organized children's sports. The pioneering, San Francisco–based New Games Foundation, for example, invents new games and modifies old ones so that the element of winning or losing is either eliminated or sharply de-emphasized. The ultimate goal: to teach all of us that play should be for the sake of playing.

In foundation-created games such as "Monster Monopoly," "Infinity Volleyball," and "Dho-dho" (a kind of yoga tag), the emphasis is on players working together. Sometimes, in fact, the principles of competition are reversed. In "Monster Monopoly," for instance, the player–property owners must band together or be gobbled up by the "monster." In "Earth Ball," perhaps the foundation's most famous game, two teams cooperate in keeping aloft a six-foot ball, painted to resemble the earth, while still trying to move toward their respective goals. Games like "Monster Monopoly" and "Earth Ball" can be played anywhere, require little or no special equipment, and leave no permanent marks on the environment.

Alternative games will not eliminate the troubles and shortcomings found in interscholastic and junior sports, which are inherently competitive. They do, however, represent a new option for the millions of younger and older athletes who ask only that their games be fun. And the New Games motto could well be applied at all levels and forms of athletics. As explained in a recent New Games Foundation training booklet:

• Play hard. We can play competitively or cooperatively just for the fun of it. We can see games as a chance to play at the limits of our abilities, not just as a chance to win.

• Play fair. Together we can choose rules for games everyone wants to play. We can share the power to say what will happen.

• Nobody hurt. We try to make our play safe, both physically and emotionally. Knowing a game is safe makes it easier to have fun.

So far we have considered what we as parents, spectators, participants, and rule makers might do to improve athletics. Urgent action also is needed on a much larger scale.

The government must establish a publicly funded, national resource center for the collection and dispersal of sports-injury information. *Sports Illustrated* has recommended that the National Football League finance a central computer registry of football injuries at all levels of the game, with print-outs available to parents and schools. However, this suggestion seems like a bad idea for two reasons. First, such an effort would further scatter sports-injury recordkeeping, already split up among states, private insurance carriers, and federal agencies. An NFL-funded football registry would merely postpone the creation of a cohesive injury picture for all sports. Worse, it would leave control of such information in private hands. The National Federation of State High School Associations and the National Athletic Head and Neck Injury Registry, the country's main repositories of continuing information about interscholastic football deaths and paralyzing spinal-cord injuries, respectively, follow restrictive policies in releasing their data. Both routinely decline to discuss or release their findings, requiring, in the case of the federation at least, prior assurances as to how their material will be used.

Policies such as these not only are unfortunate, they seriously impede efforts to improve the situation. The public must have access to the best, latest, and most unbiased information about sports injuries. Informed consent has been established as a bedrock legal right for even the most routine surgical procedures. When thousands of youngsters have been seriously injured in a single sport, when hundreds of others have been killed or paralyzed, why shouldn't the same principle prevail in amateur athletics? And how can it prevail unless the latest findings are made available to those who take the risks?

Until recently, we were little troubled by such questions. A United States Congress which routinely spends $630,000 for a single M-60 tank coughed up only $75,000 for the country's first nationwide sports-injury study, completed in 1979 (see Chapter 2, "Players," and also Chapter 3, "Coaches"). Times, however, just may be changing. In 1978 Congress created the Office of Physical Fitness and Sports Medicine. It remains to be seen how effective this effort will be; but even if it is disappointing, some states are showing an increased willingness to act on their own.

In New York, the state assembly approved $9 million for, among other things, construction of a new sports physiology and human performance center, major refurbishing of dilapidated inner-city playgrounds, and establishing a pilot training program for suburban volunteer coaches. The state revitalized its dormant New York State Sports Authority, tainted with scandal during its stadium-building days of the early 1970s, and gave the agency a new mandate: promoting the development of amateur athletics.

In Michigan, a massive, $340,000-plus research project (see Chapter 3) ended with the creation of a publicly financed Youth Sports Institute. During 1979, its first year of operation, the institute held forty six-hour clinics throughout the state. Designed to better inform adult volunteers and participants in "agency-sponsored" (i.e., Pop Warner, Little League, Midget Hockey, etc.) sports, the sessions covered such subjects as childhood growth and development, psychology, basic first aid, training, conditioning, and even included advice for parents on how to better control their own emotions. This extensive effort—which placed Michigan years ahead of most other states—was prompted by a state legislator critical of the youth hockey programs in which his own sons had taken part.

Besides conducting its clinics, the institute plans to track six hundred children in a detailed, five-year study to determine the physiological and psychological impact of adult-supervised sports programs. "We want to find out what happens to the personality of an eight- or nine-year-old swimmer who is practicing two or three hours a day," says Dr. Vern Seefeldt, head of the Michigan State University–based institute. "We want to know about the physiological impact on an eight- or nine-year-old wrestler who has cut his caloric intake in half, in effect starving himself without medical supervision, because a coach has told him he needs to lose weight. We want to study the future performance of a ten-year-old hockey player trying to play a ninety-six-game-a-year schedule, too tired to go to school the day after a weeknight game that ended at 1 A.M. fifty miles from home." Admittedly extreme, each of these examples was turned up in the earlier Michigan study. They represented a situation condoned, as Seefeldt puts it, by parents "caught up in an overly competitive situation."

We need desperately to change our attitudes about the sports we play and watch. Ice hockey, a beautiful sport—a sport of skill, speed, endurance, and strength—has been robbed of its grace, stripped of its symmetry, by coaches and managers convinced that fans want only fights and violence. Is it so difficult to believe that we can enjoy sports in another way? Must we forever bow to those who can only repeat that football, hockey, soccer, and so on are inherently "violent" games? Cannot our games be competitive without being cruel? There is a horrible contradiction working here. The pros provide the awful models for savagery, the really skilled teaching of viciousness, but the little guys, the kids who play at adults' games, supply just about all the heavy statistics.

Who is to blame? The owners, coaches, and players of professional athletics are win crazy and money crazy, and the youngsters simply imitate what they see before them. Professional athletes could make a difference by speaking out against what they know is wrong. That so few do is a tale of 2,500* small scandals. At the very least they might cease their mockery of those who try to improve conditions. "Put the quarterbacks in dresses," sneered one of our national role models when an interviewer asked how to protect an entire group of athletes from systematic annihilation.

On two occasions, Bobby Hull stood taller than anybody in his blood-drenched, money-grubbing business. Hull said no to hockey violence and refused to play. He sat out two full games because the cheap-shot board checking, slashing, and outright bludgeonings in his sport finally had become too much. "I never thought it could be so bad," Hull said after a teammate, hit from behind during a fight, suffered an eye injury. "If something isn't done soon, it will ruin the game for all of us."

Golfer Johnny Miller has shown himself to be another professional capable of viewing sport with a sense of proportion. In a long slump after a reign as the game's top money winner in 1974, Miller has learned he'd rather spend his time fishing Montana streams with his son than sampling the pro tour's staple of women, booze, and drugs. And he has had the maturity to admit that the rewards of being at the top had their limits. "I don't like the pressure—not at all," Miller told the *Los Angeles Times*. "Our priorities in this country are all turned around. I'll probably never be the best golfer again. But I will be a good person. At the end of time, will they say of Johnny Miller: 'He told the truth,' or, 'What do you know—he broke par.'"

---

* The approximate number of professional baseball, football, basketball, and hockey players in the United States.

We need more Johnny Millers and Bobby Hulls. We need more forthright television commentators like Merlin Olsen, who, hopefully with thousands of pairs of wide young eyes in mind, resolutely condemn acts of playing-field violence *when they occur.* We need commissioners and other sports leaders who will kick the rowdies and bullies out of their games for good. We need newspaper reporters and magazine writers who are repulsed by sports violence and say so.

Listen to what coach Joe Paterno* told author Paul Gillette during a series of public-television interviews:

When a coach tells a player, "All right, you've got to go out and win. I don't care how you do it"—whether it's a question of being so brutal you try to injure the other person . . . there's certainly nothing character building about that. The winning-is-the-only-thing philosophy, in my opinion, ruins the game. I like to tell my squad, look, we're going to work as hard as we know how, but when we play on Saturday, we're going to enjoy it. It's only a game. It isn't life or death.

. . . Look at it this way: a young man gets to play maybe thirty-five or forty games in his college career. Very few go on to play pro football. Contrary to what people think, not more than three or four kids out of a squad of fifty or sixty each year go on to the pros. It's not like golf. You can play golf all your life, or tennis, or go fishing, but you've only got so many football games. So I tell my squad, don't worry about losing. Just enjoy the game, think about doing your best, and either you can do it or you can't, period.

. . . I'm awfully upset about all kinds of organized play for kids. I don't think there's been a society in history that tried to organize children's games for them. Play is something they should do if they feel like it and when they feel like it. I hate to see the parents of an eleven- or twelve-year-old sitting in the stands saying, "Here comes Johnny. He's going to hit a home run and win the game." The need

---

* With a 120–25–1 (.831) record, Paterno is the winningest active football coach at the collegiate level and ranks fifth on the all-time list behind Frank Leahy and Knute Rockne of Notre Dame and premodern coaches George Woodruff and Percy Haughton.

to win—it's such nonsense! Adults should stay out of children's play lives, give them a chance to develop these things on their own. The problem is adults are bored with their jobs. They come home at night and can hardly wait until the Little League games so they can match egos with the parents across the way—and they do it at the expense of their own children.

. . . Even with gentle encouragement from coaches, it must be a devastating thing for a kid of ten or twelve to have the responsibility of performing well before a crowd. It's like the last of the ninth, the bases are loaded, his parents are in the stands, and he strikes out. Why put him through that? Why get so involved in a kid's recreation—his supposed recreation—at that age? Just let him go out and play on his own, and if he hits a home run, he comes home and tells you about it; or if he strikes out, he says nothing, and you don't ask.

This overemphasis on winning is the one thing I'd do away with if I could. There's enough glory on the field for both sides. There are enough big plays. Why is it necessary, if a team wins by a point, to make them heroes and the other guys bums? I'd like to see us watch the game for the sheer enjoyment of it—the pageantry, the beauty, the great competition going on down there on the field.

At Penn State, a player actually may learn something besides football from his coach, an English literature major who graduated from Brown. And unlike the situation at so many of the nation's big football mills, the odds are better than nine to one he'll finish with a degree of his own. A few years ago Paterno turned down a $1.3 million offer to coach the New England Patriots. "I don't think I'll ever leave here," he said recently, "as long as the alumni and administration want the same thing I want: a team that's considered a winner as long as it tries to win—regardless of whether it wins. If Penn State ever wants to be number one—or else—that's the day I'll leave."

For some time now, a group of youngsters have been playing late-afternoon baseball games in a Pomona, California, suburb. The kids have made up the rules themselves and the game changes greatly from day to day, but generally three or four skilled players on one team match up against five to eight poorer, younger players on the other. Because the games are played in a cul-de-sac, the youngsters use a tennis ball. Because some of them are too young to hit a rapidly moving target, they balance the ball atop a traffic cone. Because each has different abilities, the players can choose their hitting instruments to suit themselves—a broom handle, a regulation bat, a somewhat indescribable stick. Depending on the power in a given day's line-up, the boys and girls reroute the game's boundaries around lampposts, trees, or a neighbor's cactus.

Cal Poly's Don Morris has been observing the games from a distance, listening to what the children say, watching how they refashion each meeting to suit themselves. "Basically," he says, "it's nothing more than the old sand lot with pavement. The kids are just accommodating the games to themselves, to their own skills, so they can enjoy it more and be more successful physically."

More important for the rest of us, however, the youngsters are demonstrating a basic truth: only we ourselves can determine the ultimate quality of any human activity, including our games. In recent years we have not demanded enough from our sports and have permitted them to become tarnished with a lust for victory and violence. But there is one unique characteristic of sports that offers hope to us all: they allow for redemption. "Wait until next year" provides far more than comfort to an athlete; it gives us all another chance.

The future beckons with a new chance to end the brutality in our games. It must not be missed. As James Reston has said, "Sports in America are something more than a diversion. They are a unifying social force and a counter to the confusion and complexities of our lives."

Glossary

Beanball—A baseball deliberately thrown by the pitcher at a batter's head.

Board checking—In ice hockey, throwing an opponent violently against the "boards," the wall which forms the boundary around the rink.

Brushback—A baseball deliberately aimed by the pitcher at a batter's body, ostensibly to force him back from the plate.

Butt-ending—Poking an opponent with the butt end of a hockey stick.

Chop block—An especially vicious football technique in which one player, usually a lineman, straightens an opponent up while a teammate blocks down on his knees.

Clothesline—A football tackle in which the ball carrier is hooked from one side or behind by an arm around the neck.

Crackback—A football block in which an offensive player, usually a receiver feigning movement away from his own backfield, doubles back and at the last moment throws himself in front of the charging defensive player.

Crosschecking—Using the hockey stick with both hands to block across the upper body of an opponent.

Earholing—In football, a player's deliberate aiming of the top of his helmet at the hole in the side of an opponent's helmet.

Elbowing—Using the elbow to hit an opponent, especially in ice hockey and basketball.

Enforcer—A term used in arena sports such as ice hockey and basketball to describe a player skilled in intimidating or, if need be, actually fighting with opponents.

Giving the bone—In football, using the outside of the forearm to smash an opponent, usually in the head, as he runs toward the aggressing player.

Hand checking—In basketball, using hand contact to control the movement of an opponent.

248

Head slap—In football, using the open hand to hit the side of an opposing player's helmet.

High sticking—In ice hockey, striking an opponent with the stick carried above shoulder height.

High tagging—In baseball, purposely trying to hit a base runner in the head while tagging him out.

Jamming—In football, hitting or running into an opposing pass receiver to throw him off his pattern.

Leg whipping—In football, a lineman's use of his leg to trip an oncoming rusher from the side or behind.

Rake blocking—In football, a technique in which a lineman jerks up his head from an opponent's chest, raking his face mask into the opponent's chin.

Raking—In rugby, deliberately running over a fallen opponent with cleated rugby shoes.

Rip-up—In football, a forearm uppercut, usually administered by either an offensive or defensive lineman with the intent of catching an opponent under the chin.

Roundhouse—In football, smashing an opposing player in the head with the inside of the forearm, usually from behind.

Spearing—In ice hockey, poking an opponent with the point of the stick; in football, driving the top of the helmet into a player who is down.

Spikes high—In baseball, trying to avoid being tagged out by aiming the spikes high while sliding into a base.

Tunneling—In basketball, hitting a shooter or rebounder in the lower body while he is off the floor.

Acknowledgments

I should like to express special thanks to the staff at *The Physician and Sportsmedicine* magazine, especially Dr. Allan J. Ryan, editor-in-chief and an early leader in the attack against head tackling and blocking in football, who generously provided assistance with technical medical questions; Frances Caldwell, an early supporter of the idea of a journalistic examination of the then generally unrecognized problem of athletic violence; and Jack Martin whose excellent interviews of Johnny Bright and Gary W. Flakne contributed greatly to the book.

A partial list of fellow correspondents who made especially helpful contributions must include Darrel Maddox, Tom Baake, Marcia Opp, Brenda Lloyd, Dorsey Woodson, and Peter Sinton. My special thanks to Lois Bolton of Milan.

Those who ventured beyond the call to supply me with reports and materials include Susan Gerberich of the Institute of Athletic Medicine at Fairview Hospital in Minneapolis; Dr. James P. Knochel of the Veterans Administration Medical Center, Dallas, Texas; Don Morris of California Institute of Technology in Pomona; Gordon W. Russell of the University of Lethbridge, Alberta, Canada; Dr. Dick Moriarty of the University of Windsor, Ontario, Canada; Chris Lightbown, sportswriter for the *Sunday Times,* and John Langin of London. My deep appreciation to Donn R. Bernstein, media director for college athletics at ABC-television in New York, an understanding network sports executive who more than once came through in the clutch.

I would like to thank Dr. Thomas Tutko of San Jose State University for his early help and continuing contributions and insights, and Paul J. Moura, who, besides friendship and encouragement, provided an invaluable and encyclopedic knowledge of sports.

Without the initial support, direction, and enthusiasm of three persons this book might never have become a reality. My deep gratitude is due authors Min S. Yee and Paul Gillette, as well as my editor, Ernest L. Scott. Finally, I offer loving thanks to my wife, Judi, who, regardless of the pressing demands of her own work or the lateness of the hour, could be counted upon to edit, criticize, suggest, and—through it all—believe.

250

Notes and Bibliography

Wherever possible, considering readability, I have attributed quoted material from signed newspaper and magazine articles, reports, and books within the main body of this book. In general, unsigned wire-service stories, newspaper briefs whose origins are unknown or uncertain, and comments obtained in interviews conducted by me or by others at my request are identified and documented here rather than in the main text. This section also provides the titles and sources of a number of technical reports and professional articles that have been influential in the writing of *Seasons of Shame*.

1. Troubles

This chapter has been greatly expanded from my article in *The Physician and Sportsmedicine* for May 1977, under the title "The Savage State of Sports," pp. 94–100.

Steve Owens's comment about the changes since he entered the pro game appeared in a brief wire-service story in the *Los Angeles Times* on December 12, 1976. Owens also claimed coaches were putting more emphasis on gang tackling and that the pro game today contains a higher number of cheap shots, a view that seems to be widely shared.

The Investigation and Inquiry into Violence in Amateur Hockey, commonly known as the McMurtry report, was issued in 1974 by the Ontario (Canada) Ministry of Community and Social Services. This report, written by William R. McMurtry, is a classic and unusual response by a national government to concern over mounting athletic violence. "Fighting is not a safety valve," the report states, aptly summarizing the major issues of sports

251

252 SEASONS OF SHAME

violence. "On the contrary, it becomes an approach to the game whereby a desirable end, victory, can be achieved by illegal and violent means. You cannot blame a Dave Schultz for his approach to the game; when you consider it is a direct result of the training he received. . . . When young boys see that a Schultz is not only tolerated, but rewarded, then it is inconceivable that he would not be emulated."

Guatemala incident: Associated Press and United Press International reports for February 19, 1977, indicate that as many as thirty fans used machetes on the soccer players as they tried to board a bus. *Florida incident:* Associated Press reports, October 19 and 25, 1975, and interviews conducted at my request by Brenda Lloyd of the Atlanta Bureau of McGraw-Hill World News. *Italy incident:* reported to me by McGraw-Hill Milan bureau chief Lois Bolton. *Texas incident:* various wire-service accounts in 1977 and my own interview with the manager in 1979 (see Chapter 7). *Hockey incidents:* various news and magazine accounts, including remarks by Boston Bruin general manager Harry Sinden quoted in an antihockey violence article in *Sports Illustrated,* March 5, 1979.

The comment by Al DeRogatis was made during an interview with me in January 1977. DeRogatis, a former broadcaster and member of the New York Giants, is among a small but persistent group—which includes a growing number of physicians—who think football might benefit from a reversal of its late-nineteenth-century decision to permit below-the-waist tackles. That would help reduce the game's epidemic knee injuries, though DeRogatis admits it would not correct some of the less tangible sources of violence in the game. Another key problem, according to DeRogatis, is the vast differences in player salaries. "When you've got a $300,000 fullback playing against a $45,000 defensive back, anything can happen. Maybe those salaries—and the differentials—need reconsideration."

The attendance figures for major sports events appeared in the September 8, 1975, issue of *U.S. News & World Report.*

Dr. Charles M. Pierce's views were expressed to me in a 1977 interview and were stated in his paper entitled "Mental Readiness in Sports," written with fellow psychiatrist Dr. H. James Stuart. "One of the most difficult tasks for the coach," the physicians wrote, "is to dilute out much of the culture's insistence that it is wrong to kill. . . . On the football field the successful person is mentally ready to kill his dehumanized opponent with ruthless efficiency. . . . The team physician and trainer must be part of a solid group of family members who indicate their acceptance that such behavior—which is against societal norms off the football field—is not only expected and cherished but even necessary for the successful player on the field."

Foxboro, Massachusetts, incident: Associated Press accounts at the time and reports to me by Boston journalist Paul Giguere. An Associated Press brief almost two years before had recounted a parking lot knifing at the Foxboro facility. "It was the first stabbing reported at the stadium," according to the story, "but the fights in and around it have become as commonplace as touchdowns."

Dr. John L. Marshall declined written and telephoned requests for elaboration on the estimate of teenage athletic injuries I have cited, but he is not the only sports-experienced doctor who uses large numbers when discussing the problem. Dr. James A. Nicholas, New York Jets team physician and founding director of the Institute of Sports Medicine and Athletic Trauma at Lenox Hill Hospital in New York City, told me that in any given year 33 per cent of children between six and seventeen years of age require the services of a physician for recreational injuries. All told, as many as seventeen million Americans a year suffer mishaps in a variety of activities from backpacking to football to archery. Dr. Nicholas agrees that football is among the most injury-prone sports, but believes much of the critical emphasis on the gridiron has been misplaced. Physical injury rates in Pee Wee and Pop Warner football remain low, and injuries at higher levels of the game could be reduced by proper screening techniques, rules, and equipment, he says. His important early work on the relationship between tightness of ligaments and knee injuries was published in the *Journal of the American Medical Association,* June 29, 1970, pp. 2236–39. I am grateful to Dr. Nicholas for the opportunity to review a draft of a paper he is writing entitled "Risk Factors, Sports Medicine and the Orthopedic System . . . An Overview."

In an extensive, five-year study in the state of Washington, sponsored by the U.S. Consumer Product Safety Commission, Dr. James Garrick found that approximately 70 per cent of high school football injuries occurred during practice sessions.

The reference to thirty football deaths per year is based on the figure of 795 "direct" (i.e., head and neck) and 384 "indirect" (heat stroke, heart failure, etc.) fatalities in the 1931–1973 period, as compiled in 1974 by the American Football Coaches Association, the National Collegiate Athletic Association, and the National Federation of State High School Athletic Associations. The average works out to 28.07 deaths per year (the statistic of 30 deaths allows for what I believe is a conservative estimate of one or two deaths a year being missed in the newspaper clips on which the annual football survey relies). It should be noted that high school deaths accounted for more than 60 per cent of the total. Even more significant is the incidence of high school fatalities in the post-1960 period. Nearly half (47 per cent) of high school football players who were killed during the period covered by the forty-two-year study died in its last twelve years—the time when head tackling and blocking and the hard-shell plastic helmet were at a peak in popularity. Put another way, the average of twenty-four high school football deaths a year after 1960 was roughly double the 1931–1959 rate. By comparison, the fatalities among professional players, which had been high in the 1930s, were greatly reduced—only twelve pro and semi-pro players died from 1960 through 1973. A shocking indicator of the influence of tackling techniques and headgear on high school injuries is shown by the fact that 100 per cent of all direct fatalities in 1973 were attributed in the football survey to head and neck injuries.

In fairness, it should be noted that football is not the only sport in which higher injury rates correlate with more aggressive style of play. The U.S. Consumer Product Safety Commission reports that annual hockey injuries jumped from 30,000 to 50,000 between 1973 and 1975, a leap of almost 70 per cent in two years. *The Physician and Sportsmedicine* has published a number of articles on problems in hockey: see especially the January 1977 issue, which contains "'Too Great' a Risk Spurred Hockey Mask Development," by Dr. Paul F. Vinger; "Facing the Mask Question," an editorial by Dr. Allan J. Ryan, editor-in-chief of *P&SM;* and "Hockey Masks Go On, Face Injuries Go Down," by Joseph C. Capillo. See also "Hockey's Most Visible—and Vulnerable—Player," by Will Shapira, in the issue for November 1975.

The quotation from *Instant Replay* appears on page 190 in Kramer's book.

2. *Players*

The description of the injury to Darryl Stingley on August 12, 1978, is based on my interviews with two eyewitnesses, reports of the incident appearing in the *Oakland Tribune,* the *San Francisco Chronicle,* and the *San Francisco Examiner,* and accounts carried by the Associated Press and United Press International.

Concerning the comments about Raider Jack Tatum's ten-dirtiest-players ranking, it should be noted that he finished behind Conrad Dobler (New Orleans), Harvey Martin (Dallas), Ernie Holmes (Pittsburgh), George Atkinson (Oakland), Jack Lambert (Pittsburgh), Joe Greene (Pittsburgh), and Emmitt Thomas (Kansas City) on the list compiled by *The Sports Page,* a San Diego publication, and reprinted by the *Los Angeles Times* in December 1976. In fact, Tatum built his reputation as a devastating but legal tackler. In material supplied to me by the National Football League, *Oakland Tribune* writer Tom LaMarre recounted Tatum's exploits in an October 3, 1976, article headlined "Jack Tatum Holds the NFL Record for the Most Knockouts in One Season." LaMarre wrote: "Tatum is feared throughout football for his vicious hitting ability, in the legal sense. He knocked out seven players in one season. . . . He once got Frank Pitts twice in one game."

The Raiders' free safety reportedly was deeply troubled by the Stingley tragedy, a state of mind that could not have been helped by charges of "butchery" made against him by Green Bay Packers coach Bart Starr a few weeks later. Starr claimed Tatum smashed a Green Bay running back in the face with a forearm, but the NFL ruled the hit had been made with Tatum's shoulder and was legal.

The quotation from Dan Jenkins's *Semi-Tough* appears on page 17 of the Signet edition of the novel.

The three-part series in *Sports Illustrated,* by John Underwood, began with the August 14, 1978, issue and continued in consecutive issues. My own article in *Reader's Digest* appeared in the July 1977 issue. Joseph B. Treaster wrote about violence in sports for *Penthouse* in March 1979.

The estimate of injuries in 1905 is from page 246 of *Annals of American Sport,* vol. 15 in the *Yale Pageant of America* (New Haven: Yale University Press, 1929), by John Allen Krout. This is a superb history of early American sports.

Dr. Allan J. Ryan's remarks on the residual effects of knee surgery are from an interview with me in 1979.

Dr. Hasib Tanyol's findings on hypertension in football players were reported on May 24, 1978, at a Philadelphia meeting on "exercise and stress" sponsored by the American Heart Association. Dr. Tanyol discussed his report in personal correspondence with me dated April 18, 1979.

Regarding violence at soccer matches in England: Frederick Baron, a native of Scarsdale, New York, was spending his junior year at Oxford University when his article appeared in the *New York Times* on March 30, 1975; see also "Hooliganism at Soccer Games Is a Growing Concern in London," by Joseph Collins, the *New York Times,* October 17, 1976.

My account of the injury to Rudy Tomjanovich on December 9, 1977, is based on wire-service stories at the time. The estimate of fifty brawls a season in the NBA is from a column entitled "Vicarious Violence" in the *San Francisco Examiner,* January 1, 1978, by Dwight Chapin. "The NBA claims that its games now are no rougher than they used to be," wrote Frederick C. Klein in the *Wall Street Journal* on March 7, 1978, "but as a fan who has attended roughly ten games a year over the past dozen seasons, and watched several times that many on television, I disagree. So much pushing, holding, and elbowing has come to be permitted that the line between fair and foul is all but indistinguishable."

It should be noted that Don Atyeo does not cite a source for his statement in *Blood and Guts* that more than thirty American football players are rendered paraplegic each year. I was unable to confirm this figure in checks with the National Spinal Cord Injury Foundation. The foundation's data is admittedly incomplete.

The federal government's sports injury report mentioned throughout the text is officially titled *Athletic Injuries and Deaths in Secondary Schools and Colleges, 1975–1976, a Report on the Survey Mandated by Section 826 of Public Law 93-830.* The report was written by Robert Calvert, Jr., of the National Center for Education Statistics, Department of Health, Education, and Welfare. The comments by HEW Secretary Joseph A. Califano, Jr., were contained in his statement accompanying release of the report (February 25, 1979).

The startling estimate that one-third of entering college freshman football players display signs of previous neck injury is from an article entitled

"Nonfatal Cervical Spine Injuries in Interscholastic Football," by Dr. Joseph P. Albright, et al, in the *Journal of the American Medical Association*, September 13, 1976, pp. 1243–45. My article, "More Experience, More Neck Injury," appeared in the October 1976 issue of *The Physician and Sportsmedicine*. The survey of fifty-one colleges is from an article by Walter C. Schwank and Allan J. Ryan entitled "Stopping Spear Tackling—Will the Challenge Be Met?" in the September 1975 issue of *P&SM.*

The comments by Fred Rensing were reported in an unsigned Associated Press story in the *Oakland Tribune* of December 26, 1977.

The description of winter video-sports programming is based on a February 21, 1978, television log entry by the *San Francisco Examiner's* television critic, Bill Mandel.

The rugby injuries in Japan were reported in "Head–Neck Injuries Predominate As Rugby Gains Popularity," an unsigned article in the *Medical Tribune* for January 5, 1977. Regarding the injuries in the National Football League, Dr. Robert Kerlan was quoted by William N. Wallace in the *New York Times* for November 4, 1977. "We are getting different kinds of injuries," said Dr. Kerlan, referring to injuries caused by impact on synthetic surfaces as well as with other players.

Jim Bouton's revelations about drugs are from *Ball Four* (New York: Dell Publishing Co., 1970).

The following newspaper and magazine articles and reports were especially helpful to me in preparing the section on drugs: *Washington Post:* "The Choice of Playing with Pain," by Leonard Shapiro, August 20, 1978; *Los Angeles Times:* "Coke Is the Real Thing for More and More Athletes," by Ron Rapoport of the *Chicago Sun-Times,* August 25, 1978; *Oakland Tribune:* "Beating Drug Habit Boosts Oiler's Career," by Dave Newhouse, October 7, 1978; *San Francisco Examiner:* "In Defense of the Pep Pill Martyrs," by Richard Saltus, September 17, 1978; "Siani: Raiders Shot Me Up to Play," by Frank Blackman and Frank Cooney, September 6, 1978; "Body Builders Enjoy Lifestyle of Pain," by Stephanie Salter, March 2, 1977; *San Francisco Chronicle:* "Ex-Football Doctor's Warning," by Jack Lynch, September 16, 1978; "Drugs in NFL Still Problem," unsigned Associated Press story, June 12, 1975; "Defector Links Drugs to East German Athletes," unsigned Washington Post Service story, December 29, 1978; "50 Percent on Drugs—Tour Cyclist," unsigned United Press International story, July 18, 1978; "Warriors and Bill Walton," by Ron Thomas, August 7, 1978; "Scot Soccer Star Banned—Drugs," unsigned AP and UPI reports, June 7, 1978; "How Drugs Influence Horse Races," by Larry Stumes, March 24, 1977.

The Physician and Sportsmedicine: "Injections for Tendon Injuries, Cure or Cause?" an editorial by Dr. Allan J. Ryan, September 1978; "Bill Walton and the Novocaine Mutiny," by Lan Barnes, October 1978; "Anabolic-Androgenic Steroids in Sports," a position statement by the American College of Sports Medicine, March 1978; "Anabolic Steroids: the Myth Dies Hard," an editorial by Dr. Ryan, March 1978; "For 'Ideal Football

Weight' Assess Fat, Not Poundage," by John M. Kelly and John D. Wickkiser, December 1975. *Medicine and Science in Sports:* "The Association of Oral Androgenic-Anabolic Steroids and Life-Threatening Disease," by F. Leonard Johnson, vol. 7, no. 4, pp. 284–86, 1975. *Lancet:* "Androgenic Steroids and Hepatocellular Carcinoma," by Jerry T. Guy and Miles O. Auslander, and "Association of Androgenic-Anabolic Steroid Therapy with Development of Hepatocellular Carcinoma," by F. Leonard Johnson, et al., January 20, 1973.

Assembly [California] *Interim Subcommittee on Drug Abuse and Alcoholism:* "Drug Abuse in Athletics," transcript of proceedings beginning October 20, 1970, Exposition Park, Los Angeles, California.

The court testimony quoted from *Atkinson vs. Noll* appears on pp. 429–43 of the official trial transcript (U.S. District Court, Northern California).

Regarding my references to growth in the physical size of athletes, see the statement by Dr. James A. Nicholas in "Sports Medicine," in the October 1974 issue of the *New York State Journal of Medicine,* page 2040.

Reports of the deaths of Felix German Torres and José Morales were carried by both the Associated Press and United Press International on March 10, 1975, and January 15, 1975, respectively.

Interviews and discussions with the following individuals contributed to the writing of this and the foregoing chapter: Dr. Allan J. Ryan; Dr. Hasib Tanyol; John W. Joyce and John P. Nucatola of the National Basketball Association; Susan Gerberich; Robert Francis Mudd, Jr., and his family; Dr. Harley G. Feldick; Kenneth S. Clark; Elaine H. Beeson of the U.S. Consumer Product Safety Commission; John Brodie; Dr. James M. Glick; Ian Morrison of the National Hockey League; Dr. James A. Nicholas.

The interested reader may wish to consult some of the following articles, which cover subjects mentioned in this chapter:

Alley, Richard H. "Head and Neck Injuries in High School Football." *Journal of the American Medical Association,* May 4, 1964, pp. 418–22.

Clark, George. "A Little Less Mayhem on a Sunday Afternoon." *Job Safety and Health* (OSHA), vol. 3, no. 9, September 1975.

Damron, C. Frazier. "Accident Surveillance Systems for Sports" (monograph). Washington, D.C.: American Alliance for Health, Physical Education, and Recreation, 1977.

Kraus, Jess F., et al. "Incidence of Traumatic Spinal Cord Lesions." *Journal of Chronic Disability* 28 (1975): 471–92.

Martin, Jack. "Is Spear Tackling 'Safe and Effective'—Or 'Abusive and Illogical'?" *The Physician and Sportsmedicine,* September 1975, pp. 83–86.

Robertson, William C., Jr., et al. "Upper Trunk Brachial Plexopathy in Football Players." *Journal of the American Medical Association,* April 6, 1979, pp. 1480–82.

Ryan, Allan J. "Can We Stop Spearing?" *The Physician and Sportsmedicine,* September 1975, p. 88.
Schneider, Richard C., et al. "Serious and Fatal Football Injuries Involving the Head and Spinal Cord." *Journal of the American Medical Association,* August 12, 1961, pp. 106–11.
Sciera, John L. "Spear Tackling, the Most Dangerous Game." *Scholastic Coach,* September 1966, pp. 48–49.
Torg, Joseph S., et al. "The National Football Head and Neck Injury Registry, Report and Conclusions, 1978." *Journal of the American Medical Association,* April 6, 1979, pp. 1477–79.
———. "Severe and Catastrophic Neck Injuries Resulting from Tackle Football." *Journal of the American College Health Association,* April 1977, pp. 224–26.
———. "Unusual Fractures Caused by Football Helmet Impact." *The Physician and Sportsmedicine,* November 1976, pp. 73–75.
———. "Collision with Spring-Loaded Football Tackling and Blocking Dummies." *Journal of the American Medical Association,* September 13, 1976, pp. 1270–71.
Yeager, Robert C. "Spearing Goes to Court." *The Physician and Sportsmedicine,* September 1975, pp. 15–16.

Last, reference is made to the following U.S. Consumer Product Safety Commission publications: "Hazard Analysis Football: Activity and Related Equipment." USCPSC, Bureau of Epidemiology (NIIC 1211-74 HO1O), December 1974.
"Football." *NEISS* (National Electronic Injury Surveillance System) *News,* December 1975, vol. 4, no. 3.
Current NEISS Matrix reports for Product No. 1211, "Football, activity and related equipment."
Consumer Product Hazard Index, Fiscal Year 1977, December 1977.

3. Coaches

The account of Richard Alagich's use of film clips of Auschwitz is based on a Reuters report of July 12, 1978, and a story, "Films of Nazi Atrocities Aid Soccer Team," which appeared on July 13, 1978, in the *Daily Telegraph* (London).

Cornell–Dartmouth "fifth down" game: Glenn Dickey of the *San Francisco Chronicle* wrote an excellent column about this incident on October 6, 1978, under the title "Winning Wasn't Everything." Dickey cited *Ivy League Football Since 1872* (New York: Stein and Day, 1977), by John D. McCallum, as his source.

The story of the coach who bit the heads off frogs was told in two articles that appeared on October 14, 1977: "Parents Hop to Defense of EG's Frog-Biting Coach," by Billy Cox, *Today Newspaper,* Cocoa, Florida; and "They Toad the Line," unsigned, *New Orleans Times Picayune.*

The following articles provided useful illumination on the problem of coaching stress: *The Physician and Sportsmedicine:* "Tranquilizers, Towel Chewing, Tantrums: All Are Part of Coach Stress," by Mike Kolbenschlag, January 1976; "'Happy To Be Alive,' Says Schembechler," unsigned, January 1977; "Heart Rates of Basketball Coaches," by David T. Porter and Philip E. Allsen, October 1978. *Modern Medicine:* "Personality Traits of Competitors and Coaches," by Bruce C. Ogilvie, June 26, 1972. *San Francisco Chronicle:* "Heart Attacks Kill Raider, UCLA Aides," unsigned, April 28, 1979; "Nugget Coach Brown Quits—Poor Health," unsigned, February 2, 1979; "Detroit's Dick Vitale—a Queasy Stomach and a Losing Team," by Ron Thomas, January 1979.

Especially helpful in preparing the material on heat stress were discussions and personal correspondence in November 1978 with Dr. James P. Knochel, Professor of Internal Medicine and Associate Chief of Staff for Research, and Chief, Renal Section, Veterans Administration Medical Center, Dallas, Texas. Dr. Knochel, academically affiliated with the Southwestern Medical School of the University of Texas, is the author of a widely reprinted article, "Dog Days and Siriasis—How To Kill a Football Player" (*Journal of the American Medical Association,* August 11, 1975). I also am grateful for the opportunity to review a reprint of "How To Recognize and Prevent Heat Illness," by Robert J. Murphy, which appeared in *Consultant* magazine in 1978, and other materials by Dr. Murphy, team physician at Ohio State University. According to Dr. Murphy, the improving awareness of coaches to the dangers of heat illness can be seen in a sharp decline in reported heat stroke deaths in the 1973–1977 period (a total of four) compared to 1968–1972 (a total of twenty-five). Unfortunately, the average rose again in 1978, when four players died during that single season.

The training practices—and the reactions of team medical personnel—of George Allen were described in detail in articles in July and August 1978 by Ted Green and John Hall of the *Los Angeles Times.* Joe Kuharich's approach to training and his recollection of fullback Rich Columbini "turning to stone" were recorded in an article by Bruce Jenkins, "The Coach They Called 'Barracuda'," in the *San Francisco Chronicle,* December 30, 1977.

Gordon Jeppson's remarks to me in a 1978 interview are reflected in his booklet *Inservice Education Programs for Coaches,* an April 1978 publication of the American Alliance for Health, Physical Education and Recreation. The estimate of the number of certified trainers in public schools was supplied by the National Athletic Trainers Association, Greenville, North Carolina.

It should be noted that, according to the United Press International story in which their remarks appeared (June 28, 1978), neither Bob Devaney nor

Paul (Bear) Bryant suggested deliberately lying to the public. At the same time, however, they saw nothing wrong in concealing pregame information about the condition of their teams.

Various rules pamphlets and instructional materials published by the National Federation of State High School Athletic Associations were useful in the preparation of this chapter.

The following books and articles influenced this chapter and are recommended for further reading:

Blythe, Carl S., and Mueller, Frederick O. "Injury Rates Vary with Coaching." *The Physician and Sportsmedicine,* November 1974, pp. 45–49.
Brondfield, Jerry. *Woody Hayes and the 100-yard War.* New York: Random House, 1974.
Cope, Myron. "When the Whistle Blows,They Come Out Biting, Kicking and Gouging." *TV Guide,* October 9–15, 1976, pp. 12–14.
Edwards, Harry. *Sociology of Sport.* Homewood, Ill.: Dorsey Press, 1973.
Hair, Judson E. "Intangibles in Evaluating Athletic Injuries." *Journal of the American College Health Association,* April 1977, pp. 228–30.
Meggyesy, Dave. *Out of Their League.* Berkeley: Ramparts Press, 1970.
Redfearn, Richard W. "Are High School Athletes Getting Good Health Care?" *The Physician and Sportsmedicine,* August 1975, pp. 34–39.
Tutko, Thomas, and Bruns, William. *Winning Is Everything and Other American Myths.* New York: Macmillan, 1976.
Yeager, Robert C. "Medical Care for Young Athletes: Pretty Barbaric, But That's the Way It Is." *The Physician and Sportsmedicine,* November 1974, pp. 75–80.

4. Fans

Excellent reports of the tragic Lima riots were contained in two unsigned *New York Times* stories of May 25 and May 26, 1964, under the headlines "300 Dead in Lima As Rioting Erupts at Soccer Match" and "Peru Will Assist Riot Victims' Kin—Toll Put Officially At 318."

The quotation from D.H. Lawrence is from "Pornography and Obscenity," *This Quarter* (Paris), 1929.

The hostilities between Central American soccer rivals are described in a story headlined "Salvador and Honduras Cut Tie; Soccer 'War' Sharpens Dispute," by Benjamin Welles, in the *New York Times* for June 28, 1969, and in an unsigned United Press International report the same day.

The comments by Wayne Williamson and Alan Baker regarding the tragic incidents in Florida were made in interviews conducted for me by Brenda Lloyd of the Atlanta Bureau of McGraw-Hill World News.

The incident in which an aircraft smashed into Baltimore's Memorial

Stadium was related to me in a 1977 interview with Jack Danahy of the National Football League. A detailed description was published in an unsigned front-page story, "Light Plane Crashes in Stadium," in the *Baltimore Sun* of December 20, 1976.

Dr. David Bachman's comment on raucous fan behavior is from an interview conducted for me by Chicago writer Marcia Opp. Dr. Thomas Tutko's remarks were the subject of my own article for the New York Times Service in 1977.

Events at the 1976 College All-Star game in Chicago were described in a commentary by Cooper Rollow headlined "Unruly Mob, Not Rain, Stopped All-Star Game," in the *Chicago Tribune* for July 25, 1976.

Attendance figures for major league sports can be found in the *World Almanac & Book of Facts,* updated each year. The information regarding FANS (Fight to Advance the Nation's Sports) is from a press announcement (October 27, 1977) by Ralph Nader telling of the formation of the new group and from a story by FANS executive director Peter Gruenstein, "Scalping in the NFL," that appeared in the June 1978 issue of the organization's official publication, *Left Field.*

The observations about the 1977 World Series by Reggie Smith appeared in an unsigned wire-service story of October 13, 1977. Other accounts of New York's fans can be found in a story of the same day by the Associated Press's Will Grimsley and in "The Bronx 'Animals' Go Wild," by *San Francisco Chronicle* sports reporter Ira Miller.

The Burns study, officially titled "Report, A Panel Discussion on Security for Big Crowd Sports Events," is published by Burns Security Institute, Briarcliff Manor, New York.

Professor Michael D. Smith's extensive research is summarized in "Violence in Sport: A Sociological Perspective," *Sportwissenschaft,* January 1974, pp. 164–73. Regarding assaultive behavior leading to fan outbursts, he writes: "The most frequent assaults were player attacks on opposing players. In the majority of cases these were explicitly identified as precipitants of the collective action which followed. . . . Numerous other reports support the claim that sport-crowd violence is often 'touched off' by individual or small-scale violence: A 'Football Association News' editorial (Smits, 1968), in an analysis of 361 player offenses in English First Division soccer, associated widespread player violence with crowd outbreaks; likewise the Harrington Report (1968) on British soccer noted a connection between spectator misbehavior and violence on the field. . . . Unpopular referees' decisions comprise a second class of precipitants . . . player violence usually is the cause of the official's decision. Player violence, then, if not always the 'last straw,' seems frequently to be part of the chain of precipitants that culminates in collective outbreaks."

It is difficult not to notice the contrast in the treatment of fighting athletes, who frequently escape even game penalties for their deeds, and fans, who often are arrested and jailed for doing the same thing. A hockey contest in Oakland between the California Seals and the Toronto Maple Leafs on February 19, 1975, provides an example. Players flailed away with their fists throughout the National Hockey League match, which ended in a 3–3 tie. The Toronto goalkeeper left the arena on a stretcher. At one point Maple Leaf Dave Williams swung his stick with both hands at foe Rick Hampton, but received no penalty. However, when a fan allegedly threw an ice-cream container at a referee, he was hauled out of the stands and booked for assault and battery.

The observations about Army–Navy football fans are based on the study "Effects of Observing Athletic Contests on Hostility," by Jeffrey H. Goldstein and Robert L. Arms, published in *Sociometry*, Vol. 34 (1971), pp. 83–90.

I am grateful for the opportunity to review a 1978 draft of a forthcoming paper by Robert L. Arms, Gordon W. Russell, and Mark L. Sandilands entitled "Effects of Viewing Aggressive Sports on the Hostility of Spectators." Also helpful to my understanding were "The Perception and Classification of Collective Behavior," by Gordon W. Russell, *Journal of Social Psychology*, vol. 87 (1972), pp. 219–27; "Crowd Size and Competitive Aspects of Aggression in Ice Hockey," by Gordon W. Russell and Bruce R. Drewry, *Human Relations*, vol. 29 (1976), pp. 723–35.

Postscript I: England

The full title of the Westhill College of Education report cited in this chapter and elsewhere in this book is *Football Hooliganism and Vandalism*. The authors are Dr. Fred Milson and Russell Swannell of the Community and Youth Department at Westhill (Selly Oak, Birmingham, England).

My efforts to recount the events at Wembley Stadium were assisted by actress Dame Anna Neagle, a family friend, and writer Chris Lightbown of the *Sunday Times* (London), in conversations with my wife, Judi. The writings in the subway station were recorded by my wife in diary entries for July 1978. Helpful in preparing the material dealing with soccer mayhem outside England were the transcript of a BBC radio report (June 24, 1978) entitled "Trouble on the Terraces" and reporting conducted for me by Lois Bolton of Milan. The estimate of the number of hockey fans who died in Moscow was contained in a March 13, 1975, dispatch by United Press International.

The following articles and reports proved useful in preparing the section: "Football and Society's Bad Day," by Chris Lightbown, *Sunday Times,* June 2, 1974; "A Sick Game: Who Is Guilty?" by Chris Lightbown, *Sunday Times,* September 1, 1974; "Football Gangs," by Chris Lightbown, *Time Out,* April 28, 1976, pp. 15–18; "Goodwill Game Turns into Riot," unsigned, *Sunday Mail* (London), December 26, 1976; "Chelsea Riot Fans 'Savages'," *Evening News* (London), December 30, 1976; "The Soccer

Hooligans: Angry Britain Seeks Answers," by R.W. Apple, Jr., *New York Times*, April 21, 1978; "Hooliganism at Soccer Games Is a Growing Concern in London," by Joseph Collins, *New York Times*, October 17, 1976; "Behind British Soccer Violence," by Bob Driscoll, *San Francisco Chronicle*, May 17, 1978; "Goals of Christmas Past," by Benny Green, *What's On In London*, December 24, 1976, page 11; "The World of Football Hooligans," by Peter Marsh and Rom Harré, *Human Nature*, October 1978, pp. 62–69.

"Football Clubs Given Advice on Crowd Control" (press notice and text of recommendations), Department of the Environment, London, July 29, 1975; "Report of the Working Party on Crowd Behaviour at Football Matches," Ministry of Housing and Local Government, London, November 21, 1969; "Working Party on Crowd Behaviour—Circular for 1976/1977 Season, unbound mimeographed report; "Report of the Working Group on Football Crowd Behaviour," Scottish Education Department, Edinburgh, 1977; "Guide to Safety at Sports Grounds," Home Office/Scottish Home and Health Department, 1973; "Public Disorder and Sporting Events," by a Joint Panel of the Sports Council and the Social Science Research Council, London, 1978.

The following books have been helpful to me and are recommended:

Cohen, Stanley, ed. *Images of Deviance.* Harmondsworth, Middlesex, England: Penguin Books, 1977. (See the superb essay by criminologist Ian R. Taylor, "Soccer Consciousness and Soccer Hooliganism," pp. 134–64.)

Ingham, Roger, et al. *Football Hooliganism.* London: Inter-Action Imprint, 1978. (See especially "Football and Working Class Fans," by John Clarke, pp. 37–60.)

Marsh, Peter; Rosser, Elizabeth; and Harré, Rom. *The Rules of Disorder.* London: Routledge & Kegan Paul, 1978.

Robins, David, and Cohen, Philip. *Knuckle Sandwich: Growing Up in the Working-Class City.* Harmondsworth, Middlesex, England: Penguin Books, 1978. (See especially "The Sporting Life" through "We Gotta Get Out of This Place," pp. 126–64.)

Postscript II: An American Stadium

It must be strongly emphasized that the problems discussed in this section are by no means unique to Candlestick Park. Indeed, Roger Staubach, his wife, and the wife of a Minnesota Vikings coach were mugged as a group in the Los Angeles Coliseum parking lot following the Pro Bowl in 1979. The Dallas Cowboys quarterback was placing his four-year-old son in the family car when the youths attacked. The coach's wife was knocked down, her eyeglasses were broken, and her purse was snatched. One of the youths took Staubach's wallet and fled while others grabbed his wife and tried to rip a pendant from her neck. No one was injured, and the pack of thieves finally was dispersed, but only after another player, Archie Manning of New Orleans, charged into their midst.

A few years ago, New York City assistant police chief Anthony Bouza coined the term "feral youth" to describe the hundreds of young punks who went on a mass mugging spree outside a Muhammad Ali–Ken Norton fight at Yankee Stadium.

Two other articles that may be of interest for further reading in relation to this chapter are "Stop the Fans!" by Jack Clary, *TV Guide,* November 19–25, 1977, pp. 2–4, and "Among Spectators, 'Trait' Anxiety and Coronary Risks," by Charles B. Corbin, *The Physician and Sportsmedicine,* September 1973, pp. 55–58.

In the preparation of various portions of this chapter, talks with the following individuals were valuable: John F. Ream of the Oakland Police Department; William A. Cunningham of the Oakland Coliseum; Raider fans Dwayne Bracey and Thearon Lawton; Henry A. Fitzgibbon and Frank A. Torpey, directors of security for major league baseball and the National Hockey League, respectively; Robert Bruce (interviewed for me by Frances Caldwell), formerly of the Metropolitan Sports Facilities Commission in Minneapolis; Lieutenant Diarmuid Philpott, Sergeant Mario Busalacchi, and other members of the San Francisco Police Department; and Chuck Wood of Burns International Security Services, Inc.

5. Hucksters

The material quoted from *The Physician and Sportsmedicine* regarding box lacrosse appears in a September 1975 article by Bonnie Ginzburg entitled "You Think Hockey Is Rough? Take a Look at Box Lacrosse!"

The *Los Angeles Times* article concerning tavern patrons boxing in Arizona was written by Mark Purdy and reprinted in the August 15, 1978, edition of the *San Francisco Chronicle* under the headline "Fight Night—Blood, Sweat and Beer."

The extract regarding female wrestling enthusiasts is taken from page 73 of *The Hidden Persuaders* (New York: Pocket Books, 1965), Vance Packard's classic portrayal of the ad game.

Actor John Cassavetes' remark about violence appears in "Movie Violence, the Ultimate Obscenity," by Gene Shalit, *Ladies Home Journal,* January 1977.

The material dealing with the sports business during ancient times is based on sources cited in the notes for Chapter 6. One especially helpful source was the column "Decline and Fall: Lesson for U.S. from Ancient Rome," by Wells Twombly, *San Francisco Examiner,* March 3, 1975.

Among the most useful sources of data and interpretation concerning the entire issue of money in sports is the excellent *Sports Illustrated* series entitled "Money: the Monster Threatening Sports," by Ray Kennedy and Nancy Williamson, a three-part special report beginning in the July 17, 1978, issue of the magazine. Other helpful sources include: *Government and the Sports Business* (Washington, D.C.: The Brookings Institution, 1974), edited by Roger G. Noll; *Sociology of American Sport* (Dubuque, Iowa: William C. Brown, 1978), by Stanley D. Eitzen and George H. Sage; *The All-American Dollar* (Boston: Houghton Mifflin, 1971), by Joseph Durso.

The following government reports, which may be difficult to obtain, offer further insight into the influence of big business on athletics: *Hearings Before the Subcommittee on Antitrust and Monopoly* (U.S. Senate, Eighty-sixth Congress, July 28–31, 1959) documents one of the many attempts by Congress to reexamine the position of organized sports with regard to antitrust laws. These hearings covered legislation introduced by the late Senator Estes Kefauver and others in the wake of conflicting Supreme Court decisions—specifically, the high court's ruling in *Radovich vs. National Football League,* which held that professional football was subject to antitrust laws despite the exception that had been granted baseball in 1922. The growing impact of television is evident in testimony before the same subcommittee six years later (February, 18, 19, 23, and 24, 1965), which includes a concise guide through the legislative maze which culminated in the exemption of professional sports from antitrust provisions in the negotiation of league television contracts. An excellent basic source on government interest and involvement in the business of sports can be found in *Hearings Before the Subcommittee on Antitrust and Monopoly* (U.S. Senate, Ninety-second Congress, September 21–23, 1971).

The extract concerning the Vancouver coliseum appears on page 39 of Paul Hoch's *Rip Off the Big Game* (Garden City, New York: Anchor Books, 1972).

The *TV Guide* poll regarding the public's appetite for video sports appears in the magazine's August 19–25, 1978 issue.

Roger Kahn's comment about televised sports is taken from his fine article "Can Sports Survive Money?" published in the October 1975 issue of *Esquire*.

Wells Twombly's remarks about the future of televised athletics originally appeared in his January 14, 1977, column for the *San Francisco Examiner* entitled "The Evil Eye."

The importance of television to college athletics was described by Frederick C. Klein in the *Wall Street Journal,* April 18, 1978.

The discussion of problems in college recruiting is based, in part, upon an excellent article by the Associated Press's Fred Rothenberg entitled "Why Colleges Cheat to Recruit Athletes," published in the *Los Angeles Times* on December 20, 1978. Mustering a somewhat dubious defense, an NCAA official told Rothenberg that no more than 20 per cent of its Division One institutions were involved in cheating. Others put the figure as low as 15 per cent, but Rothenberg's story painted a picture of widespread abuses. A March 1, 1978, article by Al Moss in the *San Francisco Chronicle*, "The Season for Dirty Tricks," told of college players receiving vans, rent, even tickets to the King Tut exhibition in exchange for their talents. According to Moss, the mortgage on a southern California lineman's family's home was paid off by a southeastern university. Stu Black's "The Most Ruthless Game in Sports," appearing in *New West* on November 20, 1978, offers an excellent account of the basketball recruiting scene.

The quotes from professional sports figures regarding their playing tactics were made by, respectively, Joe Frazier (1975), Bobby Clark, captain of the Philadelphia Flyers (1971), and Alex Karras (1976).

The reference to a collegiate "Super Bowl" concerns a unanimous proposal by the NCAA's Extra Events Committee to support a four-team playoff to decide the number-one college team in the country. If approved by the full NCAA convention, the proposed event could become a reality in the early 1980s.

6. *Origins*

The selected excerpt from Robert Graves' *I, Claudius* (New York: Penguin Books, 1977) appears on pages 122 through 125 of that work.

The following books were helpful in preparing this as well as other chapters:

Beisser, Arnold. *The Madness in Sports.* 2nd ed. Bowie, Md.: The Charles Press, 1967.

Bennett, Tom. *The Pro Style.* Englewood Cliffs, N.J.: Prentice-Hall, 1976.

Bennett, Tom, et al. *The NFL's Official Encyclopedic History of Professional Football.* .New York: Macmillan, 1977.

Boyle, Robert H. *Sport—Mirror of American Life.* Boston: Little, Brown, 1963.

Brasch, R. *How Did Sports Begin?* New York: David McKay, 1970.

Denney, Reuel. *The Astonished Muse.* Chicago: University of Chicago Press, 1957.

Diagram Group, *The Rules of the Game.* New York: Bantam Books, 1976.

Dunning, Eric. *Sport: Readings from a Sociological Perspective.* Toronto: University of Toronto Press, 1972.

Edwards, Harry. *Sociology of Sport.* Homewood, Ill.: Dorsey Press, 1973.

Gardiner, E. Norman. *Athletics of the Ancient World.* Oxford: Clarendon Press, 1930.

Gibbon, Edward. *The Decline and Fall of the Roman Empire.* New York: Random House, Modern Library Giant, 1954.

Gipe, George. *The Great American Sports Book.* Garden City, N.Y.: Doubleday, 1978.

Gorney, Roderick. *The Human Agenda.* New York: Simon and Schuster, 1968.

Guttmann, Allen. *From Ritual to Record: The Nature of Modern Sports.* New York: Columbia University Press, 1978.

Hamilton, Edith. *The Greek Way.* New York: W.W. Norton, 1942.

Hart, Marie. *Sport in the Sociological Process.* Dubuque, Iowa: William C. Brown, 1976.

Hole, Christina. *English Sports and Pastimes.* London: B.T. Batsford, 1949.

Hughes, Thomas. *Tom Brown's Schooldays.* London: A & C Black, 1914.

Huizinga, Johan. *Homo Ludens: A Study of the Play Element in Culture.* Boston: The Beacon Press, 1955.

Leonard, George. *The Ultimate Athlete.* New York: Avon, 1977.

Lipsyte, Robert. *SportsWorld: An American Dreamland.* New York: Quadrangle/The New York Times Book Co., 1975.

Loy, John W., and Kenyon, Gerald S., eds. *Sport, Culture, and Society.* London: Macmillan, 1969.

Lunde, Donald T. *Murder and Madness.* San Francisco: San Francisco Book Co., 1976.

Murray, J. Alex, ed. *Sports or Athletics: A North American Dilemma.* Windsor, Ontario, Canada: Proceedings of the 15th Annual University of Windsor Seminar on Canadian–American Relations, 1973.

Nance, John. *The Gentle Tassaday, A Stone Age People in the Philippine Rain Forest.* New York: Harcourt Brace Jovanovich, 1975.

Novak, Michael. *The Joy of Sports.* New York: Basic Books, 1976.

Schlesinger, Arthur, Jr. *Violence: America in the Sixties.* New York: Signet Books, 1968.

Scott, Jack. *The Athletic Revolution.* New York: The Free Press, 1971.

Silverman, Al, ed. *The Best of Sport 1946–1971.* New York: Viking Press, 1971.

Tiger, Lionel. *Men in Groups.* London: Panther Books, 1971.

Umminger, Walter. *Supermen, Heroes and Gods: The Story of Sport Through the Ages.* New York: McGraw-Hill, 1962.

Yee, Min S., and Wright, Donald K. *The Sports Book.* New York: Bantam Books, 1976.

The following articles and papers were useful in preparing this chapter:

Bryan, Clifford, and Horton, Robert. "School Athletics and Fan Aggression." Paper presented at the annual meeting of the American Educational Research Association, San Francisco, April 1976.

Hofstadter, Richard. "The Future of American Violence." *Harper's,* April 1970, pp. 47–53.

Lasch, Christopher. "The Corruption of Sports." *New York Review of Books,* April 28, 1977, pp. 24–30.

Montagu, Ashley. "Is Man Innately Aggressive?" In *Neurological Symposium on Neural Bases of Violence and Aggression, Houston, 1972,* compiled and edited by William S. Fields and William H. Sweet. St. Louis: William H. Green, 1975.

Runfola, Ross T. "Violence in Sport: Mirror of American Society?" *Vital Issues,* vol. 24.

Smith, Michael D. "The Legitimation of Violence: Hockey Players' Perceptions of Their Reference Groups' Sanctions for Assault." *Canadian Review of Sociology and Anthropology* 12: 72–80.

The Humanistic and Mental Health Aspects of Sports and Recreation, a 1976 publication of the American Medical Association's Committee on the Medical Aspects of Sports, includes the following articles of interest: "Human Aggression," by Roderick Gorney, pp. 37–42; "Sports as a Control for Aggression," by Richard Grey Sipes, pp. 46–49; "The Relationship Between Sports and Aggression," by Barry Alan Smolev, pp. 49–54.

7. *Victims*

The interviews as they appear were edited by the author from more than three hundred pages of tape transcripts. Every effort has been made to preserve the speakers' original words while ensuring that the material flowed in a readable fashion. The interview with Johnny Bright was conducted for me by Jack Martin, former managing editor of *The Physician and Sportsmedicine.*

8. *Kids*

Douglas A. Kleiber's remarks appeared in an unsigned article in the *San Francisco Sunday Examiner & Chronicle's This World* magazine on January 7, 1979. I also have drawn insight from psychologist Kleiber's "Games and Sport in Children's Personality and Social Development" (Champaign, Ill.: Leisure Research Laboratory, University of Illinois, September 1978).

James A. Michener's far-ranging *Sports in America* (New York: Random House, 1976) is invaluable to any researcher looking into the state of American sports, and his section on children in sports, pp. 123–54, is among the best available. His critical look at Little League baseball is found on pp. 140–46. The soap-box derby gets a baleful examination on pp. 149–52. Professor Jonathan Brower is quoted on pp. 137–38. Michener's thoughts on "Competition and Violence," pp. 519–46, are particularly pertinent.

The comment by William R. McMurtry is from *The Investigation and Inquiry into Violence in Amateur Hockey* (the McMurtry report, previously cited in the notes for Chapter 1), p. 34, under the heading "Undue Pressure from Parents and Coaches." The remarks of Professor Harvey Scott appear on pp. 34–35 of the report.

David N. Campbell's observations are from his article, "On Being Number One: Competition in Education," *Phi Delta Kappan,* pp. 143–46, October 1974.

The research by Linden L. Nelson and Spencer Kagan originally was reported in *Psychology Today,* September 1972, p. 53, under the title "Competition—the Star-Spangled Banner." I interviewed Professor Nelson while preparing this book in January 1979.

"Some Detrimental Effects of Competitive Sports on Children's Behavior," by Utah psychologists Donna M. Gelfand and Donald P. Hartman, was included in a 1976 publication (cited in the notes for Chapter 6) by the American Medical Association's Committee on the Medical Aspects of Sports, pp. 42–45.

Hockey coach Richard Girard was quoted in an unsigned *New York Times* article on January 18, 1978, under the headline "Pee Wee Hockey: Reflection of Big-Time Abuses." See also "How Sports Can Hurt Your Child," by Elizabeth Jean Pascoe, *McCall's,* May 1978, pp. 49–50.

The remarks of high school coach Bob Morgan, whose team witnessed the OSU–Minnesota fracus, originally appeared in a story by Nolan Zavoral and Bill Dwyre, "Some Inverted Values, Lost Perspective," in the *Milwaukee Journal,* February 18, 1972.

Dr. George Sheehan's comment about the Lombardi mentality pervading the ranks of kid marathoners was made at a Buffalo fitness symposium reported by the Associated Press on June 3, 1979.

Dean George Gerbner's scientific analysis of television violence is explained in his "Living With Television: The Violence Profile," written with Larry Gross, *Journal of Communications,* Spring 1976, pp. 173–99. See also "Proliferating Violence," by George Gerbner, in *Society,* September/October 1977, pp. 8–13.

George Comstock's exploration of the linkage between television and aggression is discussed in his paper "Television Portrayal and Aggressive Behavior" (Santa Monica, Calif.: Rand Corp., December 1976).

The lessons of television mayhem as compiled by the University of Washington's Ronald Slaby appeared in the *San Francisco Chronical* on January 24, 1979, under the headline "What We Learn from TV Violence."

The three physicians who wrote in *Pediatrics* were quoted in *Time* for May 31, 1976. See also "Does Watching Violence on Television Cause Apathy?" by Ronald S. Drabman and Margaret Hanratty Thomas, *Pediatrics,* March 1976.

The work of L. Rowell Huesmann and Leonard D. Eron is described in detail in "Learning Violence Via TV," by Jane Bosveld, *Science Digest,* March 1977, pp. 27–30.

The study by Dr. Dick Moriarty and his colleagues at the University of Windsor is officially titled "The Effects of Pro-Social and Anti-Social TV models on Children and Youth in Selected Sports/Athletics." It was funded by a grant from the Ontario Royal Commission on Violence in the Communications Industry. A national opinion poll conducted by Moriarty's Sport Institute for Research/Change Agent Research (SIR/CAR) indicated that more than 40 per cent of those surveyed felt they had been affected by televised athletic violence, with 85 per cent of that group saying they felt "more aggressive" behavior resulted. A questionnaire undertaken as part of the Royal Commission project suggested that a majority of parents ignored the aggression content of shows their children watched and that violent programming was viewed with regularity and by more members of the family—parents as well as children—than nonviolent shows.

Other materials relating to the work of the Royal Commission were invaluable to me, specifically: personal correspondence of January 20, 1977, with Sheila Kieran, director of public participation for the commission; "The Royal Commission on Violence in the Communications Industry, Interim Report," January 1976; "Ontario Hockey Council Brief to the Royal Commission on Violence in the Communications Industry," presented by Lloyd Davidson, May 18, 1976; handwritten letters by grade school students to the commission, stamped "Received May 26, 1976"; "Television, Sports and the Audience," by L.M. Leith, presented to the commission on March 5 and 6, 1976; "Brief to the Royal Commission on Violence in the Communications Industry," by J.A. Colvin, president, Fanshawe College, London, Ontario, May 7, 1976; "Monkey See, Monkey Do," an undated report to the commission by May Van Stolk.

I am grateful to the American Medical Association for supplying a thick packet of background information that included some of the articles I have mentioned above. An intriguing AMA survey, announced on June 20, 1977, found that more than half the doctors polled believed or suspected that their patients were presenting behavioral symptoms related to television violence. And twice as many children presented such symptoms as the populace at large, the doctors noted.

See also: "The Clamor Against TV Violence Gets Results" in *Business Week* for January 10, 1977, pp. 68–69; "Imitation of Film-Mediated Aggressive Models," by Albert Bandura, Dorothea Ross, and Sheila A. Ross, the *Journal of Abnormal and Social Psychology,* vol. 66 (1963), pp. 3–11.

Eric Monroe's painful recollections appeared in the *New York Times* on October 12, 1977.

The brief prepared by attorneys for the Western Center on Law and Poverty, Inc., was filed in Los Angeles County Superior Court on December 26, 1978.

San Francisco 49ers coach Bill Walsh made his remarks about recruiting in a January 23, 1979, *San Francisco Chronicle* story by Bruce Anderson.

Interviews and discussions with the following individuals were helpful in the preparation of this chapter: Kenneth Dolan, Victor L. Grant, Karen Tootle, and other Livermore soccer parents, who, though genuinely convinced of the benefits of organized soccer for youngsters, spoke openly and candidly with me about some of the problems surrounding the sport in their town. Needham Cheely, Jr., Linden L. Nelson, John F. McCarthy, Dr. Roy M. Whitman, Anne R. Somers, Albert Bandura, Dick Moriarty, and Donn R. Bernstein also were helpful as noted here and in the main text.

9. *Solutions*

Data on professional hockey and football fines are from *The Complete Handbook of Pro Hockey* (New York: Signet Books, 1977), edited by Zander Hollander, and from an unsigned *Sports Illustrated* news brief from November 1978.

Art Spander of the *San Francisco Chronicle* wrote about basketball officiating in "An Official NBA Problem," December 13, 1977.

Commissioner Lawrence O'Brien of the NBA told *Los Angeles Times* writer Earl Gutskey that "I have assurances from all our clubs that this will not occur" when Gutskey noted that, in the case of league fines, there is no way to be certain an individual team will not reimburse players.

The Department of Health, Education, and Welfare report cited in the chapter is the same 1979 study by Robert Calvert, Jr., referred to in the notes for Chapter 1. According to the report, tackle football accounted for about half of all injuries in varsity sports and, besides its unfavorable comparison with other contact sports, experienced an injury rate eight times higher than that for noncontact sports. See "Highlights" section of the report.

The SRI report cited in this chapter is by Joe Grippo and is titled "National Football League 1974 Injury Study" (Menlo Park, Calif.: SRI International—formerly the Stanford Research Institute—June 1975).

For more information on artificial turf and cleats, see "Football Shoes and Playing Surfaces: From Safe to Unsafe," by Dr. Joseph S. Torg, Theodore C. Quedenfeld, and Steven Landau, *The Physician and Sportsmedicine,* November 1973, pp. 51–54.

The McCourt case is recounted in *Slashing* (New York: Thomas Y. Crowell Co., 1974), Stan Fischler's account of hockey violence. The reader who is interested in exploring the legal implications of sports violence is referred to the following sources:

Trial magazine, January 1977. This is a special issue on sports litigation, a superb effort by this legal newsmagazine and one that is, in the main, fully comprehensible by the general reader. See especially "Responsibility Is Also Part of the Game," by Samuel Langerman and Noel Fidel, pp. 22–26, and "Sports Violence and the Prosecution," by Gary W. Flakne and Allan H. Caplan, pp. 33–38.

Commonwealth vs. Collberg, 119 Mass. 350 (1876). "The common law recognizes as not necessarily unlawful certain manly sports calculated to give bodily strength, skill and activity," the Massachusetts court said, "and to fit people for defence, public as well as personal, in time of need." Even so, the court ruled that prize fighting served no useful purpose in upholding the conviction of two amateur boxers.

Wisconsin Law Review, 1975: "Violence in Professional Sports," by Walter Kuhlmann, pp. 771–90.

The American Criminal Law Review, 1975: "The Consent Defense: Sports, Violence, and the Criminal Law," by Richard L. Binder, pp. 235–48.

Don Morris's ideas are fully detailed in *How to Change the Games Children Play* (Minneapolis: Burgess Publishing Co., 1976). See also "Let's Give the Games Back to the Children" in the *Journal of Physical Education and Research,* September 1977, pp. 26–27.

The New Games motto was explained in a spring 1979 announcement of the foundation's training program. My articles on New Games appeared in *Nation's Schools & Colleges* magazine in 1977 and were carried by the New York Times Service.

Michigan's mammoth study of youth and sports appeared in three volumes under the title *Joint Legislative Study on Youth Sports Programs,* November 18, 1976; January 17, 1978; and November 15, 1978. The second and third volumes, Phase II and Phase III, respectively, deal almost exclusively with community sports—e.g., Pop Warner as distinct from public school sports.

Bobby Hull's comments on hockey violence appeared in Associated Press and United Press International reports of October 25, 1975. Johnny Miller's comments appeared in "Johnny Miller's Life without Compromise," an unsigned *Los Angeles Times* story carried by the *San Francisco Chronicle* on January 30, 1979.

Coach Joe Paterno's comments to writer Paul Gillette were made during a series of Public Broadcasting System programs in September 1974. Paterno's intention to remain at Penn State indefinitely was noted in an article by Bob Oates in the *Los Angeles Times* for November 3, 1978.

The James Reston quotation is taken from pg. 29 of *Sports: A Mirror of Our Society?* (New York: Scholastic Book Services, 1975), edited by Charles Wyre.

Talks with the following individuals aided me in preparing this chapter: Thomas Tutko, Bobby Hull, Michael D. Smith, Gary W. Flakne (interviewed for me by Jack Martin), Don Morris, Lewis Crowl, and Vern Seefeldt.

Index

NY

①

②

③

BRKYN

①

②

③

NY — _____

BROO _____

TOTAL _____

7c 796
Y

FIVE CORNERS BRANCH

Yeager, Robert C.

Seasons of shame

no. aca. no.

DATE DUE   C054 12.95

3/28/80

Fc 796 y   no. aca. no.